Debating the Presidency

W9-CNK-915

DATE DUE

SEP 1 1 2006	
OCT 2 7 2008	

Debating the Presidency

CONFLICTING PERSPECTIVES ON THE AMERICAN EXECUTIVE

EDITED BY

RICHARD J. ELLIS
Willamette University

AND

MICHAEL NELSON
Rhodes College

CQ PRESS

A Division of Congressional Quarterly Inc.
Washington, D.C.

CQ Press
1255 22nd Street, NW, Suite 400
Washington, DC 20037

Phone: 202-729-1900; toll-free, 1-866-427-7737 (1-866-4CQ-PRESS)
Web: www.cqpress.com

Cover image art by Kimberly Glyder; photo by Charles Dharapak, Associated Press.

☉ The paper used in this publication exceeds the requirements of the American National Standard for Information Sciences—Permanence of Paper for Printed Library Materials, ANSI Z39.48-1992.

Printed and bound in the United States of America

10 09 08 07 06   1 2 3 4 5

Library of Congress Cataloging-in-Publication Data

Debating the presidency : conflicting perspectives on the American executive / edited by Richard J. Ellis and Michael Nelson.
    p. cm.
  Includes bibliographical references.
  ISBN 1-56802-914-4 (alk. paper)
  1. Executive power—United States. 2. Presidents—United States. I. Ellis, Richard (Richard J.) II. Nelson, Michael, 1949- III. Title.

  JK516.D43 2006
  352.230973--dc22

                                          2006000769

To the memory of Francis E. Rourke,
professor of political science,
Johns Hopkins University

CONTENTS

Preface ix

Contributors xi

1 Resolved, the framers of the Constitution would approve of the modern presidency 1
PRO: DAVID NICHOLS 3
CON: TERRI BIMES 8

2 Resolved, political parties should nominate candidates for the presidency through a national primary 14
PRO: MICHAEL NELSON 17
CON: ANDREW E. BUSCH 23

3 Resolved, the president should be elected directly by the people 30
PRO: BURDETT LOOMIS 32
CON: BYRON E. SHAFER 38

4 Resolved, the presidential impeachment process is basically sound 45
PRO: KEITH E. WHITTINGTON 48
CON: BENJAMIN GINSBERG AND MARTIN SHEFTER 54

5 Resolved, the media are too hard on presidents 60
PRO: MATTHEW R. KERBEL 62
CON: BARTHOLOMEW H. SPARROW 68

6 Resolved, the president is a more authentic representative of the American people than is Congress 75
PRO: MARC J. HETHERINGTON 77
CON: RICHARD J. ELLIS 86

7 Resolved, presidents have usurped the war power that rightfully belongs to Congress 92
PRO: NANCY KASSOP 95
CON: RICHARD M. PIOUS 101

8 Resolved, the president has too much power in the selection of judges 110
PRO: DAVID A. YALOF 112
CON: JOHN ANTHONY MALTESE 119

**9 Resolved, a broad executive privilege is essential
to the successful functioning of the presidency** **125**
PRO: MARK J. ROZELL 127
CON: DAVID GRAY ADLER 132

**10 Resolved, a president's cabinet members should have a
larger role in the formation of public policy** **141**
PRO: ANDREW RUDALEVIGE 144
CON: MATTHEW J. DICKINSON 151

**11 Resolved, psychological character is a powerful
predictor of presidential performance** **159**
PRO: STANLEY A. RENSHON 162
CON: STEPHEN SKOWRONEK 167

**12 Resolved, great presidents are agents of
democratic change** **179**
PRO: MARC LANDY 181
CON: BRUCE MIROFF 191

Notes **199**

PREFACE

In 1969 the political scientist Aaron Wildavsky published a hefty reader on the American presidency. He prefaced it with the observation that "the presidency is the most important political institution in American life" and then noted the paradox that an institution of such overwhelming importance had been studied so little. "The eminence of the institution," Wildavsky wrote, "is matched only by the extraordinary neglect shown to it by political scientists. Compared to the hordes of researchers who regularly descend on Congress, local communities, and the most remote foreign principalities, there is an extraordinary dearth of students of the presidency, although scholars ritually swear that the presidency is where the action is before they go somewhere else to do their research."

Political scientists have come a long way since 1969. The presidency remains as central to national life as it was then, and perhaps even more so. The state of scholarly research on the presidency today is unrecognizable compared with what it was thirty-seven years ago. A rich array of new studies has reshaped our understanding of presidential history, presidential character, the executive office, and the presidency's relationship with the public, interest groups, parties, Congress, and the executive branch. Neglect is no longer a problem in the study of the presidency.

In addition, those who teach about the presidency no longer lack for good textbooks on the subject. A number of terrific books explain how the office has developed and how it works. Although students gain a great deal from reading these texts, even the best of them can inadvertently promote a passive learning experience. Textbooks convey what political scientists know, but the balance and impartiality that mark a good text can obscure the contentious nature of the scholarly enterprise. Sharp disagreements are often smoothed over in the writing.

The primary purpose of *Debating the Presidency* is to allow students to participate directly in the ongoing controversies swirling around the presidency and to judge for themselves which side is right. It is premised philosophically on our view of students as active learners to be engaged rather than as passive receptacles to be filled. The book is designed to promote a classroom experience in which students actively debate and discuss issues rather than simply listen to lectures.

Some issues, of course, lend themselves more readily to this kind of classroom debate. In our judgment, questions of a normative nature—asking not just what is, but what ought to be—are likely to foster the most interesting and engaging classroom discussions. So in selecting topics for debate, we generally eschewed narrow but important empirical questions of political science—such as whether the president receives greater support from Congress in foreign policy matters than on domestic issues—for broader questions that include empirical as well as normative components—such as whether the president has usurped the war power that rightfully belongs to Congress. We aim not only to teach students to think like political scientists, but also to encourage them to think like citizens of a democratic nation.

Each of the twelve issues selected for debate in this book poses questions on which thoughtful people differ. These issues include whether a broad executive privilege is essential to the successful functioning of the presidency, whether the president should be elected directly by the people, whether the presidential impeachment process works well, and whether great presidents are agents of or impediments to democratic change. We invited twenty-three accomplished scholars to take sides on these issues—just as in a formal debate—and asked them to make strong cases for their positions. Their arguments are forceful and provocative, as well as thoughtful and responsible. Indeed, sometimes the cases they make are even stronger than their personal views on the issue.

We hope that teachers and students have as much fun using these debates as we and the other contributors had in writing them, whether they are used to spark lively in-class discussions or to stimulate out-of-class writing assignments.

The pleasure we experienced compiling this volume owes much to the close and friendly cooperation of the book's two editors and to the splendid work of the staff at CQ Press. We are deeply grateful to chief acquisitions editor Charisse Kiino for her encouragement and guidance in developing this volume and to copy editor Sabra Bissette Ledent, whose involvement in any book is a surefire guarantee that it will be well and clearly written. We also thank Robin Surratt, the book's project editor, and Jessica Forman, who handled the book's composition. Our deepest thanks go to the contributors, not just for their essays, but also for their excellent scholarship on the presidency.

CONTRIBUTORS

David Gray Adler is professor of political science at Idaho State University. He has published and lectured widely on the Constitution and presidential power. His most recent book is *The Presidency and the Law: The Clinton Presidency* (coedited with Michael Genovese, 2002).

Terri Bimes is the associate director of the Center for American Political Studies and a lecturer in the Department of Government at Harvard University. Her forthcoming book, *The Metamorphosis of Presidential Populism*, examines the evolution of presidential rhetoric from Andrew Jackson through George W. Bush. Before teaching at Harvard, Bimes was a research fellow and lecturer at the University of California, Berkeley, to which she will return in fall 2006.

Andrew E. Busch is professor of government at Claremont McKenna College, where he teaches courses on American politics, elections, and public policy. He has written nine books on American politics, including most recently *Reagan's Victory: The Presidential Election of 1980* (2005), *Red over Blue: The 2004 Elections and American Politics* (with James W. Ceaser, 2005), and *The Front-Loading Problem in Presidential Nominations* (with William G. Mayer, 2004). He received his doctorate from the University of Virginia in 1992.

Matthew J. Dickinson is professor of political science at Middlebury College. He is the author of *Bitter Harvest: FDR, Presidential Power, and the Growth of the Presidential Branch* (1996) and has published numerous articles on the presidency, presidential decision making, and presidential advisers. His current research examines the growth of presidential staff in the post–World War II era.

Richard J. Ellis teaches American politics at Willamette University. He has written widely on the history of the American presidency and American political culture. His most recent books are *To the Flag: The Unlikely History of the Pledge of Allegiance* (2005) and *Democratic Delusions: The Initiative Process in America* (2002).

Benjamin Ginsberg is the David Bernstein Professor of Political Science at Johns Hopkins University. He is the author of a number of books, including *We the People: An Introduction to American Politics* (with Theodore J. Lowi and Margaret Weir, 5th ed., 2005), *Downsizing Democracy* (2002), *Politics by Other*

Means (with Martin Shefter, 3d ed., 2002), and *The Fatal Embrace: Jews and the State* (1993).

Marc J. Hetherington is associate professor at Vanderbilt University. He was the 2004 recipient of the Emerging Scholar award from the Elections, Public Opinion, and Voting Behavior section of the American Political Science Association. He has published numerous articles and book chapters on political trust and is the author of *Why Trust Matters: Declining Political Trust and the Demise of American Liberalism* (2005).

Nancy Kassop is professor in and chair of the Department of Political Science and International Relations at the State University of New York at New Paltz. Her research addresses issues of the presidency and law. Her most recent articles are "Not Going Public: George W. Bush and the Presidential Records Act," in *In the Public Domain: Presidents and the Challenges of Public Leadership* (edited by Lori Cox Han and Diane J. Heith, 2005), and "When Law and Politics Collide: Presidents and the Use of the Twenty-Fifth Amendment," in *Presidential Studies Quarterly* (March 2005). She is the president of the Presidency Research Group section of the American Political Science Association.

Matthew R. Kerbel is professor of political science at Villanova University and the author of five books on politics, the mass media, and the presidency, including the textbook *American Government: Your Voice, Your Future* (2006) and *If It Bleeds, It Leads: An Anatomy of Television News* (2000). He has worked as a news writer for television outlets, including the Public Broadcasting Service in New York City. He received his doctorate from the University of Michigan.

Marc Landy is professor of political science at Boston College. He is the co-author (with Sidney Milkis) of *American Government: Balancing Democracy and Rights* (2004) and *Presidential Greatness* (2000). His most recent essay on the presidency is "The Bully Pulpit and the War on Terror," in *New Challenges for the American Presidency* (edited by George Edwards III and Philip John Davies, 2004).

Burdett Loomis is professor of political science at the University of Kansas. A former American Political Science Association congressional fellow and recipient of a Kemper Teaching Award, he has written extensively on legislatures, political careers, interest groups, and policymaking. He is the co-editor of *Choosing a President* (with Paul D. Schumaker, 2001).

John Anthony Maltese is the Josiah Meigs Distinguished Teaching Associate Professor of Political Science at the University of Georgia. His books include *Politics of the Presidency* (with Joseph A. Pika, rev. 6th ed., 2006), *The Selling of Supreme Court Nominees* (1995), and *Spin Control* (2d ed., rev. 1994). He was named the 2004 Georgia professor of the year by the Carnegie Foundation for the Advancement of Teaching and the Council for Advancement and Support of Education (CASE).

Bruce Miroff is professor and former chair of political science at the State University of New York at Albany. His books include *The Democratic Debate* (with Raymond Seidleman and Todd Swanstrom, 4th ed., 2005), *Icons of Democracy: American Leaders as Heroes, Aristocrats, Dissenters, and Democrats* (2000), and *Pragmatic Illusions: The Presidential Politics of John F. Kennedy* (1979). He is currently writing a book on the McGovern insurgency and the transformation of American liberalism.

Michael Nelson teaches courses on U.S. politics, the presidency, and the Constitutional Convention at Rhodes College. In addition, he participates in the college's humanities course entitled The Search for Values in the Light of Western History and Religion. Before joining the Rhodes faculty in 1991, he taught at Vanderbilt University for thirteen years and was the editor of the *Washington Monthly.* His most recent books are *The Presidency and the Political System* (8th ed., 2006), *The Elections of 2004* (2005), *The Evolving Presidency* (2d ed., 2004), *The American Presidency: Origins and Development, 1776–2002* (with Sidney M. Milkis, 4th ed., 2003), *Governing Gambling: Politics and Policy in State, Tribe, and Nation* (with John Lyman Mason, 2001), and *Celebrating the Humanities: A Half Century of the Search Course at Rhodes College* (1996).

David Nichols is associate professor of political science at Baylor University and the author of *The Myth of the Modern Presidency* (1994) and numerous articles on the presidency and constitutional issues. He is currently completing a book on party realignments, presidential leadership, and political community.

Richard M. Pious is the Adolph and Effie Ochs Professor at Barnard College and the Graduate School of Arts and Sciences, Columbia University. He is the author of *The War on Terrorism and Rule of Law* (2006) and *The Oxford Guide to the United States Government* (with John Patrick and Donald Ritchie, 2001). His articles in political science journals and law reviews include studies of legal services for the poor, prerogative power and the presidency, the constitutional law of impeachment, and the public law approach to presidential power.

Stanley A. Renshon is professor of political science at the City University of New York Graduate Center and a certified psychoanalyst. His biography of Bill Clinton, *High Hopes* (1996), won the American Political Science Association's 1997 Richard E. Neustadt Award for best book on the presidency. He also is the author of *In His Father's Shadow: The Transformations of George W. Bush* (2004). His most recent book is *The 50% American: Immigration and National Identity in an Age of Terror* (2005). He is now at work on a book on the Bush Doctrine and American national security policy.

Mark J. Rozell is professor of public policy and the director of the master's in public policy program at George Mason University. He is the author of nine books, including *Power and Prudence: The Presidency of George H. W. Bush* (with Ryan Barilleaux, 2004) and *Executive Privilege: Presidential Power, Secrecy, and Accountability* (2d ed., rev., 2002).

Andrew Rudalevige is associate professor of political science at Dickinson College and a visiting scholar at Princeton University's Center for the Study of Democratic Politics. He is the author of *The New Imperial Presidency: Renewing Presidential Power after Watergate* (2005), which explores presidential-congressional relations since the 1970s, and *Managing the President's Program* (2002), which won the 2003 Richard E. Neustadt Award presented by the American Political Science Association.

Byron E. Shafer is the Hawkins Chair of Political Science at the University of Wisconsin, Madison. Before teaching at Wisconsin, he was the Mellon Professor of American Government at Oxford University. He specializes in the politics of presidential selection and has written extensively about campaigns and elections, political parties, and policy conflicts in American politics. His most recent book is *The Two Majorities and the Puzzle of Modern American Politics* (2003) and his next one is *The End of Southern Exceptionalism: Class, Race, and Partisan Change in the Postwar South*.

Martin Shefter is professor of government at Cornell University and the author of *Politics by Other Means* (with Benjamin Ginsberg, 1999), *Political Parties and the State* (1994), and *Political Crisis/Fiscal Crisis: The Collapse and Revival of New York City* (1992). He is the editor of *Shaped by War and Trade* (with Ira Katznelson, 2002) and *Capital of the American Century* (1993).

Stephen Skowronek is the Pelatiah Perit Professor of Political Science at Yale University. He has written extensively about American political development and the American presidency, including *The Politics Presidents Make: Leadership from John Adams to Bill Clinton* (1997).

Bartholomew H. Sparrow is associate professor of government at the University of Texas. He is the author of *Emergence of Empire: The "Insular Cases" and the Territorial Expansion of the United States* (2006), *Uncertain Guardians: The News Media as a Political Institution* (1999), *From the Outside In: World War II and the American State* (1996), and numerous articles and book chapters. He is coeditor of *Politics, Discourse, and American Society: New Agendas* (with Roderick Hart, 2001).

Keith E. Whittington is professor of politics at Princeton University. He has published widely on American constitutional theory and development, federalism, judicial politics, and the presidency. He is the author of *Political Foundations of Judicial Supremacy* (forthcoming).

David A. Yalof is associate professor of political science at the University of Connecticut. His first book, *Pursuit of Justices: Presidential Politics and the Selection of Supreme Court Nominees* (1999), won the 2000 Richard E. Neustadt Award as the best book on the presidency from the American Political Science Association. His articles on connections between the branches of government have appeared in, among other publications, *Political Research Quarterly, Judicature,* and *Constitutional Commentary.* He is currently completing a book on the politics of investigating executive branch officials in the absence of an independent counsel.

RESOLVED, the framers of the Constitution would approve of the modern presidency

PRO: David Nichols

CON: Terri Bimes

Americans are supposedly a forward-looking people, devotees of progress who have scant respect for traditions or customs. But, at least when it comes to politics and government, Americans are, arguably, the most backward-looking people on the face of the earth. What other nation spends so much time trying to decipher the intentions of people who lived more than two centuries ago? Few people in Great Britain, France, or Germany care about what politicians of the far distant past would say about today's political debates. Nobody in England asks, "What would Pitt the Younger say?" Even fewer care what George III would say. But Americans care a great deal about what James Madison, Alexander Hamilton, and the other "founders" would say about the ways in which Americans order their political lives.

One reason Americans care is that the United States, unlike Britain, has a written constitution that is a touchstone for how it resolves legal and political disputes. In deciding constitutional questions, federal and state judges regularly rely on the words of the framers to decipher the meaning of the Constitution. Politicians, too, frequently appeal to the framers to support their interpretations of what is and is not constitutional. Those who wish to defend or indict a contemporary practice, whether it be the Senate's filibuster or prayer in public schools, reach for the framers.

The Constitutional Convention was conducted in the summer of 1787 behind closed doors—no cameras, no reporters, no observers. The fifty-five delegates were sworn to secrecy. One might think this secrecy would make it difficult for anyone to say today what the framers had in mind when they were creating the Constitution. But, fortunately, the convention was blessed with an energetic young member who was determined to leave a detailed record of the proceedings. Every day that the convention was in session, Virginia's James Madison sat directly below the president's chair, facing the delegates and taking detailed notes of what they said. Every evening, he would write out the notes he had scribbled down during the day. It was a labor, he said, that almost killed him; yet it was also a labor that succeeded in bringing the framers' deliberations to life for subsequent generations.

Even with Madison's heroic labors, the task of determining what the framers intended remains difficult. To begin with, "the framers" were hardly a unified group. They were a diverse collection of individuals with many different ideas and interests. Some were slaveholders; some abhorred slavery. Some were wealthy; some were of modest means. Some favored democracy; others feared the masses. Moreover, whose intent matters the most? Is it the intent of the fifty-five men who attended the convention or only that of the thirty-nine who signed the document? Or should the intent of the hundreds of delegates at the state ratifying conventions matter the most? Or should the intent as interpreted by the most articulate or the most prolific of the framers be accorded special importance? New York's Alexander Hamilton, who penned the essays in *The Federalist Papers* that focus on the presidency, is often read as the authoritative framer, but he missed well over half of the convention's proceedings.[1]

Complicating matters still further, the decisions reached in the convention often were not what any delegate or group of delegates intended. Many decisions were the product of compromise and bargaining. Such decisions might be defended and rationalized after the fact, but, as the political theorist Michael Walzer points out, they reflected, as political decisions often do, "the balance of forces, not the weight of arguments."[2]

David Nichols and Terri Bimes are well aware of the difficulties in ascertaining a single intent, but in their pro and con arguments they gamely try to reconstruct as best they can what the framers believed about the presidency. According to Nichols, the framers envisioned a strong and democratic presidency. Although he does not ignore the undeniable differences between the presidency of 1787 and the presidency of today, Nichols argues that today's presidency is a natural outgrowth of the presidency created by the framers. Bimes's understanding of the framers' intent is diametrically opposed. In crucial respects, she argues, the modern presidency is unrecognizable from the relatively weak office intended by the framers. They would neither recognize nor approve of the office that exists today. Short of bringing Madison, Hamilton, and the rest of framers back from the grave, this is not a question that can be answered definitively. But it is a question that Americans will certainly continue to ask.

PRO: David Nichols

The framers of the Constitution would approve of the modern presidency, because to a great extent they created it. The essential elements of that presidency—executive discretion, legislative leadership, a substantial administrative apparatus directed by the president, and the president's role as popular leader[1]—originated in the institutional arrangements and incentives the framers established in Article II of the Constitution. Important changes in society and technology, as well as in the size, scope, and purpose of government, have occurred since the time of the founders, but these changes only accentuate the importance of a powerful popular president to the successful operation of the U.S. constitutional system.

A common assumption among presidential scholars is that the Constitution, reflecting the founders' fear of monarchy, created a relatively weak chief executive or, at most, provided a vague outline of the office that would only be filled in by history. The debates that surrounded the creation of the presidency reveal, however, a different and more complex picture.

The men who gathered in Philadelphia in the summer of 1787 had learned much about the problems of democratic government in the eleven years since the signing of the Declaration of Independence. Among other things, they had learned that overthrowing British rule was only the first step toward establishing a free and independent nation. Such a nation required a competent government, and the Articles of Confederation were inadequate to the task. The equal representation of the states in the Continental Congress, the requirement that major structural changes receive unanimous approval, and the inability of Congress to levy taxes were all important defects of the Articles, but perhaps their most fundamental flaw was the absence of a mechanism to enforce decisions of the national government. There was no national executive authority under the Articles, and from the beginning of the Constitutional Convention most delegates agreed that an independent executive was essential to the success of a new constitution.

None of the delegates entered the convention with a definite plan for accomplishing this goal. Many were not fully aware of the enormity of the task, and even by the end of the convention most did not appreciate the originality and scope of their invention. The presidency evolved gradually over the course of three months of debate. This debate focused on specific practical problems involving the structure of the executive, and it occurred in the context of a host of other debates, not the least of which were states' rights and slavery. The creation of the presidency required compromise and improvisation. Through this process, however, a deeper and more complex understanding of executive power emerged, so that by the end of the process the framers were able to deliver a new institution to the world—the popular modern presidency.

The Virginia Plan provided the starting point for the debate on the executive. It called for the creation of a national executive that would be elected by the legislature for an undetermined number of years. The executive would receive a fixed salary, would be ineligible for reelection, would possess a general authority to execute the national laws, would enjoy the executive rights vested in Congress by the Articles of Confederation, and, together with "a convenient number" of the national judiciary, would form a council of revision with the power to veto all laws subject to override by a vote of the legislature.[2]

This plan was only an outline—it did not even specify the number of executives. Edmund Randolph of Virginia wanted a plural executive, claiming that a unitary executive would be the "fetus of monarchy." Roger Sherman of Connecticut argued that because the executive was to be a servant of the legislature, the legislature should be free to determine the number of executives it desired at any time. No other delegate, however, agreed with Sherman. Even Randolph stressed that the executive must be independent of the legislature.[3]

What powers would this independent executive possess? Article II does not present an extensive list of specific powers, but this has more to do with the framers' understanding of the character of executive power than with any desire to create a weak presidency. Article I begins, "All legislative Powers *herein granted* shall be vested in a Congress . . ." (emphasis added), whereas Article II begins, "The executive Power shall be vested in a President. . . ." Legislative powers could be enumerated in the Constitution, but the executive power could not be so easily delineated. The legislature makes laws, or general rules, but the executive must implement these laws in an infinite number of possible circumstances. No rule can cover all cases, the framers realized. That is why an independent executive was needed.

The framers did, however, recognize that the president would need assistance. Some delegates suggested that the Constitution include a list of officers who would help the president to carry out the law. They wanted there to be no doubt but that the president was to be the head of the administrative offices of the government.[4] But their proposal was rejected because it might interfere with executive independence. It was feared that constitutionally created offices would undermine the unity of the executive branch. The president was to be the only constitutional officer responsible for the execution of the laws. The framers, then, created the structure of an executive branch under the direction of a president, leaving later presidents to expand it as the times required.

The framers' understanding of executive power is most apparent in two of the powers listed at the beginning of Article II, Section 2: the commander in chief power and the pardoning power. The commander in chief power involves the use of force, and the pardoning power involves the need for discretion. Together, these two provisions are a good description of executive power. Because of its many members, Congress is not suited to quick action, and because it makes laws that must apply to all citizens, it does not have the discretion to deal with particular circumstances. Force and discretion are the essence of executive power. Congress has often complained about the executive's unilateral use of force or discretion, but when President George Washington issued a Proclamation of Neutrality during the war between Great Britain and France in 1793, he understood the place of executive discretion in the Constitution, and when he led the militia in 1794 against an uprising by farmers in western Pennsylvania against a federal tax on liquor and distilled drinks (it was known as the Whiskey Rebellion), he understood the need for forceful action. The framers did not want the president to be a servant of Congress.

The framers also wanted the president to play an independent role in the legislative process. The Virginia Plan had called for the executive to share the veto power with the judiciary, but the convention delegates excluded judges because they feared such a scheme would undercut executive responsibility and independence. They wanted a president who could stand up to Congress and thereby play an active role in the legislative process.

The framers also specified that the president "shall from time to time give to the Congress Information of the State of the Union, and recommend to their Consideration such Measures as he shall judge necessary and expedient." The initial version of this provision began with the word *may* rather than *shall*. The change was made at the suggestion of Gouverneur Morris, a delegate from Pennsylvania who wanted to ensure that the president would play an active role in the legislative process. If recommending legislation was merely an option, a president might be reluctant to do so for fear of arousing the jealousy of the legislature. By making it mandatory, the framers enabled presidents to defend their actions as an obligation of their office.

Their constitutionally prescribed authority to help to set the agenda at the beginning of the legislative process and their right to cast a veto at the end of that process have enabled presidents to exert tremendous legislative influence. Not all presidents have taken full advantage of this potential, but it exists because of the efforts of the framers.

Although they concede that the framers wanted an independent president, most scholars have concluded that the framers did not want a popularly elected one. Early in the Constitutional Convention, James Wilson of Pennsylvania called for the popular election of the president, claiming that it was necessary to guarantee executive independence from the legislature.[5] But during most of the convention, a majority of the delegates supported legislative election.

Political scientist Charles Thach has argued that the preference for legislative election was based more on the fears of the small states than on any theory of executive power. The small states supported legislative selection, because they thought it would give them more power than they would have in a direct popular election. They hoped to use their control of the Senate to veto any candidate of whom they disapproved. However, when the delegates turned their attention to the specific mechanism for legislative election of the president, it became clear that a majority supported a joint vote of the House and the Senate. Because the influence of the small states would be greatly diminished in such an election, the small states became open to a compromise.[6]

The compromise was, of course, the electoral college. The idea of an electoral college was first introduced by James Wilson on June 2, who saw it as only a minor modification of his plan for a direct popular election. Recent commentators, however, often portray the electoral college as a product of the framers' distrust of democracy. They go on to argue that if the framers distrusted democracy, they certainly would not approve of what is arguably the most important element of the modern presidency—popular leadership.

To be sure, some convention delegates did speak disparagingly of popular election. George Mason of Virginia said, "It would be as unnatural to refer the choice of a proper character for chief magistrate to the people, as it would be to refer a trial of colors to a blind man."[7] Roger Sherman of Connecticut said the people would be ill-informed, and South Carolinian Charles Cotesworth Pinckney complained that the people would be led by a few "active and designing men."[8] None of these delegates, however, supported the electoral college; they were all proponents of legislative election. It was the delegates who defended the principle of popular election, such as James Madison, James Wilson, and Gouverneur Morris, who were the prime supporters of the electoral college.

If these framers supported popular election, then why (apart from Wilson) did they not favor direct popular election? The reason was the need for compromise on two issues not directly related to executive power: federalism and slavery. Because the number of electors each state received in the electoral college would be based on the number of representatives and senators from a state, the small states would have a little more weight in the electoral college than they would in a direct popular election. The desire to protect the interests of their states, not distrust of democracy, motivated these delegates.

Madison also argued that the different election laws in the states made direct popular election virtually impossible.[9] Madison was gently reminding the delegates that direct popular election would reopen the question of slavery and potentially rip the convention apart.[10] The South wanted its entire slave population to count in apportioning seats in the House of Representatives, whereas the northern states argued that because the South did not recognize the rights of slaves as human beings slaves should not count for purposes of apportionment. The Three-Fifths Compromise allowed the South to gain some representation in Congress based on its slave population, but no such compromise would be possible in a direct popular election of the president. Either the South would lose a substantial part of its power in the election because its slaves could not vote, or it would have to allow its slaves to vote. Neither option was acceptable to the South. The electoral college, however, incorporated the Three-Fifths Compromise into the selection of the president, because it based the number of electors for each state on the size of its congressional delegation.

One can debate the merits of the Three-Fifths Compromise, but its importance to the creation of the electoral college cannot be ignored. The electoral college represented the best approximation of direct popular election the framers could achieve considering the political realties they faced. The framers who were the most influential in creating the electoral college wanted a popular election, and, in practice, that is what they got. Presidential electors have seldom exercised any independent judgment—and never in a way that affected the outcome of an election. The electors have been a conduit for, not a filter of, popular opinion.

The most far-sighted of the founders, Gouverneur Morris, understood the potential for popular leadership inherent in the constitutional presidency: "The Executive Magistrate should be the guardian of the people, even the lower classes, against Legislative tyranny, against the great and the wealthy who in the course of things will necessarily compose—the Legislative body. . . . The Executive therefore ought to be constituted as to be the great protector of the mass of the people."[11]

Morris also predicted the rise of political parties, explaining that two parties would soon form, one in support of the president and one in opposition. Not all of the framers were as prescient as Morris, and even he undoubtedly would find many aspects of modern American politics strange and disagreeable. But the framers were the first to see the need for a powerful, popularly elected executive in a modern republic, and they would certainly approve of the modern presidency they did so much to create.

CON: Terri Bimes

The job description of the modern president revolves around three central domestic roles: chief legislator, popular leader, and chief executive of the federal bureaucracy. Today, presidents are expected to offer extensive domestic legislative programs, which then become the basis for Congress's agenda. When President Dwight D. Eisenhower decided not to propose a legislative package in 1953, he was broadly criticized for falling short of the standard set by Presidents Franklin D. Roosevelt and Harry S. Truman. In pursuit of their programs, presidents now routinely barnstorm the country, delivering speeches to all manner of audiences. Indeed, "going public"—the strategy of rousing the people to put pressure on Congress to enact the president's priorities—has become a routine feature of the modern presidency.[1] Finally, modern presidents lead the immense federal bureaucracy, which provides the substantial resources needed to launch presidential initiatives independent of Congress. Within that bureaucracy, a "presidential branch" has emerged that is especially responsive to an administration's priorities. Executive orders and other mechanisms are increasingly being used to shape bureaucratic decision making. None of these three central roles of the modern presidency is spelled out in the Constitution. The framers would certainly be surprised at what they have wrought.

In fact, the Constitution says very little about executive power. The "vesting clause" of Article II states that "the executive Power shall be vested in a President of the United States of America." It is followed by a list of specific presidential powers. In the domestic policy realm, the most important are the duty to report on the state of the Union to Congress from time to time, to recommend "necessary and expedient" legislation to Congress, and to nominate officers to the various departments with the approval of the Senate. As spelled out in Article I, the president also is empowered to veto legislation, subject to override by a two-thirds majority of each chamber. This terse description of executive power constitutes the extent to which the Constitution gave the nation's first presidents formal guidance on domestic policy making.

This scarcity of guidance is not surprising, however. The debates at the Constitutional Convention focused more on how presidents would be selected than on the proper scope of presidential power. This emphasis likely reflected the delegates' view that the legislature would be the most powerful branch of government, at least in domestic policy making. As noted in *Federalist* No. 51 by James Madison, "the legislative authority necessarily predominates" in a republic.[2] The legislative branch enjoyed two critical advantages: its close ties to the people and its authority to make laws. Thus the most important question of executive design was how to provide a mode of election that ensured some independence from Congress, while still leaving the president accountable to the public. The obvious answer—popular election—was advocated by a handful of the founders—notably James Wilson and Gouverneur Morris—but it was widely regarded as impractical. In the view of most of the founders, the people would be unable to judge candidates for the presidency and would have trouble agreeing on a single candidate. Election of the president by the legislature was repeatedly, if controversially, approved by the Constitutional Convention, but this plan foundered upon a basic dilemma: unless the president was ineligible for reelection, legislative selection would give presidents a strong incentive to defer to congressional whims in the hope of securing another term. Yet limiting each president to a single term was inadvisable, because reelection was regarded as a vital incentive for good behavior by the president.

The electoral college emerged as the solution: it gave the president a power base independent of Congress, while providing a measure of accountability. Although several of the founders expected the ultimate selection of the president to often end up in the hands of the House of Representatives (the Constitution-mandated solution when a single candidate failed to obtain a majority in the electoral college), this mode of election afforded at least a partial barrier to legislative domination of the president. The electoral college also solved the dispute between large and small states by granting each state a number of electors equal to its representatives and senators.

The president's role as popular leader was not at stake in these debates. By delegating the decision on how electors would be chosen to each state legislature, the framers neither precluded nor required a substantial role for ordinary voters in selecting the president. In the first presidential election in 1788, the state legislatures divided equally on the issue of how popular the presidential vote should be. Six states (Delaware, Maryland, Massachusetts, New Hampshire, Pennsylvania, and Virginia) opted for various sorts of direct popular election of electors, and five states (Connecticut, Georgia, New Jersey, New York, and South Carolina) opted for legislative appointment of electors.[3] Thus the framers' endorsement of the electoral college cannot be interpreted as a stamp of approval for modern popular presidential leadership.

It is highly unlikely that even the two main supporters of popular election, Gouverneur Morris and James Wilson, envisioned the president going out on the hustings to rally voter support. Instead, Morris and Wilson conceived of the president as a "patriot king"—that is, as a leader who would rise above politics and not engage in aggressive popular leadership appeals. Morris described the president as the "guardian of the people" and the "great protector of the people" against legislative tyranny.[4] Wilson, in his defense of the executive at the Pennsylvania convention held to consider ratification of the Constitution, contended that the president would "watch over the whole with paternal care and affection."[5] Meanwhile, throughout *The Federalist Papers* Hamilton and Madison described campaigning as the "art" of flattering prejudice and distracting people from their true interests.[6] In *Federalist* No. 10, for example, Madison argued that a large republic would make it more difficult for "unworthy candidates to practice with success the vicious arts by which elections are too often carried."[7] In *Federalist* No. 71, Hamilton lamented that, although "the arts of men" can delude the people, the executive would be their "guardian," rescuing them from the "fatal consequences of their own mistakes."[8] The president would not respond to "every sudden breeze of passion," but instead would take a more reflective view of the public good. In short, these framers portrayed the executive as a trustee who exercises his own judgment rather than as a delegate who slavishly follows the opinions of the people.

Most of the framers supported a more limited conception of executive power than Morris, Wilson, and Hamilton. Certainly many of the convention delegates would have been uncomfortable with the notion of the president as a guardian protecting the public interest against legislative excesses. Distrust of executive power still ran deep in a nation that had only recently fought a war against the British king. But there was no disagreement among the framers that the role of Congress was to initiate legislation and that presidents would not actively cultivate mass support in order to pressure Congress to cater to their priorities. The supporters and opponents of a strong executive agreed on this much.

Although the framers anticipated a more direct role for the president in leading the executive branch, their conception of presidential administrative leadership was limited when judged by the standards of the modern presidency. At first, convention delegates granted the power to make appointments, one of the president's most important tools in controlling the bureaucracy, to the Senate. But toward the end of the convention that idea fell by the wayside, in part because the Senate now represented states rather than population. The convention voted instead to give the power of appointment to the president, preserving an important role for the Senate in providing "advice and consent." As historian Jack N. Rakove has noted, "The growth of the presidency owed more to doubts about the Senate than to the enthusiasm with which Hamilton, Morris, and Wilson endorsed the virtues of energetic administration."[9] In *Federalist* No. 51, Madison clarified why the president and the Senate were linked in this manner, explaining that the "qualified connection between this weaker department [the executive] and the weaker branch of the stronger department [the Senate]" would enable "the latter . . . to support the constitutional rights of the former, without being too much detached from the rights of its own department."[10] The presidency needed the support of the Senate, because otherwise it would lack the firmness to withstand the initiatives of the House, the more popular legislative branch.[11]

In summary, the framers anticipated a division of powers in which Congress would be the leading legislative force and the president would provide a limited check. The House would be the branch closest to the people, and as such would have a critical advantage in battles with the president. As a trustee for the nation, the president would not be entirely divorced from the people, nor would he wield public opinion as a weapon in institutional or policy battles. Even in the area of administration, where the president had the appointment power, the framers expected close consultation and cooperation with the Senate to be the norm.

The modern presidency has overturned each of these expectations. Strains in the founders' model could be seen even in the conduct of the first presidents, but for the most part George Washington and his immediate successors sought to abide by the model of the restrained patriot king.[12] Washington played a vital role in defining appropriate presidential behavior, helping to resolve some of the ambiguities left by the framers. In many ways, Washington was the republican embodiment of a "patriot king." His two tours of the country as president were not the modern-day campaign swings in which presidents kiss babies and shake hands.[13] Rather, great formality and aloofness marked these affairs. Washington also stuck to a script devoid of comment on public policy issues, and his remarks were strictly ceremonial. The most common criticism of the tours was that they were "monarchical" in nature—more befitting a king than an elected president. Partly as a result of such criticism, Washington's successors generally did not go out on tour and assiduously avoided monarchical gestures. Above all, the first generation of presidents generally steered clear of explicit appeals to the public to support their policies.

In the capital, Washington often entertained public visitors, but these events, or levees as they were called, resembled his tours of the country. Washington stood at the fireplace and greeted each visitor with a bow. After making some brief remarks, he then resumed his place in front of the fireplace and each visitor then bowed to the president as he or she left the room.[14] By holding these levees, Washington acknowledged that it was important for the president to be accessible to the public. At the same time, the regal choreography of the event imposed a respectful distance between the president and the people.

Even Washington's one bold public appeal, which appeared in his Farewell Address, showed the vitality of the patriot leadership model. In the address, Washington dealt with the rise of political parties—entities that are crucial to the operation of the modern presidency but were disparaged by the framers.

Even though by the end of his administration Washington had cast his lot with the Hamiltonian Federalists and against the Jeffersonian Republicans, he used this stance of nonpartisanship to attack those who opposed his administration's foreign policy. He warned Americans about a "small but artful and enterprising minority of the community" who sought to replace the "delegated will of the nation" with the "will of party."[15] The fact that Washington attacked the Jeffersonian Republicans in the language of nonpartisanship reveals the power of the patriot king model in the early republic. It is also noteworthy that Washington waited until he was leaving office to launch an explicitly political attack in an address that is now widely regarded as a "campaign document."[16] Only then could he offer such criticisms without appearing to promote his own self-interest.[17]

The early presidents were also circumscribed in how they practiced legislative leadership. The president was expected to leave most of the initiative and maneuvering of the legislative process to Congress. Even when the president and his allies lobbied for legislation, they used "hidden-hand" leadership techniques that were consistent with the norm that made it unacceptable for the president to aggressively push his program through Congress.[18] Thomas Jefferson, for example, drafted bills behind the scenes and had members of Congress introduce them as their own. He also quietly appointed floor leaders to be his personal lieutenants in Congress, directed cabinet members to act as political liaisons with Congress, lobbied members of both parties at White House dinners, and anonymously penned editorials supporting his administration's policies in the official government newspaper.[19] The Federalists attacked Jefferson for his backstage dominance of Congress, but Jefferson's public deference to the legislature limited the damage.

Finally, in part because the federal bureaucracy was so small, the president's administrative role was limited in the early Republic. The general expectation was that departments would be staffed by people chosen for their good character and that they would serve during good behavior. Even Jefferson, who took office after the acrimonious election of 1800, did not purge many Federalists from the bureaucracy. John Quincy Adams, one of the last presidents to adhere to this character-based norm when staffing the bureaucracy, promised in his inaugural address to base his appointments on "talent and virtue alone."[20] With the election of Andrew Jackson in 1828 came an avowedly partisan approach to administration. Bureaucratic appointments would now be distributed on the basis of party loyalty and service. But this partisan approach did not necessarily empower the White House. Instead, presidents became brokers, forced to respond to the aggressive patronage demands of state and local party organizations. Not until the twentieth century did presidents begin to build an extensive bureaucratic apparatus that they could control, the Executive Office of the President. The rise of presidential administration has been a relatively recent process, not something foreordained by the Constitution.[21]

In general, then, the most important features of the modern presidency were neither anticipated nor desired by the founders. They did not want or expect the president to become the chief legislator, setting much of Congress's agenda. Nor did they want or expect the president to be a public opinion leader, aggressively rallying the people to the administration's side in battles with the legislative branch. Nor, finally, did they desire or anticipate that the president would become the leader of an extensive administrative apparatus. These elements of the modern presidency, which took shape over many decades, have created an office that neither the founders nor early presidents would recognize, let alone embrace.

2

RESOLVED, political parties should nominate candidates for the presidency through a national primary

PRO: Michael Nelson

CON: Andrew E. Busch

Americans celebrate that the United States has had the same constitution for nearly its entire history: more than two centuries and counting. No other democracy in the world can make the same claim. But constitutional stability does not mean the nation has undergone no fundamental institutional changes. Indeed, some American institutions have been characterized by almost perpetual change. Nowhere is that truer than elections—specifically, the ways in which political parties nominate presidential candidates.

The framers were smart men, but they did not foresee the rise of political parties. They anticipated that the electoral college would both nominate and select presidential candidates. Yet almost as soon as the Constitution went into effect, it became clear that this system would not work. Groups with common interests and values must be able to come together and agree on a candidate. If they were unable to do so, their votes would be spread among too many candidates, and they would lose the election to those groups that had agreed to direct all their votes toward a single candidate.

The first nominating process centered in Congress. Each party's members of Congress got together and decided who would be their party's nominee. But almost as soon as the congressional caucus system emerged, it began to attract criticism. That criticism intensified when the Federalist Party went into decline, leaving the Jeffersonian Republicans as the only national party.

Nomination became equivalent to election. Onlookers complained that the congressional "King Caucus" was undemocratic, because it was conducted by just a few individuals behind closed doors. Moreover, they pointed out that legislators had no business nominating presidential candidates.

In 1824 the congressional caucus system fell apart. Dissatisfaction with the caucus's choice, Secretary of the Treasury William H. Crawford, propelled state legislatures to nominate their own favorite son candidates, including John Quincy Adams of Massachusetts, Henry Clay of Kentucky, and Andrew Jackson of Tennessee—all Democratic-Republicans. The result was a fractured general election in which the winner of the popular vote—Jackson—failed to receive a majority of the electoral vote and the election was sent to the House of Representatives. Clay then threw his support to Adams, and Adams prevailed on the first ballot. Three days later, Adams chose Clay to be his secretary of state, igniting charges that the new president had made a "corrupt bargain" with Clay. The outrage was aimed not only at Adams and Clay but also at the nominating system that had made the election of Adams possible.

The congressional caucus system was soon replaced by national nominating conventions. In 1831 and 1832, the National Republicans (soon to become the Whigs) and the Democrats followed the lead of the Anti-Masons in holding national nominating conventions made up of delegates from each state. Although more inclusive than the congressional caucus system, the conventions were made up of delegates selected by the state parties, not by popular vote. The conventions were often long, contentious affairs, especially those in the Democratic Party, which required its presidential nominee to receive at least a two-thirds vote of the delegates (this requirement remained in place until 1936). In 1924 the Democrats met for eighteen days and endured 103 ballots before nominating John W. Davis, who was promptly thrashed in the general election by the Republican nominee, Calvin Coolidge.

In the early twentieth century, the national convention system came under attack for being undemocratic and corrupt. Reform was in the air again—this time in the call for presidential primaries that would enable voters to have a direct say in selecting the parties' nominees. In the 1912 election, twelve states, including California, Illinois, Massachusetts, New Jersey, Ohio, and Pennsylvania, held primaries. Former president Theodore Roosevelt's challenge of President William Howard Taft for the Republican nomination generated intense excitement. In virtually every primary state, Roosevelt defeated Taft, including in Taft's home state of Ohio. Although Taft won the nomination anyway because his allies controlled the convention, his victory was an empty one. In the general election, Taft received only 23 percent of the popular vote and 1.5 percent of the electoral vote. He finished a distant third behind the winner, Democrat Woodrow Wilson, and Roosevelt, who ran at the head of the Progressive Party.

Unlike the 1824 election, the 1912 election did not transform the way presidential elections were conducted. Despite calls by prominent national figures, including President Wilson, for a national primary, the parties decided to retain the national nominating convention. Primaries were still held, but as late as the 1960s they remained a subordinate part of the nominating process. A primary occasionally played an important role in demonstrating a candidate's strength—in 1948, for example, Thomas E. Dewey's victory over Harold E. Stassen in the Oregon primary helped to secure Dewey the Republican nomination. Still, winning primaries was no guarantee of victory. In 1952, for example, Adlai E. Stevenson II did not enter a single primary, and yet he secured the Democratic Party's nomination anyway, besting Estes Kefauver, who had received two-thirds of the votes cast in Democratic primaries.

Not until 1972 did primaries become the linchpin of the nominating process. As primary voters displaced party officials in selecting the parties' presidential nominees, the national convention ceased to be the theater in which the nominating process played itself out. This transformation led to yet more change. After the triumph of the largely unknown Democratic nominee, former governor Jimmy Carter, in 1976 and his defeat by another former governor, Republican Ronald Reagan, in 1980, Democrats changed their rules to ensure that around one-seventh of convention delegates (dubbed "superdelegates") would be state governors and members of Congress and the Democratic National Committee.

A more consequential change has been that states, jockeying for advantage in the selection process, have advanced the dates of their primaries and caucuses to earlier in the election year, creating the "front-loading" that Michael Nelson and Andrew Busch discuss. Both Nelson and Busch agree that front-loading is a problem. They disagree, however, about what should be done about it. Nelson favors a national primary; Busch opposes such a plan. It is difficult to say whether a national primary is in the nation's future, but one thing is certain: the nominating process will continue to change, sometimes dramatically and often unexpectedly.

PRO: Michael Nelson

How about this for an idea? Because we Americans have to elect a president every fourth November, let's choose the Democratic and Republican nominees eight or nine months earlier, in February or March, when most voters aren't paying much attention. Let's start the process in two small, rural, nearly all-white states—Iowa and New Hampshire would be perfect—and give them the power to weed out all but a couple candidates from each party so that voters in the rest of the country don't have so many choices. Then, before we've had a chance to learn much about even these few candidates, let's get as many other states into the game as we can in the shortest time possible. And because there's no real way to keep score in such an accelerated and far-flung contest, let's trust the news media to decide who's winning, who's losing, and who isn't even worth paying attention to. Then, after we know who the nominees are, let's sit back and relax for half a year, until September when the final campaign begins. If during that time we learn things about one or both major-party candidates that make us want to change our minds and nominate someone else, let's stick with them anyway.

Bad idea, right? Considering the stakes—the choice of the two finalists for the most powerful job in the world—no one ever would adopt such an approach if given the choice. And, the truth is, no one ever did. The current system for nominating presidential candidates is one that the United States stumbled into blindly.

It happened like this. In the early 1970s, both parties decided that every state's delegates to the presidential nominating conventions should be chosen through a process in which the rank-and-file members of each party can participate. In practice, that meant choosing the delegates through either primaries or caucuses. (In a primary, one votes by secret ballot; in a caucus, one attends a meeting and votes openly.) New Hampshire, which began holding the first primary of the election year in 1952, when primaries were unimportant, now found itself in the privileged position of holding the first primary when primaries were very important. Iowa quickly jumped to the head of a different line, becoming the earliest caucus state and voting even before New Hampshire.

Both states have reaped the harvest of going first ever since. Nearly all the candidates campaign endlessly in Iowa and New Hampshire, promising them the moon (or in cornfield-laden Iowa's case, ethanol subsidies) and infusing their economies with huge doses of campaign spending. The news media also camp out for months in Iowa and New Hampshire and, depending on how scholars do the counting, devote between one-fourth and three-fourths of their coverage of the entire nominating process to these two small states.[1] A candidate who does not win Iowa or New Hampshire has hardly any chance of being nominated, and candidates who do not finish in the top three are finished, regardless of how popular they may be elsewhere in the country.

Iowa and New Hampshire deserve credit for quickly figuring out what most other states realized only slowly: the earlier a state votes, the more influence it has in the nominating process and the more benefits it derives.[2] For a time, California and New Jersey held their primaries in June, at the very end of the process, thinking that going last would make them the decisive states. Instead, it made them irrelevant, because the winners were determined weeks or even months before. Eventually, succumbing to "New Hampshire envy,"[3] nearly every state advanced its primary or caucus to as close to the start of the year as possible, a process called "front-loading." In the 1972 election, the first held under the reformed nominating system, 17 percent of delegates had been chosen by the first Tuesday in April. In the 2004 election, 80 percent were.[4]

Faced with the current mess, some thoughtful observers want to try to undo the reforms of the early 1970s and revive the nominating process that existed during most of the nineteenth and twentieth centuries. "Under the old system," writes *Washington Post* columnist David Broder, "running for president involved taking a few months off from your public office in the election year to present your credentials largely to political peers—other officeholders, party leaders, leaders of allied interest groups—and then persuade them that you were best qualified to carry the party banner." As it happened, argues political scientist Jeane Kirkpatrick, the qualities those "political peers" were looking for were the very qualities that made for good presidents: "the ability to deal with diverse groups, ability to work out compromises and develop consensus, and the ability to impress people who have watched a candidate over many years."[5]

All this may sound good, but, unfortunately, nostalgia more than history marks these and similar accounts of the prereform system. Writing in the late nineteenth century, James Bryce noted in his classic book *The American Commonwealth* that party professionals indeed had a talent for choosing electable candidates. But he also felt compelled to explain "Why Great Men Are Not Chosen President" in terms of that very talent: "It must be remembered that the merits of a President are one thing and those of a candidate another thing. . . . It will be a misfortune to the party, as well as to the country, if the candidate elected should prove a bad President. But it is a greater misfortune to the party that it should be beaten in the impending election, for the evil of losing national patronage will have come four years sooner."[6]

The indifference of party professionals to nominating good presidents extended to an occasional inability to weed out dangerous ones. Of the presidents from William Howard Taft onward analyzed by James David Barber in his study *The Presidential Character,* four of the eleven who were nominated under the old rules (Woodrow Wilson, Herbert C. Hoover, Lyndon B. Johnson, and Richard Nixon) fell into the category of "active-negatives"—that is, persons who tended to turn political crises into personal crises and "persevere in a disastrous policy." Only three of the eleven—Franklin D. Roosevelt, Harry S. Truman, and John F. Kennedy—qualified as "active-positives," or leaders with "personal strengths specially attuned to the presidency." The other four presidents were mediocre—or, in Barber's terminology, "passive"—presidents.[7] So much for the party professionals' much vaunted talent for peer review.

Even the party pros' ability to choose electable candidates may have been overstated. Bryce wrote at a time of unusually close electoral competition. But in the twentieth century, twelve of the eighteen presidential elections held before the reforms of the early 1970s were landslides in which the loser won less than half as many electoral votes as the winner. At least one set of party pros in each of these elections must have poorly judged their candidate's electability. In all, then, the good old days of the past were no better than the bad new days of the present, at least when it comes to nominating candidates for president.

Fortunately, Americans are not bound by either the past or the present—they can shape the future. In designing a new presidential nominating process, two criteria should be foremost in our thinking: simplicity and clarity.

To be sure, complexity in a political system need not mean that it is undemocratic, just as simplicity and clarity alone do not guarantee a democratic process. For example, a lottery drawing would be a clear, simple, and awful method for nominating a presidential candidate. The Constitution, by contrast, is a complex system of "separated institutions sharing powers," in which citizens exercise limited authority, chiefly by voting in elections.[8]

In the design of the presidential nominating process, however, Americans are squarely in the center of that domain in which citizens get to exercise their limited authority, and that is where simplicity and clarity come in. As Henry Mayo argues in *Introduction to Democratic Theory,* "If [the] purpose of the election is to be carried out—to enable the voter to share in political power—the voter's job must not be made difficult and confusing for him. It ought, on the contrary, to be made as simple as the electoral machinery can be devised to make it."[9] In other words, whenever the Constitution opens the door to citizens, walking through it should be a clear and simple process.

Federalism, like complexity, is another vital constitutional principle that is irrelevant to the presidential nominating process. The states not only are constitutionally sovereign in their own domain, but also are embedded in Congress, where the people are represented according to where they live. Although the president, uniquely among elected officials, is meant to represent the entire country, federalism is even woven into the electoral college, in which presidential candidates seek electoral votes state by state. Federalism does not need to be entrenched in the nominating process as well.

The best way to remedy the problems with the current nominating process and replace it with one that is clear and simple (as well as democratic and practical) is to create a national primary.

Here is how a national primary could work. Any candidate trying to get on the Republican or Democratic national primary ballot would have until June of the election year to round up valid signatures equal in number to 1 percent of the turnout in the most recent presidential election (around 1.2 million in 2008). Each party's rank-and-file supporters would be eligible to vote for their party's nominee. The primary itself would be held on the first Tuesday in August—that is, voters across the country would all go to the polls on the same day. If none of a party's candidates receives 50 percent of the vote, a runoff election between the top two candidates would be held three weeks later. The national party conventions would meet soon afterward to approve the vice-presidential candidates, write party rules, adopt their platforms, and hear the nominees' acceptance speeches.

Most of the specific elements of this proposal are subject to tinkering. Perhaps independent voters could be eligible to vote in the primary of their choice. The 1 percent requirement could be a little higher or lower, so long as it is high enough to screen out frivolous candidates but not so high as to screen out serious ones. A further variation could make the 1 percent rule mandatory in a minimum number of states as well as nationwide. The date of the primary could be a little earlier than August. Forty percent could be defined as sufficient for victory. The conventions could take a different form. Because none of these variations would alter the essential nature of the national primary, any or all of them would be fine.

The national primary is not a far-fetched idea. It has a distinguished pedigree: both Theodore Roosevelt and Woodrow Wilson promoted it nearly a century ago. Since then, through reforms of state election laws, direct primaries have become the way Americans nominate virtually every candidate for elective office in the country except president. Every U.S. senator, every member of the House of Representatives, and every governor had to win a primary election to become the nominee of his or her party. It is hard to imagine an idea riper for extension to the presidency, or more thoroughly road-tested at the federal, state, and local levels, than the national primary.

Apart from its intrinsic democratic virtues and its deep resonance in the American experience, what beneficial effects would flow from the adoption of a national primary? First and foremost, every vote would count equally. No longer would the votes of a relatively few New Hampshirites, now so crucial in determining who can be president, count infinitely more than the votes of the many millions of people in states whose primaries are held after the race is essentially over. As a consequence, voter turnout would rise substantially. In recent elections, the turnout rate in the New Hampshire primary has been double that in the rest of the country.[10] The disparity was especially great in 2004, when the Democratic primary turnout was up in New Hampshire, but sunk even lower than usual nationwide.[11] Why the disparity? Because the people of New Hampshire know that their votes will directly affect the choice of the major-party nominees for president, and the people of most other states know that their votes will not. If everyone is allowed to vote on the same day, everyone will feel the same connection between their vote and the outcome that New Hampshirites do now. Moving the date of the national primary to August, several months closer to the November election than is the current round of crucial primaries, would mean that people would be asked to vote when they are paying attention to the election, not before—another spur not just to higher turnout, but also to a more informed electorate.

An additional beneficial effect of the national primary is that it would reduce the scorekeeping role of the news media. The national primary is its own scoreboard: when the votes are counted on primary night, everyone can see who won. Public opinion polls would continue to measure how the candidates are doing before primary day, but journalists no longer would be called on to determine, as well as to report on, the status of the race—a role journalists themselves are uncomfortable performing.

Yet another benefit of the national primary would be a shift in the candidates' focus from the local issues that preoccupy Iowa and New Hampshire to the national issues that presidents must confront. Today, candidates for president have little incentive to address, for example, the concerns of racial minorities or the residents of big cities (neither of whom are found in Iowa and New Hampshire) and lots of incentive to defend agricultural subsidies in rural Iowa and the deductibility of property taxes in high-property-tax New Hampshire. If presidential candidates are forced to compete nationwide, then national— that is, presidential—issues will rise to the fore, as they should.

Finally, adopting the national primary would mean that the American people would have the presidential nominating process they want. Since the Gallup Poll began asking voters in 1952 what they think of the national primary, they have endorsed it every time by margins ranging from two to one to six to one. Democrats, Republicans, and independents consistently support the idea, as do the people of every age, income, race, sex, region, religion, and educational level.[12] The national primary would not have to prove itself to voters, because its legitimacy has been preapproved.

The case for a national primary is strong, but what about the case against? One common objection is that only established political figures would have a chance of being nominated, because only they would be able to raise the vast amounts of money needed to wage a nationwide campaign. To the extent that this is true, would it be any different than the current system? After all, for the past quarter-century every major-party nominee for president has begun the election year as either the front-runner or a top-tier candidate.[13] But *is* this still true? As the once little-known former governor of Vermont, Howard Dean, showed in 2003, it is now possible for a political outsider to raise tremendous sums of money through the Internet, as long as he or she is saying things that strike a powerful chord with a great many people.[14]

Another objection is that by making Iowa and New Hampshire no more influential than their combined 1.4 percent of the nation's population warrants, a national primary would remove from the nominating process the kind of face-to-face scrutiny by voters (so-called retail politics) that presidential candidates must now undergo to compete successfully in those two states. That is a reasonable objection if one believes that Iowans and New Hampshirites are uniquely qualified to serve as the screening and selection committee for the rest of the country. There is good reason to doubt that they are, however, especially considering that these states do not represent the country in anything close to its variety and that they have a record of imposing locally major but nationally minor policy litmus tests on candidates.

A final objection to the national primary is that it would undermine the political parties. This tired wheeze was raised by defenders of the old nominating process when the reforms of the 1970s mandated that delegates be chosen through state caucuses and primaries—in complete disregard of the fact that the strongest party organizations in the country (for example, the Daley machine in Chicago, the Crump machine in Memphis, and the Byrd machine in Virginia) had happily coexisted with primary elections for decades. Since the 1970s, the two major parties, which had been in steep decline during the 1960s, have grown stronger in government, in the electorate, and as organizations. The historical record is clear: parties and primaries can coexist happily.

In summary, the front-loaded Iowa and New Hampshire–centric presidential nominating process is broken. Either the federal government, through simple legislation, or the two national parties, by requiring states to participate in the national primary or forfeit their say in the choice of the nominees, has the power to fix it.[15] Other proposed remedies—regional primaries, for example, in which the states of each region would vote on a different first Tuesday between February and June—are inadequate. Whichever region got to go first would have the same distorting power in the choice of nominees as Iowa and New Hampshire do now. The truth is that because more and more states are cramming their primaries into the same few early weeks of the election year, the country has already drifted into a kind of de facto national primary, but a lousy one. It is time to have a good one.

CON: Andrew E. Busch

The idea of a national primary election to choose presidential party nominees is almost as old as the primary itself. The 1912 Progressive Party platform demanded "nation-wide preferential primaries for candidates for the presidency."[1] One year later, President Woodrow Wilson endorsed the idea in his first State of the Union message to Congress.[2]

Since then, the national primary has garnered considerable support, chiefly because of its appeal as a simpler form of democracy. It is clean, straightforward, and majoritarian—or so it would seem. In more recent years, some have also advocated a national primary as a means of combating the flaws in the modern "front-loaded" primary system—that is, one in which the state primaries and caucuses are disproportionately crammed together early in the primary season. In national opinion polls, at least two-thirds of Americans typically say they would prefer a national primary to the current system.

Yet despite its seductive appeal, the national primary is a bad idea. Upon closer examination, its supposed advantages prove to be largely illusory, and its disadvantages are serious indeed.

THE VIRTUE OF SIMPLICITY?

Much of the argument for a national primary lies in its alleged simplicity, but should simplicity be the driving motivation behind reform of the nominating system?

The genius of the American political system lies in its complexity. Separation of powers, checks and balances, bicameralism, and federalism all represent a deliberate embrace of complexity, as does the very idea, outlined in *Federalist* No. 10, of a large republic filled with contending and balancing "factions." When it comes to presidential selection, the electoral college was adopted by the framers, and is defended today by its supporters, precisely because its complexity allows for a tempered democracy and a balance between large and small states. It is, as such, emblematic of the "Compound Republic" extolled by James Madison in *Federalist* No. 39, a republic whose complicated structure does not fit neatly into the category of a unitary national government or of a confederation of states, but does succeed in meeting the needs of a diverse nation.

America's previous experiments with simplicity in presidential nominations have not turned out well. By far the most straightforward system for party nomination was the congressional caucus, in which congressional members of each party met to select their presidential nominee. From 1800 to 1824, the congressional caucus was a model of simplicity, but that benefit was rapidly outweighed by various defects, including insufficient representation of party voters in the caucus and the potential for a breakdown in separation of powers brought on by Congress's involvement in selecting presidential nominees. In 1824 the system collapsed amid the conflicts among political factions that shattered its simple frame.

The congressional caucus was quickly replaced by the national convention system, a nominating mechanism that relied on local and state party meetings to supply, through a circuitous route, delegates to the convention. It was highly decentralized, depending on the actions and calculations of dozens of local party leaders and hundreds of delegates. This complex system served the nation well for the better part of a century before progressive reformers inadvertently added even more complexity by superimposing primaries in some states on top of the traditional convention system. The convention system and the "mixed" system that supplanted it were both more complicated than the congressional caucus system and more democratic. Thus there is no evidence that simplicity is inherently better.

Just as the congressional caucus threatened separation of powers, the national primary threatens to undermine central features of the complex and balanced American political system. It would weaken federalism by reducing the importance of states in the selection process, reduce deliberation within the nominating process, and strengthen the presidency by adding power to the president's claim of possessing an unmediated popular mandate. Moreover, the national primary can prevail only if the public is persuaded that simplicity is preferable to subtlety—a success that could have the side effect of lowering Americans' resistance to other reforms that seek to dismantle other, more central manifestations of the complex American system (such as the electoral college). As French political observer Alexis de Tocqueville argued long ago in *Democracy in America*, the seeking of simplicity and uniformity often drives a political centralization that, over time, can unbalance and degrade America's polity and even threaten its liberty.

NOT AS SIMPLE AS IT SEEMS

In addition to the symbolic damage it might do to federalism, the notion of limited presidential power, and national respect for the nuances of the American system, a national primary would probably not deliver on its promise to simplify American democracy. Instead, in the name of simplicity, the nation would just trade one set of complexities for another—and it is hardly obvious that the trade would be a good one.

For example, there is a potential conflict between the simplicity of the plan and its democratic nature. Nomination races often feature more than two candidates, and so the winners of early primaries frequently finish with less than 50 percent of the primary votes. In a national primary, should a plurality (more votes than those won by any of the opponents) be enough for a candidate to be declared a victor? Or must the winner win an outright majority (more than half of the votes)? A plurality rule diminishes the democratic element of the plan, making it possible for an extreme candidate who has intense but narrow support to win the nomination in a multicandidate field. But a runoff between the top two candidates, which would guarantee that someone wins a majority, would introduce a second election, thereby diminishing the plan's simplicity. Experience has shown that runoff elections almost invariably draw fewer voters.[3] Moreover, even a runoff does not guarantee that the winner will be broadly acceptable to the party. There is the possibility in a multicandidate race that two fringe candidates will finish first and second in the initial round of voting.

To avoid the problems inherent in multicandidate fields, some students of the electoral process have suggested introducing novel and complicated forms of voting, such as approval voting or cumulative voting. In such schemes, voters would vote for all the candidates they find acceptable, indicate their preferred ordering of all candidates, or allocate multiple votes in whatever proportions they wish. None of these experimental voting methods has ever been tried on a national scale in the United States, and they are certainly not simple.

There is also the question of whether the "national primary" would really be a single, unified national election, or whether it would consist of fifty-one separate primaries held on the same day. Most national primary proposals follow the first course, but in the latter case there would still be delegates and a convention. And there would be little opportunity, as there is now, for a multicandidate field to "shake out," increasing the likelihood that a convention would be split and deadlocked among numerous contenders and dominated by unseemly deal making. Although many political scientists and news correspondents might welcome the return of the brokered convention, it is not clear who in the modern era of fractured parties would have the power to broker it. More to the point, however interesting the spectacle might prove, it is the last thing that supporters of the national primary have in mind.

FRONT-LOADING REDUX

Proponents of a national primary have recently argued that such a reform is needed because of the front-loading of the contemporary primary process. However, the nation's experience with front-loading actually supplies some of the strongest arguments against the national primary.

Front-loading is a phenomenon that has been driven predominantly by the independent decisions of a large number of states to move their primary elections forward in the primary calendar. Whereas "meaningful" primaries—primaries whose results could actually have an impact on the outcome of the nomination race—were once spread out over three months or more, in 2004 the meaningful primary season began in Iowa on January 19 and ended on March 7, only six weeks later.

The front-loading of presidential primaries has been almost universally decried, including by the officials who pushed their states' primaries up. Critics have focused on four central shortcomings of the front-loaded system.[4] First, it is clear that front-loading has enhanced the importance of the so-called "invisible primary"—that is, the jockeying among candidates and the preparatory work that takes place in the year or more before the real primaries begin. Many analysts judge that a serious candidate must raise an "entry fee" of roughly $20 million before the primaries begin, and a near-consensus has developed that political insiders have thus regained most of the advantage that they allegedly had before the Democratic Party undertook reforms in 1970 that sought to open up and democratize the nominating process.

Second, because the meaningful primary season ends so soon after it begins, voters have fewer opportunities for second thoughts or careful deliberation. In the aftermath of the 2004 general election, some Democrats argued that the front-loaded system that sped John Kerry's nomination failed to allow sufficient examination of Kerry's strengths and weaknesses as a nominee.[5]

Third, as the state primaries begin to come fast and furious, candidates no longer have time for the "retail" (face-to-face) politicking they cultivated in small states like Iowa and New Hampshire. Instead, they engage in a wholesale "tarmac campaign" in which they flit from one big-city airport to another, while relying mostly on expensive and superficial television ads to reach mass audiences.

Finally, when by early March one candidate has amassed enough convention delegate votes to capture the nomination, all later presidential primaries are rendered moot. Thus roughly half of the states have no meaningful participation in the presidential nominating process, and the contests in those states, compared with those held before early March, see a marked decline in voter turnout. If the later primaries do not matter, why vote?

The national primary would worsen all but one of these problems. The irrelevance of later primaries would end, because everyone would vote at once. Modest Iowa and tiny New Hampshire could not start a stampede toward a candidate, and no state would be left out of the decision. In every other respect, a national primary—no matter how it is arranged—is sure to drastically worsen the problems that most analysts associate with front-loading. Indeed, the national primary would represent, in essence, front-loading taken to its extreme.

If there is a high entry fee for the invisible primary now, that fee will only go up in a national primary. As the stakes of primary day rise, the price of playing will rise, too. To participate in a one-day national election, candidates will have to run national campaigns from the beginning. They will have to raise more money, and all of it up front. And candidates will not be able to take advantage of an early surprise win in a small state to raise more money via the Internet, as Republican senator John McCain of Arizona did in the 2000 Republican primaries. The higher campaign costs will discourage some potential candidates from running, and more of those who do enter the race will withdraw before the primary voters have a chance to render a verdict. Long-shot candidates will have even less chance of overtaking the leader than they do in the current system. If there is a runoff provision, fund raising will become even more important, because candidates who advance will have to finance not one but two hugely expensive national primary campaigns.

If there is too little retail politicking in the front-loaded system after Iowa and New Hampshire, there would be virtually *no* retail politicking in a national primary system. The entire race would revolve around a costly and impersonal mass media effort, with little chance for the candidates to come face-to-face with the voters. No state would vote after the nominees have been selected, but many states and regions would be ignored in the rush of wholesale politics. Many issues of local significance that now receive at least some attention may be shunted to the side entirely.

Finally, if voters in today's front-loaded system have little opportunity to change their minds or to gather and reflect on new information produced in earlier primaries, a national primary decided by a plurality vote would allow for no second thoughts at all. A national primary with a runoff would be a bit better, but the second thoughts would be limited to the top two candidates.

In short, if front-loading is the problem, a national primary is most definitely not the solution. Indeed, a national primary will only exacerbate the pathologies of the current front-loaded system.

THE PROBLEM OF ENACTMENT

A final reason to oppose a national primary is the difficulty of establishing it through legitimate means. Almost all supporters of a national primary seem to assume that such a reform could be implemented by federal legislation. However, there are ample reasons to doubt this assumption.

The Constitution gives no outright authority to the federal government to intervene in the presidential nominating process. Only three provisions of the Constitution deal explicitly with elections for federal office. Two of the three (in Article II, Section 1) allocate between the states and Congress the powers related to the selection of presidential electors; Congress is given only the right to determine the "time" of such selections. The third (in Article I, Section 4) provides that "[t]he Times, Places, and Manner of holding Elections for Senators and Representatives, shall be prescribed in each State by the legislature thereof; but the Congress may at any time by Law make or alter such regulations, except as to the Places of chusing Senators."

Strictly speaking, then, the presidential nominating process for the parties is outside the Constitution—that is, in literal terms no constitutional provision touches nominations. Less strictly speaking, in "spirit" the Constitution treats congressional control of congressional elections more favorably than it does congressional control over presidential selection processes, which are mostly directed to state governments.

A handful of Supreme Court cases have permitted federal legislation affecting presidential elections beyond what a strict reading of the Constitution would seem to allow—for example, some rulings have upheld campaign finance regulations for both presidential and congressional elections. Some would go even further. Justice Hugo Black's opinion in *Oregon v. Mitchell* (1970) argued that the power of Congress to regulate presidential elections was equal to its power to regulate congressional elections. The Court, however, has never concurred with Black's view.

Indeed, two recent lines of Supreme Court interpretation have moved in the opposite direction. In one of these strands, the Court has increasingly held over the last three decades that the political parties are substantially private associations with considerable power to set their own nomination procedures.[6] This line of reasoning would limit both federal and state legislative interference in party affairs, at least in theory; all actual cases have involved state legislation. The second strand, evident especially since the mid-1990s, has reasserted the rights of the states against federal domination on the basis of the Tenth Amendment and a narrower reading of the enumerated powers of Congress.[7] Both strands have worked to limit, not expand, federal legislative powers that might be used to impose a national primary. Thus both the text of the Constitution and current judicial interpretations of that text give little reason to assume that the federal government possesses the authority to pass legislation establishing a national primary.[8] A constitutional amendment could solve this problem, but amendments are not easily ratified.

The national parties would seem to possess the legal authority to seek such a reform, but primaries are actually established by state law. The national parties can refuse to seat delegates selected in a manner contrary to party rules, but they cannot force state legislatures to change primary dates. Yet the parties rarely follow through on threats to deny seating to state delegations. The strategy may be one of the only tools of enforcement available to the parties, but it is too blunt an instrument to be used frequently. The more radical a proposed change—and a national primary is radical—the more unlikely it is that the national parties will be able to compel compliance. They may possess the authority, but they may not possess the power.

MITIGATING THE PRIMARY PROBLEM

The national primary, then, is in most respects inferior to a problematic status quo. However, a variety of measures currently available might at least mitigate the problems of front-loading. The goal should not be to collapse all primaries into a single election, but rather to spread out primaries and extend the meaningful nomination race. The place to start is reform of the campaign finance rules, which have made it difficult for all but the best-endowed candidates to raise sufficient funds to enter and continue in the race. A substantial increase (or perhaps even elimination) of the $2,000 limit on individual contributions would make it possible for more candidates to run and would extend the viability of candidates who do not win the first contests. Other steps aiming to spread out rather than consolidate primary dates could also extend the race. The national parties could mandate proportional representation in early primaries and could negotiate and encourage moderate calendar adjustments.

CONCLUSION

In summary, the national primary should be rejected. It offers a simplicity that is both illusory and undesirable. Although it would solve one problem associated with primary front-loading—the loss of meaningful participation by states that vote too late in the primary calendar—it would exacerbate the other problems. Indeed, a national primary would produce the most front-loaded schedule imaginable, with everything riding on a single day's contest. And there is no obvious way to bring about the reform: the federal government almost certainly does not have the authority to impose it, whereas the parties have the authority but probably not the power. Despite the good intentions of the proponents of the national primary, the nation can do better.

RESOLVED, the president should be elected directly by the people

PRO: Burdett Loomis

CON: Byron E. Shafer

No issue vexed the delegates to the Constitutional Convention more than how the president should be chosen. A few wanted the president to be elected directly by the people. Quite a few more (but, in the end, not a majority) preferred that Congress elect the president. Other ideas included having the governors of the states or a small group of randomly selected members of Congress choose the president. After going around and around on this question for nearly the entire length of the convention, the delegates created a committee to come up with a solution that all of them could live with. The committee's proposal—the electoral college—accomplished that goal admirably. Offered to the convention on September 4, it was adopted with only minor modifications two days later.

Further tinkering took place in 1804, when the Twelfth Amendment stipulated that each elector must vote separately for president and vice president, instead of voting (as the Constitution originally provided) for two candidates for president. Since then, more amendments have been introduced in Congress to replace or overhaul the electoral college than to change any other feature of the Constitution—about five hundred. But the only one enacted was the Twenty-third Amendment, which left the electoral college intact but enfranchised voters in the District of Columbia to participate in the election.

How does the electoral college work? To begin with, each state is assigned a number of electors equal to its number of representatives and senators in Congress. Currently, for example, California has fifty-five electoral votes, and several small states have the minimum number of three, corresponding to the one representative and two senators that a state gets no matter how few people live there. With the adoption of the Twenty-third Amendment in 1961, the District of Columbia received three electors. The Constitution leaves it up to each state to decide how its electors will be chosen and its electoral votes allocated. In practice, all of the states entrust this decision to the people. Except in Maine and Nebraska where each congressional district chooses an elector, the candidate who receives the most popular votes in the state wins all of its electors (a system known as winner-take-all).

To be elected president or vice president, a candidate must receive more than half of all the electoral votes in the country—currently, at least 270 out of 538. If no candidate does, the House of Representatives elects the president from the top three electoral vote recipients, with each state delegation in the House casting a single vote until one of the candidates receives a majority. (Meanwhile, the Senate chooses the vice president from the top two vice presidential candidates, with each senator assigned one vote.) The House has been called on to elect the president twice: in 1800, when it chose Thomas Jefferson over Aaron Burr, and in 1824, when it chose John Quincy Adams over Andrew Jackson. The latter was a highly controversial decision, because Jackson had outpaced Adams in both the popular vote and the electoral vote. Although it has been a long time since the House has had to act, every time a serious third party candidate enters the race against the Republican and Democratic nominees, the possibility arises that none of them will secure an electoral vote majority and the House will once again be called on to elect the president.

A more frequent occurrence, although still a relatively rare one, is for the candidate who receives the most votes from the people to lose the election because the other candidate receives a majority of electoral votes. This is what happened in 1876, in 1888, and most recently in 2000, when Democrat Al Gore received a half-million more popular votes than his Republican rival, George W. Bush, but Bush bested him in the electoral college by a vote of 271–266. By contrast, in every election between 1888 and 2000 (and again in 2004) the electoral college "magnified" the victory of the popular vote winner—that is, he received a larger percentage of electoral votes than of popular votes.

The electoral college has ardent defenders, including Byron Shafer. But as the many attempts to repeal it indicate, the electoral college also has its critics. In the early 1950s, Congress seriously considered modifying the electoral college by adopting a proportional system in which each state's electoral votes would be awarded in proportion to the popular vote each candidate received in the state. More recently, the leading alternative to the electoral college has been direct election by the people. This is the idea championed by Burdett Loomis.

PRO: Burdett Loomis

I live in Lawrence, Kansas, home of the University of Kansas and part of the last "blue" county for well over five hundred miles for anyone headed west. More prosaically, Kansas is a Republican state; in fact, it is so Republican that the party's two major factions energize state politics with their bloody feuds. When presidential elections roll around, however, Kansans are reliably "red," voting by large margins for every Republican nominee in the past forty years.

In 1979 I moved to Kansas from Illinois. Earlier, I had lived in Wisconsin and Pennsylvania, where the race for president meant candidate visits, lots of advertising, and a real sense of competition. But not here, where both the Democratic and Republican presidential campaigns studiously avoid the state, knowing full well that Kansas's six electoral votes will almost certainly end up in the Republican column. On occasion, a vice-presidential candidate might stop by, as Democrat John Edwards and Republican Dick Cheney did in 2004, but that's about it.

Since 1980 I have cast a Kansas ballot in each election for the Democratic presidential candidate. For all the difference it has made, I may as well have voted for the Libertarian candidate, the Socialist Workers' nominee, or the Man in the Moon. In this country's most important election, my vote, along with those of my fellow Kansas Democrats, counts for nothing.

The contrast with Missouri, just forty miles away, is stark, because of that state's highly competitive partisan makeup. Living forty miles from Missouri, within the media market for three major Kansas City television stations, I do get to *watch* an actual presidential election take place. It's great. Candidates fly in, have press conferences, and tend to any number of local Missouri issues. They raise money and spend lots of it on television advertising. Both parties seek to win every possible vote in Missouri, and its citizens benefit from a vigorous campaign, fought in every corner of the state.

Even Kansas Republicans are not part of the presidential campaign. Their job is merely to deliver the expected six electoral votes and contribute some money to a candidate whose campaign will never visit the state. All of this would be bad enough if Kansas were somehow an oddity in presidential politics. But it is not; in fact, Kansas is closer to the norm than is Missouri, because most states are not competitive and are thus ignored by presidential campaigns.

To summarize, because of the nature of contemporary presidential politics under the rules of the electoral college, millions of Americans are effectively disenfranchised in choosing the president, whose actions affect all of them. Simply put, that is just not fair.

As a student of American politics, I certainly understand, and even celebrate, the importance of the nation's political institutions. Moreover, as a political scientist I recognize that institutions affect elections and policy decisions
and that institutional rules are never neutral. But I have a hard time appreciat-
ing a system in which the cards are stacked, over and over again, so that my vote
for president does not count.

Although I am a Democrat in a GOP stronghold, this is no partisan argument. Indeed, a Massachusetts Republican might well offer the same complaint. But my argument is both personal and general, lodged on behalf of the
minority-party voters in the thirty or so states that are uncompetitive in any
given presidential election. Unlike any other statewide electoral contest in
Kansas, the presidential race is finished before it even starts. Writing in 2005, I
will venture to guess that all sides already consider it to be over for the 2008
presidential campaign.

So what? Should Americans condemn the electoral college because most
state races are not competitive? After all, presidential elections have been vig-
orously contested and competitive at the national level for more than two centuries. Even if every voter is not treated equally or fairly, the system has
worked reasonably well, producing legitimate winners for two hundred years,
despite disagreements that once rose to the level of a civil war. It is an argument worth addressing, and so I will now abandon, for the time being at least,
the frustrating story of Kansas and other similarly situated states. But I will
return to them later, because in the end the most profound critique of the
electoral college rests on its failure to give each citizen an equal voice in selecting the nation's president.

THE ELECTORAL COLLEGE AS A CONTINUING POLITICAL EXPERIMENT

The electoral college is the institutional mechanism used to select the president
of the United States. Like the legislative branch and the judicial branch, the
executive branch was conceived by the framers in their dual roles as political
philosophers and practicing politicians. Although the framers' debates about
the nature of the Constitution and the subsequent debates over its ratification
reveal many of the core theoretical underpinnings of the American system, the
framers were political reformers who were seeking institutional solutions to
actual problems of governance.[1]

Although the framers seriously considered allowing the legislative branch
to select the president, they decided that any such process would have given
lawmakers too much power, while rendering the executive less strong and independent. At the same time, direct election of the chief executive was rejected,

but largely for practical reasons rather than because of an aversion to direct democracy. To be sure, some delegates to the Constitutional Convention rejected the idea of direct election because they feared placing too much power in citizens' hands. More of the framers, however, found direct election impractical because of the difficulties of communicating effectively and knowledgeably across the entire nation.[2]

As for the electoral college, during the battle over ratifying the Constitution New York delegate Alexander Hamilton argued that it had escaped serious scrutiny at the convention.[3] In fact, it was an amalgam of various compromises, including the number of electors to be assigned to each state, the counting of slaves as three-fifths of a person for the purpose of calculating voting population, and the mediation of direct elections through the state-by-state selection of electors. The electoral college, then, is more a product of political necessity than of overriding principle. The framers also proved to be poor prognosticators when it came to the electoral college. They anticipated that electors would exercise judgment in voting for candidates, and they gave no consideration to the possibility that political parties—specifically two parties—would come to dominate the process. Rather, the framers foresaw eminent men being chosen as electors and then selecting a highly qualified president.

But their expectations about the electoral college proved wrong on almost every count. Political parties, both in their emerging form of the early 1800s and in their more mature manifestations that appeared in the Jacksonian era, proved capable of holding electors to their pledges to support the parties' choices for president and vice president. The role of electors as independent intermediaries vanished almost as soon as the first real contest for the presidency was waged, in 1796.

By 1836 the role of the electoral college had become well defined. Voters selected electors pledged to candidates who ran for president under party labels. In large part because each state adopted a "winner-take-all" rule for presidential (and most other) elections, only two major parties emerged.

Although the politics of presidential nominations and campaigns has changed greatly since the early 1800s, the basic features of the electoral college have not. So there the electoral college sits, an eighteenth-century institution, conceived in political compromise and essentially unchanged for two hundred years. Yet during those many years Congress has evolved, as has the presidency and the Supreme Court. Why then do Americans return every four years to a jury-rigged system that discriminates against millions of American voters and raises profound questions over the legitimacy of its results?

THE ELECTORAL COLLEGE: A SUCCESSFUL FAILURE

If twenty-first century Americans designed a system to select their chief executive, two values would likely emerge as especially important: equality and transparency. Each vote should count the same, and all citizens should understand easily how the process works. Over the course of U.S. history, those values have become part of the fabric of the democratic process. Today, almost no one is denied access to the polls, and in almost all elections—whether for governor or school board or on referenda—each vote counts the same. Likewise, the reforms of the twentieth century, from the Australian ballot to primary elections to campaign finance reporting rules, increased the transparency of the electoral process. Irregularities may remain, but the values of equality and transparency are essentially honored in how Americans conduct their elections—with one major exception: the electoral college. In the electoral college, the votes of individual citizens in different states do not count the same. And despite legions of newspaper stories that purport to explain the electoral college every four years, it remains notoriously misunderstood, in large part because Americans vote simultaneously for a presidential candidate *and* the slate of electors who formally cast their votes for president a month after the November general election.

So, in two major ways the electoral college falls short. But these are just the first two counts in a long indictment. Before turning to some of these other problematic features of the electoral college, I first want to flesh out the equality issue a bit more.

Many critics of the electoral college complain about the numerical inequalities among the states or about how the institution counts some votes differently from others. Many of these related concerns flow from the disparities produced by giving each state a number of electors equal to its congressional delegation. Delaware thus receives three electoral votes, while California gets fifty-five. At first blush, Delaware and the six other states with a single House member seem to be getting away with murder. After all, their electoral votes are triple the number they would receive if population (reflected in the number of House seats) were the sole criterion. At the same time, the Senate "bonus" barely changes California's electoral total; the two extra electors pale in comparison with the state's fifty-three House members.

But Delaware's citizens understand that they do not have nearly the clout held by Californians. After all, under the winner-take-all rule all fifty-five of California's electors are awarded to the candidate who carries the state; Delaware's prize is tiny by comparison. Thus even with their extra electors, small states remain at a disadvantage. Moreover, anyone wanting to look at real inequality in the American political system need look no further than the U.S.

Senate, which is by far the most unrepresentative major legislative body in the world. The inequalities of the electoral college pale before those of the Senate.

Ironically, the core inequity of the electoral college involves neither the largest nor the smallest states, but the handful of states (about fifteen or so in the past few elections) that are truly competitive—that is, are neither red nor blue. Not only do these states—such as Florida, Iowa, New Mexico, Ohio, Pennsylvania, and Wisconsin—receive the lion's share of the campaigns' attention, but the value of each vote in these states is magnified by the fact that the entire presidential election could well be decided by a relatively small number of votes in a single state.

That said, the gravest defect of the electoral college is that the candidate who receives the most popular votes can lose the election. Before the 2000 election, the last time this situation arose was in 1888, when Republican Benjamin Harrison defeated the Democratic incumbent president, Grover Cleveland, despite the fact that Cleveland received more popular votes.[4] Prior to the 2000 election, then, defenders of the electoral college could have argued that the institution, while perhaps flawed, had generally proved a success. At the same time, skeptics could look at the narrow elections of 1916, 1948, 1960, 1968, and 1976 and express wonderment that the system did not produce more presidents who won the electoral vote while losing the popular count.

The 2000 election brought the flaws of the electoral college into full view. Republican George W. Bush received fewer popular votes than Democrat Al Gore, yet Bush won the electoral vote count by five votes. In the popular vote, Gore had a narrow but clear national plurality of more than 500,000 votes. A system of direct election would have awarded him the presidency, but the electoral college—and a razor-thin margin for Bush in Florida—created a constitutional crisis and elected the candidate who lost the popular vote count.

Unfortunately, the defects of the electoral college were obscured in the shuffle of postelection court battles and vote counting in Florida. But the simple truth remains that the popular vote count was far less ambiguous than was the result produced by the electoral college, save for the Supreme Court's late intervention in Bush's behalf.

Despite some initial calls for electoral reform after the 2000 contest, the wind soon went out of reformers' sails, and the 2004 election was conducted in the same manner as the 2000 election, with candidates focusing on the ten to fifteen states that were in play. A Kansan or even a Californian had no more role to play in 2004 than in 2000. Moreover, the Bush-Kerry contest again demonstrated the potential for an electoral college "mistake," because Bush, despite winning the national popular vote by three million votes, had only a 119,000-vote margin (of almost three million cast) in Ohio, a state essential to his victory. Democrat John Kerry could easily have become the second consecutive chief executive who lost the popular vote, in which case real concerns about presidential legitimacy would certainly have surfaced.[5]

So far, I have focused on actual problems with the electoral college. Its dysfunctional nature comes into even sharper focus when one considers what happens when no candidate receives a majority of the electoral vote. This situation arose in both 1800 and 1824, but never in the modern two-party era. There have, however, been a lot of near misses, most notably in 1948, when "Dixiecrat" candidate Strom Thurmond won thirty-nine electoral votes in the South, and in 1968 when American Independent Party candidate George C. Wallace won forty-six electoral votes. In a closer election, either might have been in a position to determine the winner by negotiating a deal with one of the major-party candidates. Many states have sought to avoid such deal making by binding electors to candidates, but most constitutional scholars agree that the courts would not uphold such laws.[6]

Governments in parliamentary systems often come into existence through this kind of negotiation, but the United States does not have such a system. Americans can scarcely anticipate the possible implications of politicking for the electoral college vote, but the preparations for negotiations that third party candidate H. Ross Perot made in 1992 and the actions of both the Bush and Gore camps in 2000 are reminders of the potential for a backroom deal to decide the presidency.

And what if the deal making fails and the electoral college does not produce a majority for any candidate? As noted earlier, the House of Representatives decides who will be president; each state delegation receives one vote, with a majority (twenty-six) required for victory. Anyone who finds the electoral college unrepresentative would become apoplectic at the patent unfairness of such a decision. California would have a voice equal to that of Delaware. Indeed, California, which has more House members (fifty-three) than the smallest twenty-one states together (fifty-one), could be outvoted twenty-one to one. To be sure, small states would probably not vote as a bloc, but that does not make the process any more equitable.

The inequities of the "one state–one vote" rule pale in comparison with the political machinations it invites. Consider the following scenario: the Democratic candidate receives 260 (of the 270 necessary) electoral votes and wins 50 million popular votes; the Republican candidate wins 230 electoral votes and 45 million popular votes; and a third party candidate receives 78 electoral votes and 35 million popular votes. Republicans control the House delegations in twenty-seven states, Democrats in twenty, and three are equally divided. The Republican candidate won the popular vote in four Democratic states, while the Democrat prevailed in six GOP states. Would Republican House members toe the party line, elect a president who received only about

36 percent of the popular vote, and risk their seats in the next elections, especially in districts where the Democratic presidential candidate won? Would the third party candidate throw his or her support to one of the major-party nominees? And on and on. This, too, is the electoral college system at work.

DUMP THE ELECTORAL COLLEGE

A short essay cannot fully explore the many problems posed by the electoral college. But excellent alternatives are available that rely on a direct popular vote. A pure plurality vote election might be the cleanest alternative, but other systems, including runoffs between the top two candidates, would also count every vote equally and produce a clear winner more often than the electoral college, with its myriad possibilities for breaking down. And I could then cast my vote in Kansas, certain that it counted just as much as if I were in Ohio or New Mexico or any other of the so-called battleground states. We in the Land of Oz might even see a few ads and the presidential candidates in the flesh. Maybe it won't happen, but it should.

CON: Byron E. Shafer

"Is there any other point to which you would wish to draw my attention?"
"To the curious incident of the dog in the night-time."
"The dog did nothing in the night-time."
"That was the curious incident," remarked Sherlock Holmes.

—Arthur Conan Doyle, *Silver Blaze*

In a year of curious incidents, three of the most curious involving the presidential election of 2000 were contributed by the electoral college. One was manifest and dramatic: the electoral college, not the popular vote, determined the outcome. A second was latent and ironic: the electoral college kept pumping away as a device for majority formation in the usual manner despite a controversial outcome. And the third unfolded before our eyes but was frequently not tied back to its actual cause: the electoral college helped to restore "retail politics" to the presidential contest. How an observer feels about the practical balance among these three curious incidents goes a long way toward determining how that observer feels about the electoral college.

But first, note that neutral observers quickly came to know how the general public felt. In the face of the central fact of the 2000 outcome, whereby the winner of the popular vote and the winner of the electoral college diverged, the general public demonstrated remarkable equanimity. Before the fact, many analysts, both supporters and opponents of the electoral college as an institution, would have predicted that the next time the institution "misfired," it would be reformed out of existence. When it did misfire, electing the "wrong" president, a few political elites attempted to raise the hue and cry. But there was no great mass response, and the matter passed quickly.

Isolating the larger systemic contribution of the electoral college to American politics, especially in that long stretch between 1888 and 2000 when it did nothing but confirm the winner of the popular vote as the next president, has never been a simple task. Worse yet, the argument on both sides has had to be about things that did not happen or were not happening—about dogs that did not bark. Yet the arguments themselves are straightforward enough. Moreover, the strategic politics surrounding these arguments has changed in our time, a fact that further justifies our returning to the debate.

The last time the electoral college received sustained scholarly attention, during the late 1960s and early 1970s, it was as part of a larger debate about institutional reform. The essence of that discussion involved participatory versus representative democracy, and reached into every institutional theater: political parties, Congress, the bureaucracy, and, by way of the electoral college, the presidency as well.

- Proponents of reform focused on procedural fairness. They argued against the "distorting" effect of the electoral college on the popular will, quite apart from the ultimate risk of electing the wrong contender, and against an institutional barrier to the direct registration of the public will, distorted or not.

- Opponents focused instead on behavioral effects. They countered that the electoral college had to be judged in the full context of the institutional structure of American government and that, when it was, the college contributed important countervailing influences to *other* distortions, lodged where they could less easily be addressed.

In pursuit of these arguments, both sides used the same basic data. Proponents of reform argued that the campaign, both the activities and the positions of the presidential contenders, was being heavily influenced—distorted—by the electoral college. What proponents saw was that candidates inevitably attended to the competitive states, where a small shift in the popular vote could swing a large bloc of electors. In the process, they did *not* go to states where the partisan outcome was obvious, and thus did not stimulate participation and turnout in these neglected areas.

Opponents agreed with the diagnosis but disagreed with the conclusion. They focused on the identity of these competitive states, which tended to be larger and more socially diverse. In practice, Republicans had to reach out to the northeastern industrial states plus California, rather than to their guaranteed base in the Midwest and Rocky Mountains. In the same way, Democrats had to reach out to the northeastern industrial states plus California, rather than to their guaranteed base in the South. Ideological liberalism, coupled with energy and innovation, were thereby fostered, compensating for other conservatizing elements in the Constitution.

Opponents won the debate in the sense that reform of the electoral college did not proceed, though it was not necessarily their arguments that carried the day. The small and less competitive states were often the most actively opposed to reform. They focused on the fact that they were over-represented within the electoral college, because every state got two electoral votes for their two senators regardless of population, rather than on the fact that the big states gained leverage by being more competitive. And the larger and more competitive states often supported reform, because they were the home of many ideologically committed reformers.

Flash forward to 2000. Proponents of electoral college reform heard their clarion call. The "wrong candidate" won. Members of the general public were unimpressed. The winner in the electoral college was the "right candidate" by definition; that is how presidents are chosen. Yet if we refocus the argument on the two *other* things that the electoral college does, conducing toward majorities and encouraging retail politics, it should be possible to weigh the alternatives intelligently—that is, it ought to be possible to see whether these contributions are sufficient to compensate for the occasional year when the electoral college does not award the presidency to the contender with a plurality of the popular vote.[1]

The surface influence of the electoral college on the way we form presidential majorities was exercised in the usual way during the 2000 campaign through its hostility toward third parties and independent candidacies. Ralph Nader, Green Party candidate for president, bore the brunt of this effect, though he bore its burden lightly. During the campaign, the electoral college produced the usual argument against supporting Nader: if a third contender cannot win, then voting for him will always benefit the major-party candidate you like least. As election day approached, the stated intention of voting for Nader did decline, and it declined most in those states where the outcome was apparently closest—states where the strategic argument was truest. Afterward, in an election in which a myriad of factors could be argued to have been sufficient to alter the outcome, the remaining Nader vote in Florida certainly qualified: had the electoral college managed to repress that vote further, Al Gore would have become president.[2]

Yet this effect still grossly understates the majority-forcing aspect of the electoral college. For in fact, the college is shaping not just the fortunes but the very field of presidential candidates. And here, the question of how American politics would handle the shaping of this field, if we imagine doing away with the electoral college, becomes critical to the argument—and critical to the functioning of American democracy. For the electoral college is not just repressing the vote for announced third candidates for president, its evident surface impact. It is powerfully reinforcing the definitiveness of the processes by which the two major-party candidates are selected. In the long run, this deeper process—another dog that does not bark—may be far more consequential.

At a minimum, the electoral college reinforces the dynamic under which, by the time a national party convention confirms a major-party candidate for president, the battle within that party is over, and the other candidates who sought its nomination withdraw from the field. Because of the electoral college, all they could alternatively do is to launch a quixotic independent bid for the presidency, thereby guaranteeing victory for the other major-party candidate—the opposition-party candidate—probably while terminating any further political career of their own.

The moment the electoral college is gone, however, this dynamic changes: aggrieved candidates for major-party nominations would no longer need to withdraw. And recurrent sources of aggravation are multiple and obvious. Some candidates always believe that their positions have been distorted by opponents or by the press. Some candidates always conclude that they have lost just because other contenders had unfair resource advantages. Some candidates always have supporters who desire—and deserve—to continue the crusade. And on and on.

Fanciful? Recent campaigns suggest not. For example, it is not difficult to imagine the 2000 contest with all four main contenders—George W. Bush, John McCain, Al Gore, and Bill Bradley—continuing on to the general election. Indeed, it is not that difficult to imagine the nominating contests of 1992, with the senior George Bush and Bill Clinton as major-party nominees, with Pat Buchanan not dropping out, with Jesse Jackson entering—he certainly wanted to—and, of course, with H. Ross Perot staying in.

Moreover, the fancy helps to underline some very real facts about the operation of the electoral college. For it emphasizes how important the new rules of presidential election would be in the absence of the college. Would the general public demand a majority of the popular vote in order to affirm a president? Possibly not—we do not demand it now—though note that this is precisely because we have an alternative, majority-forcing device in the form of the electoral college. We could, of course, demand just such a majority, and we might well have to once the electoral college was gone, though note that this would almost certainly require runoff elections. Indeed, there would have had to be runoffs not just in 1992 and 2000 but even in 1996.

Most alternatives to the electoral college proceed on the theory that the plurality vote winner would become president. But this is a safe assumption only within a system that is powerfully constrained by the electoral college—that is, it assumes that the two parties will be creating the two main candidates, that this selection process will simultaneously be repressing major partisan alternatives, and that coronation of these two main alternatives will then be deterring independent candidacies. Yet these parties guarantee their two major-party nominees and deter third (fourth, etc.) alternatives by way of the electoral college. Both proponents and opponents agree that the existence of the electoral college shapes the field of candidates and their electoral strategies. Surely removing the college would likewise (re)shape them.

And here the alternatives become less fanciful. Surely there will often be presidential contenders who could expect to draw a substantial portion of their support from independents and loyalists of the opposite party. John McCain in 2000 seems an obvious example. The current system is stacked against them, all but forcing them to run within a party. A direct plurality vote system is what they need, encouraging them to run directly for president instead. Surely there will likewise—nearly always—be presidential contenders who could expect to rally a major social group. The current system encourages them not to, since they cannot win a nominating majority with such a strategy. A direct plurality vote system is what they need for rallying their group and then attempting to trade off its influence. Jesse Jackson in 1992 seems an obvious example, though there are many possibilities.

Yet if more than two serious contenders actually ran in the general election, year in and year out, would we still be willing to elect the plurality winner? How large a plurality would we require? Would you tolerate a candidate as president who had "won" with 25 percent of the vote? Twenty-two percent? Nineteen percent? The moment you establish a system in which, say, 30 percent of the vote might win, you encourage any candidate who might hope to attain that total to run as an independent rather than seeking the Democratic or Republican nomination. The moment you address this problem by having a second round of voting—a runoff—you encourage *every* candidate to enter the first round of the "real election," the general election, rather than being content with an internal party process under which all but one would be eliminated.

In the face of these alternative rules, how fissiparous is American society—that is, how many candidates can it "naturally" support? If you believe that it is quite diverse—socially diverse, economically diverse, ideologically diverse—the answer is surely, in principle, many. With the presidency, the two-party system as buttressed by the electoral college works against such a multiplication of candidacies. In its absence, at a minimum, the strategic calculations of many potential candidates would be altered. Yet the chain of impacts would likely go on and on. A presidency that is either balkanized by major ongoing social divisions, each with their own designated candidate, or "unified" by standing apart from those divisions and thus obscuring candidate attachments, will be a weakened institution: either devoid of mandate or devoid of program.

We are not, however, reduced to imagining that the interaction of social change with institutional rules might alter the character of politics. For in our time, the combination of the electoral college as the central institution for presidential elections and the changing nature of American society has already transformed the character of presidential politicking. This impact is widely recognized, though the role of the electoral college in creating it is less so. Nevertheless, this impact is yet another reason one might—or here, might not—desire to see the electoral college continue to perform its major roles. For what the electoral college has done, when imposed upon partisan shifts in the states and localities, is to restore what is known as "retail politics" to the presidential campaign.

This is a terminology more commonly recognized at the nomination stage. We say that the opening contests—Iowa, New Hampshire, maybe South Carolina, sometimes one or two others—feature "retail politics," in which candidates meet voters face to face in their localities. After this opening phase, we switch to "wholesale politics," the politics of the tarmac, in which candidates are flown from airport to airport delivering set speeches while the bulk of the campaign switches to televised advertising. There are proponents and opponents of this system as well, and it is true that we emphasize these early contests in small places at the cost of later and usually larger ones. But both proponents and opponents recognize that the country has designed a process privileging retail over wholesale politics, at least at the start.

This was long thought to be part of the impact of the electoral college too, forcing candidates to address individual states on the way to the general election. In recent years, much of this effect appeared to go away, replaced by fully national campaigns—retail campaigns, tarmac campaigns, media campaigns. Now, as evidenced by 2000 and again by 2004, the old effect is back with a vengeance. The two major contenders have focused on a small set of what are widely recognized as "battleground states," and they do so with events that are radically scaled down from those of only a few years ago. No one can deny that many states are thereby ignored. But nor can one deny that both the focus and the character of campaigns have changed.

How did this come about? Apparently through the impact of partisan shifts *as funneled through the electoral college*. In truth, what was previously viewed as a national campaign was in part illusory, resulting from the fact that the electoral college focused the campaign on the bigger (and more socially diverse) states. If you have to worry about California, New York, Pennsylvania, and Illinois, the result will *seem* like a national campaign, and it will inevitably be wholesale politics. You cannot campaign in California as you would campaign in Wisconsin; the scale alone forbids it. But if, as in 2004, you have to worry instead about Wisconsin, Iowa, Minnesota, New Hampshire, and New Mexico—even throwing in Florida and Ohio—the story is different. The fact that you are campaigning within states is no longer hidden. The retail character of that campaign is likewise evident.

The result is not as self-evidently virtuous as the majority-forcing impact of the electoral college, and the effect of removing the college is thereby not as self-evidently disastrous. But the point in closing is a different one. What needs emphasis is that the choice between electoral college or not is inherently a choice between one vision of politics and another. It is not between one set of rules and "no rules." It is not between one impact and "no impact." The choice is instead between majority-forcing and minority-inducing strictures. It is between incentives toward retail and wholesale politicking. It is between one set of institutionalized "distortions" and another. In such a world, anyone who opposes the electoral college without specifying an alternative and then elaborating the consequences cold-bloodedly is irresponsible at best, pernicious at worst.

Let me say the same thing differently. The fact that the existing dogs do not normally bark does not mean that they are not standing by the gate, protecting the commonwealth. If they are slain by accident, no less than if they are slain deliberately, the majoritarian process in American politics—a politics riddled with nonmajoritarian elements in its institutions and in its society—can hardly be said to have been reinforced. If that process is weakened, it is hard to see how government would become either more effective or more responsive. Holmes would have known how to make the proper deduction.

RESOLVED, the presidential impeachment process is basically sound

PRO: Keith E. Whittington

CON: Benjamin Ginsberg and Martin Shefter

The framers of the Constitution chose a strong, independent presidency for the new government, but they also recognized that a constitutional safety valve was needed in case a president abused the formidable powers of the office. Because the president was to serve a fixed, four-year term, the safety valve would have to take the form of an impeachment process that could remove a president from office before the term expired.

Defining the constitutional grounds for impeachment and designing the impeachment process were complex undertakings. For a time, the delegates to the Constitutional Convention specified "malpractice or neglect of duty" as the impeachable offenses. But these offenses were too broad, they decided, and so they substituted "treason, bribery, or corruption," which in turn struck them as too narrow. Eventually, the delegates arrived at "Treason, Bribery, or other high Crimes and Misdemeanors," the latter a phrase from fourteenth-century English common law that, loosely translated, meant "serious abuses of the constitutional authority of the office."

In designing the process for determining whether a president was guilty of an impeachable offense, the delegates assigned roles to all of the other branches of the federal government. The House of Representatives was charged with deciding, by majority vote, whether the president had committed one or more impeachable offenses. The Senate would then try the president, with the chief justice of the United States presiding, and decide whether to remove the president from office. A two-thirds majority vote would be required to do so. Although the penalty for impeachment could "not extend further than to removal from Office, and disqualification to hold any Office of honor, Trust or Profit under the United States," presidents who were impeached and removed from office would still be liable to "Indictment, Trial, Judgment and Punishment" in the courts for any violations of criminal law they may have committed.

No president was impeached until 1868, when the House charged Andrew Johnson with both violating the year-old Tenure of Office Act by firing Secretary of War Edwin M. Stanton and seeking to bring Congress into "disgrace, ridicule, hatred, contempt, and reproach" in a series of campaign speeches. Johnson's defenders argued that he was the victim of a partisan power grab by northern Republicans, whose real motive was to force out a president whose views on the post–Civil War Reconstruction of the South were less draconian than theirs. Thirty-five of fifty-four senators voted to remove Johnson, one fewer than the two-thirds majority required by the Constitution.

Within a few years, the Johnson impeachment was widely regarded as a politically motivated abuse of the impeachment process, so much so that the process lost much of its legitimacy. In 1898 political scientist Henry Jones Ford likened presidential impeachment to a "rusted blunderbuss that will probably never be taken in hand again."[1] In 1960, after nearly a century had passed without another presidential impeachment even being considered, historian Clinton Rossiter "predict[ed] confidently that the next president to be impeached will have asked for the firing squad by committing a low personal rather than a high political crime—by shooting a senator, for example."[2]

Ford, Rossiter, and nearly all of their contemporaries would have been astonished to learn that, within the span of a quarter-century, impeachment proceedings would be launched against two presidents, Richard Nixon in 1974 and Bill Clinton in 1998–1999. Nixon, facing certain impeachment by the House and conviction by the Senate for his role in covering up his administration's involvement in the Watergate scandal, resigned in August 1974. Clinton was charged with lying under oath about his affair with White House intern Monica Lewinsky and with urging her and others to lie as well. The House voted by a narrow margin to impeach Clinton, but the Senate handily acquitted him. Indeed, neither article of impeachment won the support of a simple majority, much less a two-thirds majority, of senators.

In their arguments, Keith E. Whittington defends the presidential impeachment process as basically sound, and Benjamin Ginsberg and Martin Shefter find the process to be seriously flawed. Both sides note that the drives to impeach Nixon and Clinton came from a legislative branch that was controlled by the opposition party. Whittington, however, attaches great importance to the fact that the effort to impeach Nixon succeeded only because it eventually became bipartisan, whereas the effort to remove Clinton foundered because it was almost a purely Republican effort. Ginsberg and Shefter believe that both impeachments were politically motivated. They fear not only that this fate will become more common for presidents, but also that the search for presidential wrongdoing will distract Congress from the larger and more important question of the excessive growth of presidential power.

PRO: Keith E. Whittington

It took a while for veterans of the American Revolution to grow comfortable with the idea of executive power. The revolutionary state constitutions expressed a lingering antipathy to the royal governors, who had collided with the locally elected colonial legislatures. Those constitutions gave few powers to executive branch officials and granted them little independence from the state legislatures. The Articles of Confederation, the predecessor of the U.S. Constitution, did not create an executive branch at all, but instead entrusted all federal powers to the Confederation Congress. Yet by the time those who favored constitutional reform to strengthen the national government met in Philadelphia in 1787, a decade of unhappy experience had weakened public trust in legislatures and strengthened the desire for a robust separation of powers.

The members of the Constitutional Convention were convinced that a new government would need a chief executive, but they were bedeviled by the problem of how best to select and remove the holder of such a powerful office. The new presidency had to be independent enough to perform its functions effectively and to act as a check on Congress, but it also had to be accountable enough to prevent it from becoming a threat to the Republic. The wrong selection mechanism could lead to the choice of a president who was unfit for the high responsibility, politically weak, or beholden to legislative factions. Too short a term of office could create a presidency whose occupant was always looking over his shoulder; too long a term could invite a kind of American monarchy. The invention of the electoral college seemed to balance the interstate rivalries, give the president a sheen of popular authority, and make him independent of Congress. A four-year term of office gave the presidency some stability, while maintaining some accountability.

To the mistrustful constitutional drafters, it seemed natural to include a removal mechanism to supplement regular elections. The British Parliament did not have the right to impeach the king, but it could and did impeach the king's ministers, deterring potential collaborators from joining with a scheming monarch. The Americans were impressed by this example of constitutional checks and balances, and, in fact, many of the early state constitutions authorized the legislature to impeach, remove, and ban from future public office governors and judges guilty of corruption, maladministration, or endangering the state. Although there was some nervousness at the Philadelphia convention about making the president answerable to anyone but the people or rendering him too timid toward the body holding the impeachment power, the framers ultimately found it safer to make the president liable to impeachment than to include no constitutional device for stripping the president of his formidable powers for the duration of his term of office. As Virginia delegate George Mason said early in the convention, "Some mode of displacing an unfit magistrate is rendered indispensable by the fallibility of those who choose, as well as by the corruptibility of the man chosen."[1] Another Virginia delegate, James Madison, later added,

> [S]ome provision should be made for defending the Community against the incapacity, negligence or perfidy of the chief Magistrate. The limitation of the period of his service was not a sufficient security. He might lose his capacity after his appointment. He might pervert his administration into a scheme of peculation or oppression. He might betray his trust to foreign powers. The case of the Executive Magistracy was very distinguishable, from that of the Legislature or of any other public body, holding offices of limited duration. . . . In the case of the Executive Magistracy which was to be administered by a single man, loss of capacity or corruption was more within the compass of probable events, and either of them might be fatal to the Republic.[2]

Most of the convention delegates came around to this point of view.

The remaining questions were who would exercise the impeachment power and under what conditions. As was often the case, those matters were resolved by compromise. The convention quickly rejected Delaware's proposal to give the states a role in removing the head of the national government. James Madison worried that the president would not be sufficiently independent of Congress if the legislature alone wielded the impeachment power, but his proposal to give the Supreme Court the power to try impeachment cases seemed to carry its own risks. The convention decided to entrust this power to the Senate, composed of representatives of the states, rather than to draw into heated political controversies the small body of justices who had themselves been appointed by the president. The convention took advantage of the bicameral structure of Congress to separate the power to impeach (or charge) the president, which was given to the House of Representatives, from the power to convict, which was entrusted to the Senate.

The scope of impeachable offenses was likewise a matter of debate. No single formula was common to all the state constitutions, and the current formulation, "Treason, Bribery, or other high Crimes and Misdemeanors," was designed to satisfy both those who worried that treason and bribery would not capture all the ways in which the Constitution might be subverted by perfidious officials and those who worried that something as vague as "maladministration" would put the president at the mercy of Congress.[3] In the end, the Constitution's impeachment provisions did not fully satisfy any of the founders, but they were the best balance of presidential (and judicial) independence and accountability likely to win widespread agreement among the convention delegates.

Since the adoption of the Constitution, the impeachment power has been used sporadically, primarily against judges.[4] Along the way, a variety of concerns have been raised about certain details of the impeachment process and about particular impeachments. Persistent arguments have arisen in both the House and the Senate about the proper rules for admitting evidence during impeachment proceedings. In the 1980s, for example, the Senate took the unprecedented step of appointing a special committee to hear evidence in the impeachments of three federal judges so that the legislative work of the full Senate would not be disrupted by an extended trial. But these concerns will not be examined in this essay.[5] Instead, it will address three big questions about the presidential impeachment process: Is the process too difficult? Is it too easy? Has it been used properly?

The Constitution places two types of hurdles in front of efforts to impeach a federal official. One type of hurdle is procedural. To remove an official, advocates of impeachment must win the support of a simple majority in the House of Representatives to impeach and a two-thirds majority in the Senate to convict. The other type of hurdle is substantive. The impeachment power is limited to cases of "Treason, Bribery, or other high Crimes and Misdemeanors." In addition, the consequences of Senate conviction cannot exceed removal from office and disqualification from future federal office holding. Advocates for the removal of a president have never successfully cleared all of these hurdles. Proponents of presidential removal have twice won impeachments from the House, but they have been unable to win conviction in the Senate. Andrew Johnson narrowly escaped conviction, and Bill Clinton retained his office by a more comfortable margin.[6]

IS THE IMPEACHMENT PROCESS TOO DIFFICULT?

For some Americans, the constitutional hurdles may appear too high, rendering the presidential impeachment process more difficult than it needs to be. Because a single political party has rarely been able to capture two-thirds of the seats in the Senate, convicting a president on impeachment charges would almost always require some senators to cross party lines to vote against him. Party loyalty thus might sustain a scoundrel in office. At the same time, those who admire parliamentary systems of government are frustrated by the gridlock that divided government is thought to produce.[7] How much easier it would be if congressional majorities could simply remove opposite-party presidents without waiting for the next election. Frustration with obstructionist, minority-party presidents fed the impeachment movements against John

Tyler, Andrew Johnson, Richard Nixon, and Bill Clinton, and some scholars think the country would be better off if such movements could be facilitated.[8]

Without question, the existence of political parties complicates the constitutional scheme in various ways, including the process of presidential impeachment. Although the founders well understood that factions and intrigue might stimulate presidential removals, they did not anticipate that Congress would be formally divided between pro-administration and anti-administration forces. Not only do party divisions create an additional source of conflict between the executive and legislative branches of government, but they also distort the deliberative capacity of the legislature. When contemplating the impeachment of a president, legislators cannot be expected to act simply as disinterested judges making impartial judgments about the public welfare. The political and policy consequences of a presidential impeachment will seldom be far removed from their minds.

Good reasons may exist to prefer a parliamentary to a presidential system of government. But those with such a preference for the United States would be better advised to engage explicitly in the wholesale constitutional reform needed to make the change than to try to sneak it through the backdoor of the impeachment clause. Even if a constitutional amendment were passed to make presidential removal by impeachment easier for the majority party in Congress, the result would only be an awkward and ill-fitting system of congressional government rather than a coherent parliamentary system.

The current presidential impeachment process effectively requires bipartisan participation in order to remove a president from office. On the whole, this is good. Overturning the people's choice for president should not be easy. The procedural requirement of a two-thirds majority for conviction in the Senate means that the constitutional specification of impeachable offenses must be honored, preventing congressional leaders from converting the impeachment process into a vote of no confidence. If allowing the president to serve until the next election really endangers the public good, then the case for removal should be clear and uncontroversial. Indeed, the case for removal should be plain not only to partisan foes of the president, but also to the president's partisan allies. For example, by the time the crimes associated with the Watergate scandals were revealed, Republicans in Congress had become convinced that President Nixon's position was no longer tenable and that the fortunes of both the party and the nation would be better served by his departure from office. Seeing his support crumble, Nixon resigned rather than face certain impeachment and conviction. Clinton, by contrast, was able to rally nearly all Democrats to his side, persuading them, and the general public, that there was more merit in his political survival than in his out-of-season departure. In the American constitutional system, with its fragmented institutions and checks and balances, important political decisions tend to require large rather than narrow majorities. Surely the decision to remove a president should require as much support in the Senate as the decision to override a president's veto of a piece of legislation.

IS THE IMPEACHMENT PROCESS TOO EASY?

The House has long been organized to facilitate action by the majority party, and a party-line vote by a narrow majority is all it takes to impeach a president. That is what happened when a slim Republican majority impeached President Clinton weeks after the midterm elections of 1998, even though it was obvious that the chances of conviction in the Senate were low.

Especially in an era of highly polarized parties and frequently divided government, the relative ease of the impeachment process in the House is worrisome. Although the House was asked to consider articles of impeachment against a president only once in its first 180 years of its existence, impeachment articles made their way to the floor twice in the next thirty years. In their book, Benjamin Ginsberg and Martin Shefter regard impeachment efforts as part of a larger shift toward "politics by other means," in which "rather than seeking to defeat their opponents chiefly by outmobilizing them in the electoral arena, contending forces are increasingly relying on such institutional weapons of political struggle as legislative investigations, media revelations, and judicial proceedings to weaken their political rivals and gain power for themselves." In such a climate, frequent impeachment movements could "impede the government's capacity to govern."[9]

However, plenty of other "institutional weapons of political struggle" are available without adding impeachment to the list. Indeed, Ginsberg and Shefter's original presentation of their theory of "politics by other means" did not even mention the impeachment process. Appropriately, they focused on more frequently used weapons, such as litigation, congressional investigations, and unilateral policy making by the executive. Making the impeachment process more difficult to initiate would do little to address concerns about governmental gridlock, while hindering efforts to bring real presidential wrongdoing to light.

At the same time, the impeachment process is self-limiting in a way that other institutional weapons are not. The House may be able to impeach relatively easily, but impeachments are of little consequence—the equivalent of a resolution of censure—if the Senate will not convict and if the public sides with the president. Senate obstruction of executive and judicial appointments and congressional and prosecutorial investigations of the executive create far greater impediments to the smooth functioning of a presidential administration than would a largely symbolic impeachment. Those weapons, moreover, can be used at little cost to those who wield them. Precisely because impeachment efforts are so visible to the general public but so pointless if there is no realistic chance of conviction in the Senate, severe political risks await the political party that routinely brings forward frivolous articles of impeachment. Cheapening the impeachment process by turning to it too often would be more likely to damage the House majority than the president.

IS THE IMPEACHMENT PROCESS MISUSED?

Even if the impeachment process is neither too difficult nor too easy, it might be misused. In their con argument that follows, Ginsberg and Shefter worry that "impeachment-like" activities are too often directed toward individual wrongdoing rather than toward institutional and policy reform, leaving excessive presidential power untouched even as they weaken individual presidents. The impeachment process, therefore, is "flawed" to the extent that it "offers no solution" to the country's more significant constitutional problems. This concern is misplaced. The fault, if there is one, lies not in the impeachment process but in those who might make use of it.

The primary purpose of the impeachment process is to deter and stop misconduct by high government officials. It was never intended to be a primary mechanism of institutional reform. The most common targets of impeachment proceedings, federal judges, have been impeached and removed from the bench for offenses such as dereliction of duty, taking bribes, recurrent drunkenness, and conviction for crimes unrelated to their judicial office. Many others in such circumstances, judges and cabinet officials alike, have resigned without the need for impeachment hearings. The impeachment process would indeed be broken if it could not be used against a president guilty of similar wrongdoing.

Presidents are rarely so careless. Their offenses tend to be less petty, but also more controversial. If a president were to suspend the writ of habeas corpus without congressional authorization or to authorize wiretaps without judicial approval, then a remedy other than impeachment would likely be more useful. Judicial review or a legislative response could correct the constitutional harm without removing an otherwise able chief executive. Although the impeachment power would be better used to remove presidents who persistently abuse their constitutional powers, there is rarely agreement on when that has occurred. One party's constitutional villain is likely to be the other party's constitutional hero.

However, the impeachment power can be used, in conjunction with other congressional powers, to engage in constitutional reform. An impeachment could help to redefine the actions that are constitutionally appropriate for a president. But the impeachment process can do this only if legislators are committed to reforming institutional relationships. When Congress impeached and tried President Andrew Johnson for interfering with congressional Reconstruction of the South, it forced him to back down and ensured that the powerful presidency Abraham Lincoln had built up during the war did not continue into peacetime. Unlike in 1868, however, Congress did not significantly pare back presidential power in 1974. The House Judiciary Committee consciously avoided raising broader constitutional issues when approving articles of impeachment against President Nixon. Congress pulled up short not because of the inadequacy of the impeachment process or the distraction of Watergate, but because it did not *want* to significantly limit presidential power, only to redirect it.[10] Similarly, in 1999 Republicans objected to President Clinton, not to presidential power as such. Indeed, the entirely personal focus of congressional Republicans both made it difficult to justify their desire to remove the president and limited the long-term significance of the impeachment.[11] Whether impeachment is used to construct new constitutional understandings and practices or merely to discipline an individual wrongdoer depends on the goals of the legislators who employ the process, not on the process itself.

Presidential impeachment was built into the Constitution as a kind of failsafe device, a backup system to stand behind the myriad other constitutional and political defenses against a wayward president. Entrusting any body of politicians with the power to remove the president carried risks, but the founders judged that the advantages of an impeachment mechanism outweighed the risks of its misuse. They expected it to play a small role in our nation's political life, and it has. The most immediate fears of those who urged the creation of an impeachment power have not come to pass. No American president has declared loyalty to a foreign prince or raided the Treasury to pad his offshore bank accounts. Even so, legislators have had occasion to turn the weapon of impeachment against the president. Whether in each particular case they were wise or unwise to do so, the presidential impeachment process itself is basically sound.

CON: Benjamin Ginsberg and Martin Shefter

Impeachment is quite atypical of politics-as-usual in the United States. After all, of the nation's forty-three presidents, only two—Andrew Johnson and Bill Clinton—were ever impeached by the House of Representatives. And not a single president has actually been convicted and removed from office by the Senate. Even classifying Richard Nixon as a case of impeachment—Nixon resigned to forestall imminent congressional action—raises the historical probability of a president's being impeached to only 3/43, or 0.07.

It is often argued that the infrequency of impeachment indicates that Congress does not deploy this weapon lightly. Thus it appears that the benefits of having a removal procedure available for those rare occasions on which a president flagrantly abuses the powers of his office outweigh whatever disadvantages the procedure may present. In this essay, we question this argument on two grounds. First, we suggest that since the Watergate hearings of 1973–1974, congressional committees and special commissions established by Congress have conducted numerous hearings and investigations that are the functional equivalents of impeachment proceedings. For example, the Iran-contra hearings in 1987 were an attempt by Democratic congressional leaders to drive President Ronald Reagan from office without the formality of an impeachment process. More recently, in 2004, the congressionally mandated National Commission on Terrorist Attacks upon the United States (also known as the 9-11 Commission) was an effort by congressional Democrats to block President George W. Bush's reelection.

Second, we point out that, like the formal impeachment process, Watergate and post-Watergate congressional inquiries have focused mainly on questions of presidential wrongdoing, or indeed criminality, rather than on the institutional and policy concerns traditionally associated with congressional hearings. This is a marked change from the pattern prior to Watergate, when the most prominent congressional hearings concentrated largely on fashioning appropriate public policies and effective government institutions. For example, in the late nineteenth century the Patterson, Cockrell, and Dockery-Cockrell Commissions were established to reform federal administrative practices. As administrative historian Leonard White notes, "These were efforts [by Congress] to improve administration, not to investigate error or wrongdoing."[1] Another noteworthy example was the Pujo Committee hearings of 1912 that led to the creation of the Federal Reserve system. A half-century later, the hearings on the Vietnam War conducted by Sen. William Fulbright sought not so much to assign blame for a failed policy as to discern flaws in the foreign policy-making process that led the United States into the quagmire of Vietnam. Even the hearings led by Wisconsin senator Joseph R. McCarthy in the early 1950s, though they smeared individuals and castigated particular officials, had the more general purpose of raising questions about the performance of the institutions that conducted American foreign policy.

The Watergate investigations of 1973–1974 were a turning point. The investigations were sparked by the Nixon administration's efforts to expand presidential power. But during the course of the probe, Congress and the news media focused mainly on the question of Nixon's personal responsibility for ordering a break-in at the Democratic Party's national headquarters. The Senate hearings paid little attention to such institutionally important matters as the president's efforts to reorganize the executive branch without obtaining Congress's approval.

Ever since Watergate, however, the most prominent congressional investigations have followed the form and displayed the tone of criminal prosecutions. These investigations have attracted coverage in the national news media by revealing misbehavior by the president, or by arguing that a major national problem resulted from the actions (or the inactivity) of the president or his top appointees. For example, after driving Nixon from office, Congress sought to discern whether there was anything untoward in Gerald R. Ford's pardon of the departed president from criminal prosecution. During the administration of Jimmy Carter, congressional hearings sought to discover whether White House aides Jody Powell and Hamilton Jordan and budget director Bert Lance were guilty of various improprieties. The Iran-contra hearings of the mid-1980s looked for evidence that President Reagan himself had been involved in, or at least had been aware of, the sale of weapons to Iran and the supply of arms to the contra forces in Nicaragua. As for Reagan's successor, George Bush, Congress asked whether any improper considerations were involved in Bush's pardon of Secretary of Defense Caspar Weinberger for his role in the Iran-contra affair. And during the Clinton administration, the most publicized congressional hearings examined the propriety of the circumstances surrounding President Clinton and his wife's investment in Whitewater, an Arkansas real estate project, as well as the president's sexual dalliances with White House intern Monica Lewinsky and other women.

In the spring of 2004, the 9-11 Commission examined events preceding the terrorist attacks on New York City's World Trade Center and the Pentagon, seeking to ascertain whether President Bush and other top officials had failed to respond appropriately to warning signs. Congressional Democrats hoped that a probe of the Bush administration's failure to anticipate the September 11, 2001, attacks would embarrass the president in an election year and undermine public confidence in his ability to protect the nation's security—an area long seen as the president's chief political asset. Because Democrats did not control either house of Congress, they lacked access to the House and Senate's formal investigative machinery. Nevertheless, they demanded an investigation and, through public pressure, ultimately forced congressional Republicans to agree to the creation of an ad hoc, bipartisan investigative panel to be appointed by the leaders of the two parties in Congress.

There had been some expectation that the members of the panel would have expertise in national security matters, and some panelists did, in fact, have such backgrounds. But Democrats placed on the panel several individuals whose expertise was prosecutorial rather than in the realm of national security. These included Richard Ben-Veniste, an attorney and Democratic activist who had helped to prosecute President Nixon in the Watergate investigation and to defend President Clinton in the Whitewater probe. The choice of prosecutors rather than national security experts underlines the role that congressional Democrats intended the commission to play.

Recognizing the president's peril and seeking to limit any political damage from the commission's findings, the GOP insisted that the investigation be completed and its report released by July 2004, some four months before the presidential election. Consistent with the pattern of contemporary congressional probes, the investigation focused mainly on the president's shortcomings rather than on broader institutional issues.

The report of the 9-11 Commission, to be sure, criticized intelligence agencies and practices and offered recommendations, some of which were the basis for bills later introduced in Congress. But Congress, riven by partisan divisions and conflicts, was unable on its own to implement any commission recommendations. Shortly after his 2004 reelection, President Bush intervened to bring about the enactment of legislation nominally based on the commission's recommendations, but that actually greatly expanded the power of the executive branch to conduct intelligence investigations, to engage in surveillance activities, and to detain suspects without bail. This expansion of investigative powers had long been sought by the administration, but had been opposed by civil liberties groups and blocked by their allies in Congress. Thus the administration was able to use the 9-11 Commission's recommendations to overcome opposition to its antiterrorism initiatives. Ironically, then, the ultimate result of a legislative investigation designed to weaken the incumbent president was an expansion of presidential power.

That is not to say, however, that the president emerged from the commission's investigations and hearings unscathed. Because of the tight time limit, the commission was not as powerful an investigative instrument as a full-blown congressional inquiry. Nevertheless, commission hearings in March and April 2004 suggested that the Bush administration had not been sufficiently attentive to the terrorist threat prior to September 2001—a finding that deeply embarrassed the president. During the hearings, the 9-11 Commission highlighted the testimony of a former national security aide, Richard Clarke, who had just published a book criticizing President Bush for his inattention to the threat of terrorism.[2] Committee Democrats led by Ben-Veniste praised Clarke, while castigating the administration's star witness, National Security Adviser

Condoleezza Rice, whose testimony the commission had demanded despite presidential claims of executive privilege. Ben-Veniste interrupted Rice repeatedly, and Democratic commission member Jamie Gorelick, who had served as an assistant attorney general in the Clinton administration, delivered a lengthy statement critical of Rice's testimony.

Indeed, long before the publication of the official report, members of the commission made numerous public and media appearances to present their own views critical of the president.[3] Ben-Veniste, Gorelick, and the others fully understood that the main purpose of the 9/11 probe was to undermine Bush's political standing—not to develop more effective antiterrorism policies. Democrats also mobilized a group of survivors of 9/11 victims—the so-called Jersey girls—to make television appearances during the hearings so that they could express their outrage at the president's failures allegedly identified by the hearings.

Republicans, for their part, launched a series of counterattacks. They demanded that Gorelick resign from the panel, charging that her own actions as assistant attorney general had hampered the FBI and now produced a conflict of interest with her service as a commission member. Republicans also mobilized their own 9/11 survivors group to make television appearances in support of President Bush.

The foregoing examples suggest that in recent years Congress has blurred the distinction between legislative investigations and impeachment proceedings. Legislative leaders have used investigations and actual impeachment interchangeably as mechanisms for seeking to weaken incumbent presidents or oust them from office. This use of congressional hearings and investigations as a quasi-impeachment process, however, has done little to advance Congress's institutional interests. In recent years, Congress has had enormous difficulty responding to presidential assertions of power, particularly in the realms of war, spending, and control of the federal bureaucracy. And, although impeachment-like investigations—to say nothing of an actual impeachment (Clinton's)—have embarrassed the presidents against whom they have been directed, they have done little to reduce the institutional power of the presidency. In driving Nixon from office, the Watergate hearings did kill Nixon's efforts to reorganize the executive branch by presidential fiat. But within a few years Reagan had increased presidential control over the nation's budget and reduced to little more than legal fiction the War Powers Act and other Watergate-spawned congressional efforts to curb the president's unilateral war-making abilities—a power grab that the Iran-contra investigations did nothing to reverse. In a similar vein, after Clinton limped out of office upon surviving a series of investigations and an impeachment, his successor, George W. Bush, did not hesitate to lead the nation into war with only the barest pretense of consulting Congress. Thirty years of impeachment-like hearings, one actual impeachment, and one resignation to forestall imminent impeachment have little muddied Louis Fisher's observation that in recent decades presidents have largely gained control of war making and spending—arguably, the two most important constitutional prerogatives of Congress.[4]

The ongoing shift in the focus of congressional investigations from institutional and policy concerns to individual wrongdoing parallels the ongoing decline of Congress as a policy-making body. Also consistent with this decline is the fact that these highly publicized congressional investigations have had few, if any, policy consequences. To be fair, Congress enacted several pieces of legislation, such as the Ethics in Government Act, in the aftermath of the Watergate investigation that were designed to curb presidential power, but they have proven to be largely ineffective. Even the Clinton investigations, apart from reminding presidents to curb their sexual appetites, have had no implications for institutional power. Indeed, while Congress was investigating sex in the Oval Office, President Clinton was developing new mechanisms of regulatory review that increased presidential control over the bureaucracy.[5] Finally, the 9-11 Commission hearings produced reforms that ultimately increased the power of the presidency. In all of these instances, congressional investigations focused on the personal rather than the political. And the dictum of the 1960s to the contrary not withstanding, the personal and the political are not one and the same.

In summary, the impeachment process is seriously flawed. The questions raised in impeachment or quasi-impeachment proceedings have invariably revolved around personal wrongdoing. But the real issue raised by the contemporary presidency is not individual misconduct but institutional power. While Congress has searched for the missing tapes or the smoking gun or the blue dress that might force a president from office, it has all but ignored the executive orders, executive agreements, and regulatory directives that have expanded the power of the presidency. The problem in the Oval Office is not excessive venality, criminality, or sex; it is excessive power. And the impeachment process offers no solution to this problem.

RESOLVED, the media are too hard on presidents

PRO: Matthew R. Kerbel

CON: Bartholomew H. Sparrow

One of the qualities that distinguishes the modern presidency from the traditional office of the eighteenth and nineteenth centuries is that modern presidents—that is, every president since Theodore Roosevelt—have been the figures most in the spotlight on the political stage. And who shines that spotlight on presidents? The mass media.

In the era of the traditional presidency, *mass media* meant local newspapers with a local focus. As a result, mayors, governors, and local representatives in Congress usually loomed larger in media coverage than presidents. But in the early twentieth century, the media expanded to include national magazines with a national focus. The editor of a popular magazine such as *Collier's* or *McClure's* knew that although his readers in Virginia probably would not care to read about the governor of Nebraska or the mayor of Buffalo, readers everywhere were interested in the president. Indeed, it was at this time that enough reporters began covering the president to form the White House press corps and presidents began to hold regular news conferences.

The next major innovation in mass media—and arguably the most important one politically—was radio. For the first time, radio brought the president into people's homes, making him not just a familiar figure but also an intimate one, the personification of the entire federal government. Although radios became a standard fixture in American homes during the 1920s, Franklin D. Roosevelt was the first president to figure out how to use the new medium effectively. In place of loud oratory—suitable for addressing large crowds but not for visiting families in their living rooms—FDR offered "fireside chats."

Television, the new technology that swept the country during the 1950s, added pictures to the words that radio conveyed. As with radio, however, it took a while before a president was able to figure out how best to use this new medium. In 1961 John F. Kennedy began holding news conferences on live television—mini-dramas in which viewers saw their president coolly fending off seemingly difficult questions from an army of reporters.

The most recent major addition to the nation's mass media is the Internet. Like radio and television, this technology spread widely over the course of a decade—roughly the mid-1990s to the present—from being a medium that a few people used to one that is used widely. But so far, no president has figured out how best to use this new medium for maximum political effect.

New media have offered presidents new tools to communicate with the American people and, in doing so, have elevated the prominence of the presidency in the political system. But with this increased prominence has come increased scrutiny. The media are not mere conveyor belts bringing presidential words and images to the American people. They are journalistic organizations whose reporters can ask challenging questions, report news that undermines the president's message, give voice to the president's political opponents, and interpret what the president says and does critically. The media spotlight shines brightly on the modern presidency, but, while doing so, it brings both the good and the bad into sharp prominence.

Are the media—newspapers, magazines, radio, television, and Web "blogs" and other political Web sites—too hard on presidents? Yes, argues Matthew R. Kerbel, and, still worse, their harshness has provoked presidents to act in ways that do not serve the national interest. Bartholomew H. Sparrow dissents from this view. To be sure, Sparrow argues, presidents may not be able to prevail in an open contest with the news media, but they have more subtle means of exercising their domination.

PRO: Matthew R. Kerbel

By going on the offensive on Afghanistan and by arranging a schedule that provides lots of colorful pictures, the President has sought to override criticism that he's a weak leader of the Western alliance while at the same time dominating the nightly television news. It may not have worked but as this trip demonstrates once again Mr. Carter's image makers know how to give this sort of thing an awfully good try.

—Sam Donaldson, *ABC World News Tonight,* June 26, 1980

Out for his morning jog, President [George] Bush dished out his own spin on how reporters should write about new figures showing surprising growth in the overall economy the last three months. . . . The president is seizing on a quarterly bump of 2.7 percent in the gross domestic product, which is the best measure of the economy's growth. Economists say that's a notoriously volatile number that does not necessarily mean a trend. . . . Voters tend to make up their minds not by statistics but by assessing their own economic situation. And for many voters who have seen plants close and safe jobs disappear, the highest of the measurable economic indicators is anxiety.

—Eric Enberg, *CBS Evening News with Dan Rather,* October 28, 1992

I think, Mary, the best thing you can say about this process right now is that it's chaotic and also that [President Bill Clinton] is having a terrible time in part because a lot of the people out in the public are more concerned about things like crime and certainly things like O. J. [Simpson] and the economy than they are about changing the healthcare program and that—here we are at the last minute. There are only a couple of weeks to go. They have to throw together something for which neither party has a majority, . . . which the public has not agreed on, and I think that this is a very, very hard row for the President.

—Julia Malone, *CNN and Company,* July 18, 1994

Back in this country, the debate over Social Security. Today another leading Republican raised doubts about [President George W. Bush's] plan to revamp the program, a sign that it may be in serious trouble.

—John Seigenthaler, *NBC Nightly News,* February 13, 2005

A sign for the president, indeed. Anyone who has paid casual attention to television news over the last three decades should find these comments so familiar as to be unremarkable, which is precisely why the media have caused presidents unlucky enough to serve during the heyday of network and cable television news vexing problems. There is nothing special about reporters pointing out the failed but determined media manipulation efforts of Presidents Jimmy Carter and George Bush, or the hopeless policy predicaments of Presidents Bill Clinton and George W. Bush. A Lexus/Nexus search on any contemporary president would generate a bonanza of negative stories about his failed or long-shot attempts at political, policy, and media control. Such negative themes bring drama to coverage in the television age.

Presidents throughout history have felt the burden of a constitutional separation of powers that requires them to cajole, threaten, charm, and otherwise manipulate those in Washington who stand in the way of their agendas. But only presidents of the television era have been subjected to having these efforts laid bare for a national audience, as well as having the results of presidential politicking evaluated against the unrealistic expectation that these presidents' efforts will end successfully. Constitutional design sets up presidents to fail by making them simply one actor in a system of competing actors with different political interests. Media scrutiny compounds this disadvantage by portraying presidents in a negative light that does little to enhance either their positions with the public or their strategic positions in Washington. This is not to suggest that the media should give presidents the benefit of every doubt, or that journalists should not be critical of presidential initiatives. But when reporters dwell on the manipulative underbelly of the political system and harp on political or policy failures, they do a disservice to everyone with a stake in the governing process, presidents included.

Television requires that presidential politics be portrayed as problematic. In a fashion that suits television's need to tell a story, media narratives since the 1960s have increasingly emphasized all manner of competition, from odds making on presidential policy efforts to dissecting the president's public standing.[1] Could President George W. Bush convince a reluctant Congress of his own party to change the popular Social Security system? Could President Clinton win ratification of the North American Free Trade Agreement (NAFTA) treaty? Could the first president Bush convince fellow Republicans to raise taxes? Could President Carter win the release of American hostages in Iran? How would President Gerald R. Ford convince the public that he could rein in inflation? If any of these presidents failed at any of these initiatives, how badly would it hurt his public standing or his chances for reelection? Suggesting the possibility of presidential failure was an integral part of each storyline. Discussing the race to replace the incumbent was an ever-present accompanying theme, along with periodic accounts of presidential missteps and scandals.[2]

Negative media frames prime the public to assess the president in the context of failed policy initiatives, unattractive strategic maneuvering, or both.[3]

Such negativity adversely affects how the president is evaluated by the public, which, in turn, constricts the president's ability to influence official Washington by virtue of his diminished public support.[4] The interplay between media frames and the public's response is self-fulfilling: the president is portrayed as trying desperately but unsuccessfully to control the news and policy agenda, which primes the public to experience the president negatively, thus validating reporters' expectations about presidential failure. Media coverage then shifts from negative reporting of presidential actions and outcomes to negative coverage of declining public support for the president, guaranteeing that public support will remain low.[5]

This dynamic has touched every president of the television age to some degree. For Presidents Ford, Carter and Bush senior, it contributed to a tailspin in public support from which the incumbent was unable to recover. A content analysis of network evening news coverage conducted by the Center for Media and Public Affairs divided the first three years of the Bush (senior) and Clinton administrations into twenty-four quarters and found that the incumbent averaged positive coverage in only three of them. Even when Bush had an 88 percent approval rating after the Persian Gulf War, his coverage barely averaged in the positive range.[6] More recently, the Center for Media and Public Affairs found that in the critical last months of the 2004 presidential campaign, almost two in three mainstream media references to George W. Bush were negative.[7]

The phenomenon of the media combating the president became more pronounced as the influence of television expanded. Although television has been around since the late 1940s and had national reach by the 1950s, it did not emerge as a dominant political force until the 1960s. At the beginning of the television era, a series of dramatic national events satisfied television's demand for gripping plot lines. They included political assassinations, the civil rights and women's rights movements, the Vietnam War, the Watergate scandal, and President Ford's pardon of Richard Nixon. But social activism dissipated as twenty-four-hour cable news emerged, leaving news producers with fewer inherently compelling news items at a time when increased media competition had upped the demand for gripping content. As captivating plot lines became harder to find in daily political events, reporters turned to the competition inherent in the political process to keep viewers engaged.

By emphasizing the political process over political events, television bolstered the personal presidency. It turned the president into "communicator in chief" in an era characterized by the struggle between reporters and presidents over message control. Incumbents had to operate in a political-media environment in which reporters cast presidents as political losers in an ongoing game of "gotcha." Presidents, not surprisingly, found governing difficult under these conditions.

One measure of the intensity of the struggle between reporters and presidents since the 1950s is the steadily increasing number of "feeding frenzies"—that is, exercises in pack journalism in which candidates or officeholders face the full wrath of a media hoard fixated on saturating the airwaves and dailies with juicy details about scandalous behavior. Sorting through major stories about presidential politics and governance, political scientist Larry J. Sabato identified one such frenzy in the 1950s, three in the 1960s, six in the 1970s, and fifteen in the 1980s.[8] And all this was before Bill Clinton, the walking feeding frenzy, came to power in the 1990s.

Presidents predictably pushed back. White House communications offices evolved into war rooms devoted to crafting, controlling, and disseminating administration-friendly messages.[9] Governance morphed into marketing. Administration officials spent most of their tenure competing with reporters over the content of the news agenda.[10]

A clear line of demarcation separates practices such as these—hallmarks of the television era—and earlier presidential efforts to shape news coverage. The differences are of type and degree. In 1960 presidential scholar Richard E. Neustadt commented that presidents could sometimes manufacture events to move opinion in their direction, but that the conditions for doing so were not readily available to them and that, in any event, the press would rarely cooperate for long in such initiatives.[11] In the political environment that developed over the following decades, however, White House–manufactured events became presidential job one. Similarly, when Neustadt wrote that "an image of the office, not an image of the man, is the dynamic factor in a president's prestige," Washingtonians were still talking to taxi drivers to sample public opinion.[12] Since then, ad hoc soundings have given way to wall-to-wall polls and media analysis of wall-to-wall polls, which presidential advisers attempt to shape by carefully crafting a positive image of their boss.

Although presidents since Franklin D. Roosevelt have paid attention to public opinion polling,[13] not until Lyndon B. Johnson did presidents actively attempt to influence opinion poll results.[14] In the 1940s, FDR used polling, then in its infancy, as a way of guiding his leadership decisions, but not as a device for image manipulation. According to his pollster, Hadley Cantril, Roosevelt did not alter or even shade his policy objectives to bring them in line with public opinion, choosing instead to use polls to find ways "to try to bring the public around more quickly or more effectively to the course of action he felt was best for the country."[15] His successor in office, Harry S. Truman, was notoriously hostile to opinion polls, and Dwight D. Eisenhower, who succeeded Truman, preferred to ignore them altogether.[16] These presidents had the luxury of operating without television reporting every strategic turn of events.

All this changed in the 1960s with Johnson, who tried to shape poll results by attacking negative public polls and attempting to influence them; he planted favorable information from in-house polls with sympathetic columnists and courted the favor of pollsters.[17] Nixon and Carter viewed negative poll results as an invitation to engage in public relations efforts to improve their public standing rather than to identify possible problems with where they were leading the nation.[18] Soon, political scientist Theodore J. Lowi contends, presidents essentially became spin machines, devoting the latter portions of their tenures to convincing the public that the early portions of their tenures were more successful than they appeared.[19]

For all his work, Johnson's effort to manipulate pollsters and their numbers was ineffectual.[20] Most of his successors fared no better. The clear direction of public support for presidents of the television age has been downward.

Yet, it was not always like this. In the 1950s, Eisenhower's support was steady and strong, resting in the 70 percent range for much of his two terms in office and falling only slightly at the end. His successor in office, John F. Kennedy, claimed comparable approval ratings for his first two years in office, and this rating hovered at about 60 percent support at the time of his death.[21] After that, things changed. Most presidents of the television era came to office with strong support, only to see it drop—sometimes sharply—during their first three years in office, never to see it return.[22] George W. Bush failed to receive even this initial burst of goodwill, coming to office in 2001 with middling approval scores, which, after skyrocketing to record levels in the wake of the 2001 terrorist attacks on the United States, followed a steady downward trajectory over the next four years.

Notably, in the 1980s, Ronald Reagan bucked the trend, turning an initial two-year decline into sustained support that lasted well into his second term.[23] The Reagan White House figured out how to wage a successful public relations and media relations battle, blending the former actor's communications skills with a disciplined message development and management apparatus to form the perfect combination for governing in the television age. But his efforts did not put an end to negative press coverage; the Center for Media and Public Affairs found that Reagan received a record 91 percent negative coverage while he was running for reelection.[24] Reagan's team responded by devoting a lot of energy to figuring out how to work around the critical media.

The positive trajectory of Reagan's public standing and his ability to win reelection and complete his second term unscathed were the calm exceptions in an otherwise turbulent era of television-centered administrations. Table 5-1 compares the fate of twentieth-century chief executives pre- and post-television. Before 1960, incumbents were returned to office nine times. A

Table 5-1

Stability and Change among Incumbent Presidents, 1900–2004

Stability	Change
1900–1956	
Elected/reelected	Defeated
1900　McKinley	1912　Taft
1904　T. Roosevelt	1932　Hoover
1916　Wilson	
1924　Coolidge	Open seat, vacated by incumbent
1936　F. Roosevelt	1908　T. Roosevelt
1940　F. Roosevelt	1920　Wilson
1944　F. Roosevelt	1928　Coolidge
1948　Truman	1952　Truman
1956　Eisenhower	

Stability	Change
1960–2004	
Elected/reelected	Defeated
1964　Johnson	1976　Ford
1984　Reagan	1980　Carter
1996　Clinton[a]	1992　G. Bush
2004　G. W. Bush	
	Involuntarily retired
	1968　Johnson
	Reelected, forced to resign
	1972　Nixon
	Open seat, vacated by incumbent
	1960　Eisenhower
	1988　Reagan
	2000　Clinton

Source: Matthew R. Kerbel.
[a] Impeached, not convicted.

change in administrations was more likely to be caused by an incumbent voluntarily stepping aside (four times) or dying (three times) than by an incumbent being voted out of office (twice). From 1960 to 2004, during the emergence of television-centered politics, three incumbents were turned out by voters, one (Johnson) was forced by political circumstances to abandon a reelection bid, and one (Nixon) was forced to resign in the face of certain impeachment and removal. One more had to confront the possibility of involuntary removal from office: Bill Clinton was impeached but survived the Senate trial.

Although George W. Bush survived a close reelection contest in 2004, he began his second term without a honeymoon and with the lowest approval ratings of any modern reelected president. His response, famously, was to claim a mandate despite receiving the narrowest reelection victory since 1916. It was a public relations effort that typifies presidential governance in this era: if a mandate was not forthcoming, Bush would try to create one via television. If enough people then believed he had a mandate, his public relations effort would render the same political benefits as if he had been reelected in a landslide. In keeping with the fates of contemporary presidents, the maneuver failed. Within one year of his reelection victory, Bush faced low job approval ratings and widespread speculation in official Washington that with three years left to his term he was already a lame duck.

It would be stretching things to say that the ascendancy of television is the cause of the turbulence experienced by modern presidents, but the two are strongly correlated. One might expect an era of enormous political, economic, and social change to lend instability to politics, and the period since 1960 has certainly been such a time. But then so was the rest of the century. Social and economic dislocation was a constant in the twentieth century, but the existence of a saturated media environment characterizes only the last several decades.

Negative process–oriented, horserace-centered, scandal-heavy coverage plays to television's competitive needs. But it is bad for the polity, because it turns politics into a spectator sport in which people are detached from their government. It is bad for governance, because the relentless focus on Washington's "winners and losers" detracts from examining the merits of policy. It is certainly bad for presidents, who find themselves caught up in a battle with reporters over message control that most have found they cannot win.

CON: Bartholomew H. Sparrow

Scholars tend to portray president–media relations as essentially balanced and two-sided. According to media observer Doris Graber, presidents "desperately" need the media, and the media need them just as much if not more. Even though presidents and the media have a love-hate relationship and are not able to live comfortably with each other, they do not dare go their separate ways.[1] In the battle between the White House and the media, agrees Richard Davis, another media observer, both are fully aware that they are mutually dependent and that neither one can dominate the other.[2]

There is validity to these views. Neither presidents nor the media *can* wholly dominate their counterparts; presidents and journalists *have* conflicting motivations and interests; and presidents and the media *are* unavoidably interdependent. But surely it is possible to be more specific about whether presidents or the media have the better of things. Whether the media are too hard on the president ultimately comes down to a question of power: which are better able to determine the political information that Americans receive—presidents or the media?

The answer to this question lies in a closer look at power in all its dimensions. As the sociologist Stephen Lukes points out, political actors may exercise power in several ways: by defining the circumstances of open conflict between persons or parties; by setting the agenda—that is, by determining what is (and is not) subject to debate and settlement; and by controlling how meaning is attributed to events and thereby effectively defining political culture.[3] Here Lukes's threefold typology is applied to media politics by considering president–media relations across three dimensions: (1) which party is dominating the determination of issues being openly contested in the media; (2) who is setting the political news agenda; and (3) who is controlling the "news framing"— that is, how new information is categorized, how it is connected to existing information, how it is linked to particular problems and solutions, and whether it implies or creates opposition.[4] In all but the first dimension, presidents dominate. And in the first dimension, presidents now hold a clear advantage.

CONTESTED ISSUES

In his first term, President George W. Bush and his administration largely received the coverage they wanted on the issues that had stirred political conflict. In other words, in covering the Bush administration's policy initiatives that spurred open disagreement, the media gave short shrift to the political opponents of the president's programs. Moreover, what opposition there was found expression in newspapers' op-ed pages rather than in the news itself, much less television broadcast or cable news.[5] This was particularly true of media coverage of the Bush administration's major initiatives—the PATRIOT Act, the invasion of Afghanistan, the Iraq War, the establishment of a Department of Homeland Security, the reform of the intelligence community, tax cuts for the wealthy, and the administration's overall budget priorities.

The Bush administration had the benefit, of course, of the Republican Party's control of both houses of Congress, of a vigorous Republican leadership in the House and the Senate, and of a disciplined White House. The president also profited from the rise on cable television of right-leaning Fox News with its large viewing audience, the growing prominence of Christian television and radio

broadcasting, the ongoing popularity of conservative talk radio, and the continued influence of the *Wall Street Journal, Washington Times, New York Post,* and
other conservative publications. Taken together, this new media order pushed
the centrist broadcast networks, other cable channels, and mainstream newspapers such as the *New York Times* and *Washington Post* more to the political right.

Most significant, the terrorist attacks of September 11, 2001, on the United
States gave instant legitimacy to the Bush administration after the controversial election of 2000. Bush's policy successes (and arguably his reelection) have
derived from his standing as the leader of the United States in the "war on terror," the Iraq War, and the war in Afghanistan. This is not to say that the Bush
administration had no choice in how it responded to the events of September
11, or that Bush did not play the war card to cultivate his standing as a wartime
president.[6] He did manage, however, to connect his policies and political programs—the Iraq war most obviously—to the events of September 11.

Because of the Republican control of both houses of Congress and the
White House, the rise of conservative media, and the wars, the Bush administration, until the summer of 2005, received only modest and brief challenges in
the media. In other words, the president was able to get the better part of news
coverage on the issues. As one White House official claimed, "We create our
own reality."[7] Although some may argue that this reality has begun to unravel
in the summer and fall of 2005 with the news coverage of the administration's
poor response to Hurricane Katrina, the withdrawal of Supreme Court nominee Harriet Miers, the indictment of vice-presidential aide I. Lewis "Scooter"
Libby, and the increasing pressure to bring the troops back from Iraq, little in
the media has seriously questioned or offered meaningful alternatives to any of
the policies introduced by the president—whether the PATRIOT Act, the commitment of U.S. troops in Iraq, the tax cuts for the wealthy, or the administration's other top priorities.

AGENDA SETTING

As the head of state, the U.S. president personifies the federal government. As
such, presidents are usually able to dictate what is and what is not the subject
of the news.[8] Presidents and other high-ranking officials and leading politicians drive the political agenda, not the news media.[9]

Modern presidents have become expert at using the routines of journalism
to set the national agenda. For example, they hold fewer one-on-one press conferences than their predecessors so that they can avoid difficult questions on
topics on which they are vulnerable to criticism. President George W. Bush
held fewer solo press conferences per month during his first term than did any
president since Woodrow Wilson. President Bill Clinton held the third fewest

number of press conferences during his second term in office (President Nixon held the second fewest number of press conferences during his Watergate-shortened second term in office).[10]

Presidents also avoid critical media coverage by making access to news inconvenient for the public, such as by releasing news statements before weekends or holidays. For example, on August 30, 2002—the Friday before the Labor Day weekend—the White House announced the appointment of Allan Fitzsimmons, a libertarian policy analyst who favors more logging, to oversee Bush's "Healthy Forests Initiative." Later, on Christmas Eve 2002, the administration announced that it was going to allow state and local governments to have more control over the roads, trails, and paths that cross the public lands overseen by the Bureau of Land Management. And on December 31, 2002—New Year's Eve—the White House announced rule changes to make it easier for manufacturing and refining companies to avoid installing expensive pollution controls when modernizing their plants.

Presidents use secrecy as well to ensure that some topics receive no media exposure whatsoever. After the events of September 11, the Bush administration took several steps to enhance governmental secrecy. The Intelligence Authorization Act of 2001, for example, criminalized the disclosure of any information that the executive branch determined to be properly classified, and it dictated that the president need not provide any review or explanation to extend "the full force of criminal law" to the classification of information. In addition, Bush removed the presumption of disclosure with Freedom of Information Act requests, allowed former presidents and their heirs to veto access to presidential papers, and further delayed the opening of federal records to journalists and the American public. "Among the documents that the Administration has refused to release to the public and members of Congress," stated a 2004 congressional report "are (1) the contacts between energy companies and the Vice President's energy task force, (2) the communications between the Defense Department and the Vice President's office regarding contracts awarded to Halliburton, (3) documents describing the prison abuse and use of torture at Abu Ghraib [in Iraq], (4) memoranda revealing what the White House knew about Iraq's weapons of mass destruction, and (5) the cost estimates of the Medicare prescription drug legislation withheld from Congress."[11] The media cannot report what they do not know.

Presidents also have other, more prosaic ways of setting the news agenda. They limit the length and number of their messages. They make speeches and release statements on targeted themes only. They stage attention-getting events, such as Bush's "Mission Accomplished" appearance on the deck of an aircraft carrier at sunset on May 1, 2003, or his Thanksgiving Day dinner with U.S. troops in Iraq on November 27, 2003. The Bush administration has also introduced the use of political slogans to serve as visual backdrops when the president appears in public—slogans that come across clearly in television footage or in still photographs, but that are less visible to the audience in attendance.[12]

Probably the Bush presidency's most successful effort at setting the news agenda was its embedding of reporters with troops in Iraq. The reporters produced stories that featured coalition soldiers, but they typically neglected to report on civilian casualties, the reconstruction of Iraq, and dead and injured coalition soldiers.[13] As a result, the media gave Americans a "sanitized" view of the war, one "free of bloodshed, dissent, and diplomacy but full of exciting weaponry, splashy graphics, and heroic soldiers."[14]

In summary, the Bush administration has set the news agenda by scheduling fewer press conferences, releasing controversial news quietly, increasing government secrecy, and employing masterful public relations strategies. The media have had little to cover in national politics except for subjects selected by the Bush White House.

NEWS FRAMING

The media framed the politics of the first years of the George W. Bush administration much like the White House wanted. News coverage portrayed the September 11 attacks as "national identity-affirming" events and followed the administration's lead on whom to blame, on the reaffirmation of American values, and on the assertion of U.S. strength. Similarly, the Iraq War was overwhelmingly framed in terms of military conflict and human interest, frames promoted by the Bush administration.[15] Rather than an independent, questioning press, the United States has been served by national media that have little room for genuine controversy, much less dissent.[16] Not surprisingly, too, most of the American public also saw the Iraq War this way: as a patriotic mission against an evil Iraq, with nice young American men and women fighting misguided and manic insurgents.

Not only have the media framed the terrorist attacks of September 11 as "war," just as the White House intended, but they also have cooperated with the administration on other matters—such as framing the estate tax as a "death tax," labeling intact dilation and fetus extraction as "partial birth abortion," and identifying the proposed transformation and privatization of the Social Security program as "Social Security reform." Indeed, the media have generally reported the administration's frames uncritically, and much of the American public, as a result, now understands these issues in terms of these frames. Presidential rhetoric "defines political reality," David Zarefsky writes, and with much of the media reinforcing the Bush administration's framing of the news, he is probably right.[17] The rhetoric used by President Bush has reversed the long trend of presidential rhetoric, dating back to 1948, of declining "certainty" in presidential speech. An example of "low certainty" speech is the following address by the President Bush senior on January 16, 1991, during the first Gulf War: "Prior to ordering our forces into battle, I instructed our military commanders to take every necessary step to prevail as quickly as possible, and with the greatest degree of protection possible for American and allied service men and women." An example of President George W. Bush's "high certainty" speech is his message of March 19, 2003: "Our nation enters this conflict reluctantly, yet, our purpose is sure. The people of the United States and our friends and allies will not live at the mercy of an outlaw regime that threatens the peace with weapons of mass murder. We will meet that threat now, with our Army, Air Force, Navy, Coast Guard and Marines, so that we do not have to meet it later with armies of fire fighters and police and doctors on the streets of our cities." For all the difference between the two speech types, however, the media have helped the George W. Bush presidency by consistently quoting President Bush's sentences and phrases containing the most certainty, while passing along none of the "low-certainty" segments of speech. According to some observers, "The press clearly preferred the raw meat Bush served up during his first 1,000 days in office."[18]

In summary, the record of media politics since 2000, and especially since September 11, 2001, indicates that the Bush presidency has been able to prevail over the media on all three dimensions of power. First, the media have minimized the conflicts and disagreements over the president's initiatives, while even the criticisms that began to emerge in mid-2005 have not posed serious challenges to the president's programs (with the exception of the scuttled plans for privatizing Social Security). Second, the media have gone along with the Bush administration's strategies to set the political agenda. And, third, the media have reflected in their news coverage the Republican and conservative political culture promulgated by the Bush administration and its political allies—notwithstanding the fact that the American public is far more ambivalent and centrist than the media would lead one to think.[19]

CONCLUSION

President–media relations now occupy uncharted waters. A remarkable convergence has occurred: a conservative president, an increasingly conservative media, and a unified Republican government. Bush has further helped his presidency through his own leadership style—highly disciplined and insistent on loyalty. But conditions can change. The United States may once again be at peace, the war in Iraq may get worse to the point of becoming unsustainable, and terrorism may subside; a future White House may be less disciplined; and the next president could face an opposition Congress. But the Bush administration has invented powerful tools of media management—its fusion of national security with control of political communication, its reliance on secrecy and simple slogans, its careful staging of appearances, and its assertive rhetorical style—that future presidents are also likely to adopt. This is not to imply that all presidents are equally skilled in using the tools at their disposal to manage the media in any given political era, only that the tools are out there should presidents choose to use them. And clearly George W. Bush is better at this than was his father; Bill Clinton was better than Jimmy Carter, particularly after he brought in communications specialist David Gergen and began to take White House reporters seriously; and Ronald Reagan was better than Gerald Ford.

Nor does the end of the "golden age of presidential communication"[20] mean that presidents have lost their advantage over the media. Fewer people may be reading newspapers, watching the nightly news, or otherwise attending to politics, but the evidence suggests that the rise of the "short attention span presidency,"[21] a less politically attentive audience, and the prevalence of soft news[22] helps presidents to manage the media. The collapse of a shared political news culture only makes the public that much more susceptible to the charms of human interest stories, the happy lessons of political theater, the attractions and simplifications of political advertising, and the manipulations of public relations. Future presidents, too, should be able to win on most of the issues that come up for political debate, control the political agenda, and frame political reality as they see it.

RESOLVED, the president is a more authentic representative of the American people than is Congress

PRO: Marc J. Hetherington
CON: Richard J. Ellis

Imagine the scene on inauguration day, the start of the new presidential term. Incoming president Jay Sulzmann strides to the front of the stage on the west front of the Capitol, faces the chief justice, places one hand on the Bible and raises the other heavenward, and takes the constitutional oath: "I do solemnly swear that I will execute the Office of President of the United States, and will to the best of my Ability, preserve, protect and defend the Constitution of the United States." Then, instead of turning to the audience to deliver his inaugural address, President Sulzmann steps back and waits as incoming presidents Carla Rodriguez and Michael Lamb, each in turn, come forward to take the identical oath.

Three presidents at the same time? The idea seems far-fetched, almost inconceivable. But to Edmund Randolph, the governor of Virginia and a delegate to the 1787 Constitutional Convention, a plural executive made perfect sense. Entrusting the executive power of the new national government to a single person struck Randolph (and some other delegates, including Benjamin Franklin) as a dangerous folly. A unitary executive would be the "foetus of monarchy," Randolph warned. To represent the thirteen states in all their variety, he proposed a three-person executive: one from New England, one from the South, and one from the Middle Atlantic states.

Randolph's fellow delegates voted down his proposal. Some, perhaps most of them, were persuaded that entrusting the executive power to more than one person would make it impossible to assign responsibility when something went wrong—each of the three co-presidents would point the finger of blame at the other two, and there would be no way to tell who was right. Besides, these delegates reasoned, the president would not be the chief representative of the people or the states anyway. That would be the responsibility of Congress, whose members would live in and be chosen by every part of the country.

A few delegates, however, saw the issue differently. Two Pennsylvanians in particular, James Wilson and Gouverneur Morris, worked throughout the convention to make the presidency a stronger office than most of their colleagues initially wanted. For Wilson and Morris, only a unitary executive could act with the "energy" and "dispatch" that are essential for strong leadership. Strong presidential leadership was important to them, because they believed the president was the true representative of the people. Wilson envisioned the president as "the man of the people," and Morris described the president as "the great protector of the mass of the people."

In practice, few eighteenth- and nineteenth-century presidents (Andrew Jackson was a notable exception) spoke of themselves as being more authentic representatives of the American people than Congress. President William Henry Harrison, for example, deemed "preposterous" the idea that a president could "better understand the wants and needs of the people than their representatives" in Congress. The rise of the modern presidency during the twentieth century, however, was propelled by a different theory of representation—one that regards members of Congress as servants of the special interests in their states and districts and sees the president, who alone is elected by the entire country, as representing the national interest. Congress's arcane and antimajoritarian procedural rules, as well as the Senate's overrepresentation of people who live in small states, were also thought by some observers to warp the legislature's representative character. Of course, at any given moment those whose political party controlled the presidency were more likely to make this argument than those whose party was stronger in Congress.

As Marc J. Hetherington, who regards the president as the people's more authentic representative, and Richard J. Ellis, who defends the representative primacy of Congress, reveal in their essays, the debate that began in Philadelphia in 1787 continues. Each author adds a new element—the contemporary era of ideologically polarized political parties—to the two-centuries-old controversy, but each finds in this development further grist for his mill.

PRO: Marc J. Hetherington

When the founders devised the new nation's constitutional structure, they wanted the presidency, House, and Senate to differ in their responsiveness to the public. Thus they varied both the lengths of the terms assigned to the offices and the constituencies that would elect them. With its two-year terms and direct election by the public, the House of Representatives was intended to be the most responsive. House members would serve and also reflect their relatively homogeneous constituencies. The Senate, with its six-year terms and indirect election, would be insulated from the public. Even so, because each state is smaller and more homogeneous than the nation as a whole, the Senate would be relatively consonant with the wishes of the public. Finally, the founders provided for the indirect election of the president through the electoral college. They wanted the president to be accountable to the public—the provision for reelection in the Constitution is proof. Yet the relatively long four-year term meant that the president would not need to reflect the public's wishes at all times.

If the founders could observe their handiwork today, they would be surprised. Most Americans are politically moderate; ideology does not structure the thinking of many voters. In Congress, however, few voices sound like those of the American people. In the last twenty years, the House has evolved, at least ideologically, into the least representative branch of the federal government. In a political environment driven by ideological activists in districts with hardly a trace of interparty competition, House members have grown increasingly extreme in their views and voting patterns. The Senate is not far behind, because specific states are becoming increasingly "red" or "blue," with little room for ideological moderation. Both chambers are headed by ideologically extreme elected leaders, ensuring that the recent impulse away from moderation will continue well into the future. This state of affairs in no way reflects the public at large.

In today's politics, then, the president best reflects the public's will—although imperfectly so. Presidents do not need to take account of public opinion on all issues and at all times. Yet in this era of partisan and ideological polarization, only the president must appeal to a broad cross section of voters. Recent presidential elections have been extraordinarily competitive, with the winner decided by a swing constituency that is ideologically moderate. Because most Americans are moderate, the president is more representative of the public than the Senate or, especially, the House of Representatives.

PARTY POLARIZATION IN CONGRESS

Perhaps the most important development in American politics in the last two decades has been the marked ideological polarization of the two major parties, especially in Congress. No matter the measure, it is clear that Democrats are becoming increasingly liberal and Republicans, at an even faster rate, are becoming increasingly conservative.

Figure 6-1 shows this change in the House using a measure called DW-NOMINATE scores. Devised by Keith Poole and Howard Rosenthal, these scores track the voting records of members of the House of Representatives

Figure 6-1

Distance between Average Members of House Party Caucuses, 1967–2005

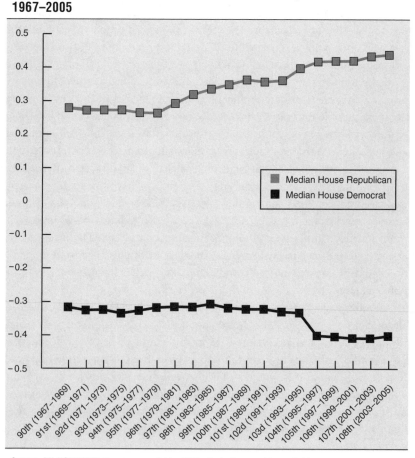

Source: DN-NOMINATE scores are available at http://voteview.com/dwnomin.htm.

over time. Each member gets a NOMINATE score for every two-year term based on the extent to which his or her voting record was conservative or liberal. Very liberal members receive very low scores, very conservative members receive very high scores, and more moderate members receive scores in between.

Sorting the Republican and Democratic members into their party caucuses reveals how remarkably ideologically distinct the parties are. Since the early 1970s, the parties have been moving apart at a breakneck pace. For example, in the Ninetieth Congress (1967–1969) the average member of each party was about 0.30 points from the ideological center, or about 0.60 points from each other. By the 108th Congress (2003–2005), the difference between the parties had increased to nearly 0.90 points, almost twice as great. Most of the polarization has taken place since the mid-1980s.

Not only is the "average" member of the House increasingly extreme, congressional leaders are even more so, which, in turn, has probably accelerated the parties' continued movement apart. Not many years ago, leaders tended to come from the ideological center of each party. For example, for most of the 1980s the House minority leader was Robert Michel, R-Ill., who had a DW-NOMINATE score that placed him in the middle quartile of his party. The majority leader, Jim Wright, D-Texas, was another moderate. His NOMINATE score placed him at the exact median of his party when he first became its leader. These ideological "middlemen" made certain that the caucuses did not stray too far to the left or to the right. Today, however, they have been replaced by ideological extremists. For example, when the Republican Party first elected Tom DeLay of Texas into the leadership along with fellow Texan Richard Armey in 1993, both were in the most extreme 3 percent of their party. Although DeLay's record moderated a bit after he became majority leader in 2002, he was still in the most extreme 20 percent of his party. Nancy Pelosi, D-Calif., who was elected minority leader of the House in 2002, was similarly extreme in her caucus. As a result, increasingly extreme parties in Congress were being led by even more extreme leaders.

The reasons for this change are many. The most important is that the once solidly Democratic South is now a Republican stronghold. In the 1950s, Republicans controlled only a tiny number of seats in what is today among the most conservative regions of the country. During that period, the large number of conservative southern Democrats in Congress ensured that their party remained quite moderate to counterbalance the party's conservative southern and progressive northern wings. But when the Democratic Party championed civil rights in the 1960s, it sparked a fundamental realignment in American politics. During the next three decades, the Democratic Party fell into disfavor in the South and was dislodged by an even more conservative southern GOP.

In 1994 Republicans won more than 50 percent of the House districts in the eleven states of the former Confederacy for the first time. In the 2004 election, they upped that percentage to 63. No longer, then, did liberal Democrats need to take account of a substantial conservative wing.

Meanwhile, a similar, although less dramatic, change was taking place in the Northeast. Traditionally, the New England and Middle Atlantic states have been liberal, but they have elected a fair share of liberal Republicans to Congress. In the decades after the civil rights revolution, these liberal northeastern Republicans were in large measure replaced in Congress by even more liberal northeastern Democrats. The results of these regional shifts have been fewer members of Congress who are ideologically in tune with the other party and thus two parties that are ideologically much more homogeneous.

The political reform movement that followed the Vietnam War and Watergate scandals in the 1960s and 1970s also contributed (unwittingly) to this trend toward more ideologically extreme parties in Congress. Campaign finance laws passed during this period were intended to minimize the role of sometimes corrupt party organizations. Indeed, initially the new streams of money opened by the Federal Election Campaign Act of 1974 provided candidates the freedom to govern in less party-centered ways. As time passed, however, elections were dominated by a disproportionate number of ideological activists whose chief desire was to implement policy objectives—a desire that ran counter to that of members produced by the old patronage-driven boss system. Because patronage depended on winning elections, party bosses tended to choose ideological moderates as candidates. The new breed of candidate values ideological outcomes more than patronage.

In the House, redistricting has also hastened the trend toward ideologically extreme parties in Congress. In its *Baker v. Carr* (1962) decision, the U.S. Supreme Court ruled that congressional districts must be of approximately equal population, and it called on each state to redraw its congressional districts after every decennial census to reflect changes in population.[1] After the 1990 and 2000 censuses, redistricters took full advantage of great advances in computer technology to protect incumbents from competition. The original concern about redistricting was that the majority party in each state would attempt to maximize its partisan advantage by drawing districts so that the other party could not compete. The more recent concern has been that redistricting officials from both parties would collude to protect as many incumbents from interparty competition as possible.

The latter concern is well founded. Although always high, the reelection rate of House incumbents is now stratospheric. In 2004 only nine incumbents tasted defeat (two in primaries, seven in general elections). Moreover, only a small handful of races were even close. The benchmark for a marginal district (one that can be won by either party) is that the winning candidate triumphs with less than 55 percent of the two-party vote. In 2004 a mere 8 percent of races were marginal, and the average House incumbent won with 70 percent of the vote. In fact, sixty-two House races featured no major-party competition at all. Open-seat races—those with no incumbent running—are ordinarily the most competitive. Yet in 2004 only five of the thirty-two open-seat races were won by the party opposite that of the retiring member, a historically very low percentage.

Because they face little competition in general elections, House members are not particularly constrained by public opinion. To the extent that real competition may arise in their districts, it is more likely to occur in a primary than a general election. But primary voters tend to be much more ideologically

Figure 6-2a

Support for Positions Held by Americans for Democratic Action (ADA) and by American Conservative Union (ACU) by Selected Senators, 99th Congress (1985–1987), First Session

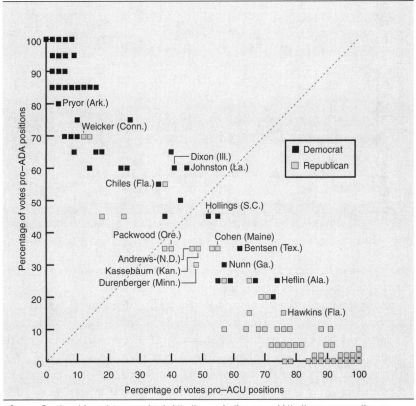

Source: Developed from data appearing in http://www.adaction.org and http://www.conservative.org.

Figure 6-2b

Support for Positions Held by Americans for Democratic Action (ADA) and by American Conservative Union (ACU) by Selected Senators, 107th Congress (2001–2003), First Session

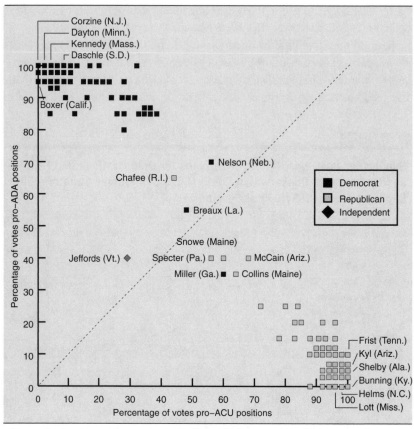

Source: Developed from data appearing in http://www.adaction.org and http://www.conservative.org.

extreme than the electorate as a whole. This fact further reinforces the polarization that is occurring in the House of Representatives.

Although it has not been as stark, the Senate has been undergoing a change similar to that under way in the House for all the same reasons except for redistricting, which does not apply to the Senate. Figure 6-2 provides two snapshots of the Senate's ideological makeup—one taken in 1985 and one taken in 2001. The x-axis in both graphs is the loyalty score awarded to House members by the Americans for Democratic Action (ADA), a liberal interest group. The score represents the percentage of time a senator votes with the ADA on bills it cares about. The y-axis is the score awarded by the American Conservative Union (ACU), a conservative interest group.

Figure 6-2a reveals that in the 1980s some senators in both parties scored about 50 percent, indicating ideological moderation. About half the time they voted with the conservatives and about half the time they voted with the liberals. In fact, some Republican senators appear on the liberal side of the figure and even more Democrats appear on the conservative side. Each party also had a fair number of ideologues, clustered in the upper left-hand and lower right-hand corners of the figure, but the important point is that the distribution of senators in both parties was widely dispersed.

The picture looks much different in the 2000s (Figure 6-2b). Only a handful of senators appear in the center. For every moderate like Ben Nelson, D-Neb., or Arlen Specter, R-Pa., there are ten ideologues like Trent Lott, R-Miss., or Edward M. Kennedy, D-Mass., who almost always vote conservative or liberal, respectively.

If the public were similarly polarized along ideological lines, then Congress's ideological polarization would be representative. The public, however, is not ideological in any meaningful sense of the word. Indeed, perhaps the most durable finding from the last fifty years of public opinion research is that Americans know little about politics and thus are unable to organize their thoughts about politics in ideological terms. Individuals' opinions about issues tend to oscillate wildly, which is inconsistent with the notion that their preferences are deeply held.

Americans do not seem to want to think of themselves as ideologues either. Since 1972, the National Election Study has asked Americans to place themselves along a seven-point ideological scale ranging from extremely liberal on one end to extremely conservative at the other. They can also call themselves "liberal," "slightly liberal," "slightly conservative," or "conservative." The midpoint of the scale is labeled "moderate" or "middle of the road." People can also indicate that they have not thought very much about their political position. In the seventeen studies since the question's debut, a minimum of 22 percent of respondents have availed themselves of the "haven't thought much about it" option. Among those who do place themselves on the scale, the most popular choice in all seventeen studies has been "moderate, middle of the road."

In 2004, for example, 25 percent of respondents called themselves moderate and another 24 percent said they had not thought much about it. In other words, about 50 percent of Americans eschewed the liberal and conservative labels altogether. A combined 20 percent of respondents said they are either slightly liberal (8 percent) or slightly conservative (12 percent). Although most members of Congress are extremely conservative or extremely liberal, only 5 percent of the public thinks of itself as such.

In general, public opinion tends to follow changes in the behavior of leaders. But such a shift has not happened to any meaningful degree with ideological identification. In 1972, for example, only 44 percent of respondents placed themselves in either of the three liberal or three conservative categories. In 2004 that percentage was 51 percent. The difference represents an increase in ideological self-identification, but not one that in any way reflects the increase that has occurred in Congress. The public, by any measure, is centrist. The House and Senate are not.

THE PRESIDENT IS A LITTLE DIFFERENT

Presidents face a different set of political imperatives that make them significantly more representative of the public as a whole than are members of Congress (especially in view of its present polarization). The last two presidential elections have been remarkably close, especially in the electoral vote count. George W. Bush's thirty-four-electoral-vote victory in 2004 may have seemed like a landslide compared with his five-electorate-vote victory in 2000, but it was still razor-thin by historical standards. Over the last fifty years, the Kennedy-Nixon and Carter-Ford elections produced popular votes that were just as close, but they also produced eighty-four- and fifty-seven-electoral-vote victories, respectively. Only one election in the twentieth century had a closer electoral vote count than the 2004 election—Woodrow Wilson's twenty-three-electoral-vote victory over Charles Hughes in 1916.

Despite the closeness of the national result in 2004, an increasingly larger number of states are uncompetitive, which is consistent with the trend toward a polarized Senate. In 1960, when the national popular vote margin was razor-thin, only six states gave one candidate a twenty percentage point victory over the other; eighteen states produced a victory margin of less than five percentage points, which is the usual definition of a battleground state. Likewise, the 1976 election, in which Jimmy Carter won a 2.1 percentage point victory in the national popular vote (about the same as George W. Bush's 2.8 percentage point victory in 2004), produced six twenty-plus percentage point blowouts and twenty battleground states. By 2004, however, things had changed. The number of blowouts had increased to seventeen, and the number of battleground states had dropped to twelve.

And what role do battleground states play in any argument claiming that the president is more representative of the public than Congress? These states are, after all, the ones that both parties know they must win to take the presidency. Thus presidential candidates spend the bulk of their time trying to carry these states. In both 2000 and 2004, the twelve battleground states were the same: Colorado, Florida, Iowa, Michigan, Minnesota, Nevada, New Hampshire, New Mexico, Ohio, Oregon, Pennsylvania, and Wisconsin. For the most part, these are moderate states with heterogeneous electorates that require presidential candidates to appeal to the political center.

Most battleground states fall into two categories. Half of them are in the Rust Belt and the upper Midwest—that is, those states that run almost without interruption from Pennsylvania in the east to Iowa and Minnesota in the west. Each of these states has a significant labor movement, and all but Iowa has a major urban center, both of which favor Democrats. But each also has large rural and suburban populations, which tend to favor Republicans. The other cluster of battleground states is in the Southwest: Colorado, Nevada, and New Mexico. All three have strong Republican traditions, but also increasingly large Latino populations. Although Bush increased his share of the Latino vote in 2004, it is still a strongly Democratic constituency. Moreover, the growth of the Latino population is increasing the heterogeneity of these states, which, in turn, is contributing to their political moderation.

Another indication of the moderation of these states can be found in their choice of senators. Only thirteen states currently have one Democratic and one Republican senator, a clear sign that their voters are comfortable voting for both conservatives and liberals. Seven (Colorado, Florida, Iowa, Minnesota, Nevada, New Mexico, and Oregon) of the twelve presidential battleground states are among these thirteen. In the face of such moderation in these battleground states, the president is compelled to tout policies that bridge the partisan divide.

In addition, as revealed in the previous section, most Americans, when considering the nation as a whole, are moderate and nonideological. A president who fails to account for this factor runs the risk of alienating a large chunk of the public. Indeed George W. Bush, a president who has often catered to his religious conservative and pro-business base on domestic policy, provides a good example of the pitfalls of an overly ideological president. It is not surprising in this polarized time that the difference in presidential approval ratings between Democrats and Republicans for Bush have never been larger in the history of polling, which dates to the 1930s. Republicans love him, and Democrats hate him. Importantly, however, the broad partisan and ideological middle has grown to dislike him as well, which accounts for his overall unpopularity in his second term. Individual members of Congress, especially in the House, face much less risk.

CONCLUSION

Presidential candidates face a different electorate than most members of Congress. House members' districts tend, by nature, to be relatively homogeneous, and redistricting has made them more so. Thus members have little incentive to embrace ideological moderation. Indeed, because the competition House members face is potentially greater in primaries, ideological extremity is almost a necessity. Most senators have moved toward one ideological pole or the other as well. Some states with especially heterogeneous populations do elect moderate senators, but they make up only a small minority of states. This relatively small group of truly moderate states is, however, decisive in determining who wins presidential elections. Thus presidential candidates must tailor their messages and policies to appeal to the most moderate voters in these moderate states.

CON: Richard J. Ellis

The notion that the president is the truest or most authentic representative of the American people is an old one, dating back at least to Andrew Jackson. Its enduring appeal rests in large part on the American people's habitual distrust of politicians, parties, and legislative bodies. Members of Congress are typically denigrated as parochial or in the pocket of powerful interests, corrupt and out of touch with the people who sent them to Washington, D.C. The chief beneficiary of this deeply ingrained skepticism of Congress is the president.[1]

To be sure, the president's claim to being the most authentic representative of the people rests on more than Congress bashing. It also stems from the fact that the president is the only government official selected by all American citizens. Members of Congress are elected in contests open only to a small fraction of the American people: those who reside in a particular state or electoral district. But the question is not whether the president is a truer representative of the nation than a senator from Rhode Island or a representative from Georgia, but rather whether the president more authentically represents the American people than does the political deliberations of 535 representatives selected from every part of the nation.

One does not have to look hard to find some of the many ways in which the will of the people—or at least the will of the majority of the people—may be frustrated in a legislature. The legislative structure provides a plethora of veto points whereby intense, well-organized minority interests can prevent action from being taken on a piece of legislation. Indeed, the halls of Congress are littered with apparently popular proposals that never made it out of committee, or that made it out only in a hopelessly watered down form. Further attenuating the connection between voter preference and congressional output is the

power of incumbency. High name recognition coupled with attentive constituency service and massive fund raising can help to insulate a member of
Congress from shifts in popular opinion. And when districts are redrawn to
make incumbents' seats safer still, Congress's responsiveness to public opinion
drops even further.

It is right, then, to reject the assumption that Congress will automatically
and accurately mirror voter preferences. That the legislative process often dis-
torts the popular will is indisputably true. In fact, to some extent it intention-
ally thwarts majority preferences—the filibuster is but one example. But it does
not follow from this observation that the president more accurately represents
the will of the people. Indeed, the president is, in many ways, less representative of the people than is Congress.

How can that be? After all, the president is elected by the people. If the people do not like what the president is doing in their name they can throw the
rascal out of office. This observation has an intuitive appeal, but it makes certain assumptions about voter behavior that turn out often not to be justified.
In particular, it assumes that voters, first, know the candidates' stands on issues,
and, second, vote on the basis of the candidates' issue positions.

But even when voters have strong views on issues, they often have a difficult
time connecting those issues to the positions taken by the candidates. In 2000,
for example, George W. Bush made tax cuts the centerpiece of his campaign,
yet polling data collected by the National Annenberg Election Survey found
that only 60 percent of respondents identified Bush as the candidate who
favors "the biggest tax cut." And when asked whether Bush or his Democratic
opponent, Al Gore, favored using the Medicare surplus to finance tax cuts, only
51 percent of respondents identified this as the position of candidate Bush.[2] If
people do not know what a candidate's issues positions are, they cannot use
their vote to express their issue preferences.

President Bill Clinton had the same problem, particularly when he took centrist positions. A 1998 poll showed that although nearly seven in ten respondents knew that Clinton supported a woman's right to have an abortion, only
about one in four knew that Clinton had not promoted a universal system of
national health insurance. A mere 13 percent knew that Clinton had signed welfare reform into law. Even when offered only two choices, fewer than a quarter
knew (or guessed correctly) that the Clinton administration opposed the international treaty banning land mines. And it was not that people were not following politics: 93 percent could correctly identify White House intern Monica
Lewinsky. But when it came to identifying the president's issue positions, particularly those in which he tacked to the center, voters failed miserably.[3]

And, of course, in presidential elections much more is at stake than issue
positions. Voters are encouraged to think about the candidate's character and

experience. Most Americans probably want voters to think about a candidate's temperament before deciding on whether that person should possess the power to destroy the world many times over. But casting a vote based on character and experience, however sensible, weakens the connection between the vote and support for issue positions. The more that character matters, the less the vote for president can tell us about the policy preferences of voters.

Finally, even if voters were perfectly informed about the issues and the candidates' positions on those issues, and voted entirely on the basis of those positions, there would still be reason to question whether a president's programmatic agenda represented the will of the people. Claims that the president has a mandate from the people are inherently implausible because, as political scientist Raymond E. Wolfinger reminds us, there are many issues but only one vote.[4] In other words, even in a hypothetical environment of informed, purely issue-oriented voters (an environment that does not exist today and has never existed in the past), a president's electoral victory reveals little about the issue preferences of the electorate. Only if these perfectly informed issue voters arrange their issue preferences in ideologically consistent packages that are identical to those of the candidate would candidate choice reflect voters' issue preferences. In the real world, presidential candidates are about as likely to win in spite of their issue positions as because of them.

In short, presidential election results are an unreliable indicator of public opinion on any given issue. The mere fact that a candidate is elected president says next to nothing about what issue positions voters favor or the issues they care about most. The only halfway reliable way to know what voters prefer is to poll them. Thus even though the president is elected by all the people, the president is not any more likely than Congress to represent voter preferences. The difference is that media pundits and Washington insiders regularly make the mistake of assuming that presidents have electoral mandates to pursue particular policies, whereas the same mistake is rarely made when those same people talk about Congress.

The real test, then, is whether the president or Congress actually pushes policies that are closer to the views of the public. One might think presidents would move closer to the views of the people in an effort to boost their popularity and gain reelection. But do presidents in fact single-mindedly seek to boost their popularity? Are they single-mindedly focused on reelection? And is their behavior significantly different in this respect from that of members of Congress?

Even if it is assumed that presidents single-mindedly seek reelection, this motivation is more likely to lead them to keep the economy purring than it is to prompt them to adopt particular issue positions. It is a long-standing precept of political behavior that in the general election presidential candidates

tack to the center to appeal to the median voter's preference. The electoral college is supposed to accentuate this tendency, because a presidential candidate's
attention is necessarily focused on the most competitive states. But is that how
presidential candidates really behave? Certainly in 2004 the candidates spent
the lion's share of their time in competitive states. But did Bush focus his campaign in Ohio on moderate swing voters? Or did he seek to turn out his evan-
gelical base, just as the Democrats in Ohio countered by turning out their
African American base? The fewer the number of undecided voters, the greater
is the incentive for presidential candidates to appeal to their base rather than
to reach for the middle.

An incumbent president has a particularly strong incentive to pay attention
to his partisan base. Since 1970, the only incumbent presidents to be defeated
were those who faced stiff primary challenges, from the right if they were
Republicans and from the left if they were Democrats. Republican Gerald R.
Ford went down to defeat in 1976 after receiving a stern primary challenge
from Ronald Reagan; Democrat Jimmy Carter was defeated in 1980 after being
pressed to the wire by fellow Democrat Edward M. Kennedy; and Republican
George Bush lost in 1992 after having to fend off a bitter primary challenge
from Pat Buchanan. The four incumbent presidents who won—Richard
Nixon, Ronald Reagan, Bill Clinton, and George W. Bush—faced no serious
primary opposition. So even a president who focuses single-mindedly on his
reelection would arguably be more concerned with placating his base than
appealing to the middle.

Even if one accepts the unlikely premise that the electoral needs of presidents push them toward the political center, that argument would only hold for
a first-term president. The Twenty-second Amendment cuts the knot between
a second-term president and the people. Second-term presidents may still
worry about their popularity, especially if they think it will improve their effectiveness (though the empirical evidence that it does is decidedly mixed), but
they have their eyes on a larger agenda: their place in history. Such a president
may pursue wise or unwise policies, but those policies will be shaped far more
by the views, beliefs, prejudices, and wisdom of the president and his closest
advisers than it is by the views of "the people."

Consider Social Security. When voters were asked in 2003 or 2004 what was
the most important problem facing the country, few said the looming crisis in
Social Security. Yet after the 2004 election President Bush made Social Security
the issue facing the country. Moreover, the president's position on the issue—
that it should be privatized and that there should be benefit cuts rather than
tax increases—was not a position shared by the American people. When
polled, the most popular answer with the American people was a modest
increase in the level at which income was exempt from Social Security taxes.

The president's position represented not the views of the people; it represented his own views and those of his advisers and some vocal Republican activists.

By contrast, members of Congress, even quite conservative members from relatively safe seats, were much more in tune with the concerns and anxieties of the American people. When members went back to their districts to talk about the president's plan, they encountered real voters with real concerns, and they immediately transmitted those anxieties back to Washington. When members of Congress held town hall meetings to talk about Social Security, they were not the carefully scripted, invitation-only affairs favored by the Bush administration. Rather, they were open to all comers, and so were louder, angrier, and more skeptical. In these meetings were heard the discordant notes of democracy, notes that the representatives of the people carried back to the capital.

Of course, presidents—even second-term presidents—look at polls. But they use polls less to make policy than to sell policy. For example, focus groups and internal polls prompted the Bush administration to stop talking about the privatization of Social Security and to talk instead about "personal accounts." Polls drove the packaging, but they did not change the policy. In short, presidents pay attention to polls not in order to follow the public's will but to mold it.[5]

Moreover, democratic responsiveness is often not even regarded as a virtue in presidents. Presidents who try to tack to the center or pay too much attention to public opinion polls are viewed as either weak or untrustworthy ("Slick Willy"). Presidents who stand by their convictions, even when those convictions are not shared by a majority of the American people, are praised as men of resolute courage and character. And if it is character that matters to voters in choosing a president, then it should hardly be a surprise that presidents do not feel a pressing need to be responsive to voter preferences on issues.

All government, as historian Edmund S. Morgan has rightly observed, "requires make-believe. Make believe that the king is divine, make believe that he can do no wrong or make believe that the voice of the people is the voice of God. Make believe that the people *have* a voice or make believe that the representatives of the people *are* the people. Make believe that the governors are the servants of the people."[6] Make believe that when presidents speak they speak as the voice of the people. Make believe that presidents have mandates from the people to enact policies. Make believe that, as political scientist Clinton Rossiter put it, presidents are "the one-man distillation of the American people."[7] Make believe—this time in the words of Woodrow Wilson—that "when the president speaks in his true character, he speaks for no special interest."[8] Make believe that when presidents act, the people rule. Elections, contrary to what these fictions would have us believe, are primarily events in which Americans choose which few individuals will rule over the rest of them.

The same is true for Congress. But in American politics there is little danger that people will uncritically accept the myth that the voice of the people expresses itself through Congress. Skepticism of politicians in Congress runs deep. Congress is the only "distinctly native American criminal class," jibed Mark Twain. But the presidency poses a qualitatively different challenge. The president speaks with a single voice, and the president claims to speak for all Americans. The news Americans read and see on television is structured around the president's agenda and the president's words. Individual presidents may be unpopular, but Americans are loath to relinquish the fiction that the president speaks for all Americans. The truth, however, is that the president is just an extremely powerful politician whose policies are about as likely to reflect public opinion as not.

To reject the idea that the president is the most authentic representative of the people is to defend not only Congress but democratic politics. It is to insist that 300 million people are more likely to be represented in all their diversity by 535 people than they are by a single person. Deliberations in Congress *are* more rancorous, but that is because Congress, for all its many failings, is a more open, democratic institution than is the modern presidency. Democracy, moreover, is not about finding an "authentic" expression of the people's voice, because "the people" do not have a single voice. Rather, the people make a cacophonous variety of sounds and utterances, and those sounds and utterances are far more likely to be heard in the halls of Congress than they are in the speeches of a president.

7

RESOLVED, presidents have usurped the war power that rightfully belongs to Congress

PRO: Nancy Kassop

CON: Richard M. Pious

War transforms nations and governments. It centralizes power. It elevates state over society, the national government over local and regional governments, and the executive over the legislature. State building in Europe—in countries such as Great Britain, France, and Germany—was a direct result of war and the threat of war. Throughout much of its early history, the United States was blessedly free of the threat of war. Separated from the European powers by a vast ocean, the United States was able to maintain a relatively small military, a weak central government, and a limited executive.

The astute French observer Alexis de Tocqueville correctly diagnosed the political significance of America's isolation from the great powers of Europe.[1] Tocqueville understood that "it is chiefly in the realm of foreign relations that the executive power of a nation finds occasion to demonstrate its skill and strength." The United States that Tocqueville observed in 1831 had "an army that consists of six thousand soldiers" and a navy of "only a few vessels." The president was empowered by the Constitution to "direct the Union's dealings with foreign nations," but the nation had "no neighbors" and "no enemies." From Tocqueville's Eurocentric point of view, the United States was "separated from the rest of the world by the Atlantic Ocean." Rarely, he observed, "do its interests intersect with those of other nations of the globe." The result was that, although "the president of the United States possesses prerogatives that are almost royal in magnitude" (especially as the commander in chief), "he has no occasion to use" such powers, "and the powers that he has been able to use until now have been very circumscribed."

For Tocqueville, these observations underlined the need to look beyond formal powers and constitutional theories. "The law," he wrote, "allows [the president] to be strong, but circumstances keep him weak." Yet "if the existence of the Union were under constant threat, if its great interests were daily intertwined with those of other powerful nations, the executive power would take on increased importance in the public eye, because people would expect more of it, and it would do more." In other words, if and when circumstances changed to diminish the importance of the Atlantic Ocean as a barrier, then the chief executive of the United States would begin to look more like the strong executives of Europe. Executive power—along with the power of the central government as a whole—would grow. Not for the only time, Tocqueville was prescient.

Of course, the United States did have its wars in the nineteenth century, none more important than the Civil War. But during the Civil War, and even during World War I, the growth in executive power and in the control exercised by the central government was followed by a period of reaction in which nearly all of the powers bestowed on the executive and the central government were dismantled. The executive powers exercised during these wars were justified as extraordinary measures necessitated by a national emergency. It was expected that after the threat passed, the political system would revert to its normal, more decentralized pattern of authority.

At first, it appeared that World War II would follow this venerable American tradition of wartime centralization and peacetime reaction. But the cold war with the Soviet Union changed that pattern. War was no longer a temporary state but a permanent condition. Anxiety about the communist threat justified the accretion of executive power. After the Berlin Wall was torn down in 1989 and the Soviet Union collapsed in 1991, it appeared that the pendulum might swing back again. With the nation no longer under threat from communism, executive power no longer seemed essential. Many scholars in the Clinton years and in the opening months of George W. Bush's presidency forecast a weakened president and a smaller central government. But the September 11, 2001, terrorist attacks on the United States changed all that. The cold war was replaced by the "war on terror," which, like the cold war, has no clear beginning or end. The anxiety about threats to the nation is ubiquitous, the state of crisis permanent. And with these feelings of anxiety about the nation's safety have come, as Tocqueville predicted, an increase in executive power.

Whether that change is good or bad, and whether it is contrary to the intentions of the framers of the Constitution, are among the subjects of the debate between Nancy Kassop and Richard M. Pious. Kassop laments that Americans have forgotten the wisdom of the framers, who placed the power to "declare war" in the hands of Congress. Pious, by contrast, sees the Constitution (in legal scholar Edward S. Corwin's famous phrase) as "an invitation to struggle" for control of foreign policy. In Pious's telling, it is not that the president has usurped the war power of Congress but that Congress, with an assist from the courts, has essentially handed power over to the president.

PRO: Nancy Kassop

"The Constitution . . . is an invitation to struggle for the privilege of direct-ing American foreign policy."[1] So wrote the constitutional scholar Edward S. Corwin in 1957. But the words of the framers of the Constitution are actually clear and unambiguous, leaving little over which to struggle. Article I gives Congress the power to declare war, along with the power to pro-vide for and maintain an army and a navy. Article II designates the president as commander in chief, whose authority, according to Alexander Hamilton in *Federalist* No. 69, "would amount to nothing more than the supreme command and direction of the military and naval forces, as first general and admiral of the Confederacy; while that of the British king extends to the *declaring* of war and to the *raising* and *regulating* of fleets and armies—all which, by the Constitution under consideration, would appertain to the legislature."[2] Thus, as with most of the other shared powers in the Constitution, the lines of authority delineated by the framers for Congress and the president seem clear.

Article II, Section 2, of the Constitution reads: "The President shall be Commander in Chief of the Army and Navy of the United States, and of the Militia of the several States, when called into the actual Service of the United States." That provision gives the president a title, commander in chief, but no specific list of powers that can be exercised in that capacity. It also suggests that the president is not "Commander in Chief" all of the time, but only "when called into the actual Service of the United States." As Hamilton wrote, also in *Federalist* No. 69, "The President will have only the occasional command of such part of the militia of the nation as by legislative provision may be called into the actual service of the nation."[3] Further evidence of Hamilton's under-standing that the president's power was to be limited is found in his proposal to the Constitutional Convention (he was a delegate from New York) that the president "have the direction of war when authorized or begun."[4] It is Congress, then, that calls the president into service as commander in chief when it declares war or authorizes the use of force by statute. The framers could not have been clearer: the decision to go to war belongs to the delibera-tive branch of government, because declaring war is a political decision to move the nation from a state of peace to a state of war. Only then does the pres-ident command the troops and conduct military operations.[5] As law professor Louis Henkin has noted, "Generals and admirals, even when they are 'first,' do not determine the political purposes for which troops are to be used; they com-mand them in the execution of policy made by others."[6]

The framers, however, were not blind to the possibility that emergency or exigent situations could arise. Notes from the Constitutional Convention confirm that the delegates' change in wording of Article I—from the power "to make war" to the power "to declare war"—indicated their intention to give the president "the power to repel sudden attacks" without specific statutory authorization from Congress.[7] But this sole exception makes the rule all the more plain: presidents can act on their own *only* in defensive circumstances. Any offensive military action, regardless of size, duration, or purpose, must be authorized by Congress. Offensive versus defensive was the crucial distinction for the framers. However, enforcement of that distinction, at least since the middle of the twentieth century, has been sorely lacking. No delegate at the Constitutional Convention, not even Hamilton, would recognize the power to use military force that presidents have wielded in the international arena since World War II.

Thus at a bare minimum the Constitution requires the following:

1. All offensive uses of military force must be authorized by Congress, either through a formal declaration of war or by specific statutory authorization. In either case, joint action by both branches is required— that is, passage by both houses of Congress and signing by the president.

2. Any independent constitutional authority the president may have to direct the use of military force without Congress's approval must be defensive in purpose—"to repel sudden attacks."

3. The president's status as commander in chief is confined to the authority to conduct military operations when Congress determines, through the mechanisms of a declaration of war or specific statutory authorization, that such operations are warranted.

4. The president's status as commander in chief confers on the president, subject to Congress's authorization, the power to conduct military operations after Congress has identified the location, purpose, scope, and, to the extent possible, anticipated duration of hostilities. Status as commander in chief does not confer a "blanket" or open-ended authority to direct domestic policy, unless Congress has delegated specific emergency powers to the president in connection with the use of military force it already has approved as law.

5. In order for Congress to make effective judgments about whether to authorize the use of military force in any situation, the president and other executive branch officials must make good-faith efforts to supply the legislature with accurate, timely, valid, and, as much as possible, complete information. Congress is at the mercy of the executive branch to provide it with information. The decisions it makes are only as good as the information it receives.

6. The constitutional requirement that Congress approve the use of military force is not satisfied by the approval of other international bodies, such as the North Atlantic Treaty Organization (NATO) or the United Nations Security Council. When an international body calls for the deployment of U.S. military forces, Congress must first give its approval.

Each of these constitutional requirements has been violated by presidents, with increasing impunity, since the mid-twentieth century. Some presidents have violated more than one of these requirements in a single decision. President Harry S. Truman's decision to send U.S. troops to Korea in December 1950 is the most-cited example of a president ordering troops into combat on the basis of inherent executive authority without any participation by Congress. Truman's action violated all of the items just listed. He sent troops to Korea without either a declaration of war by Congress or specific statutory authorization (No. 1). The purpose of the action was not to repel an attack against the United States, but rather to protect U.S. interests by defending an ally against communist aggression (No. 2). Truman based his decision to employ U.S. forces on his commander in chief authority alone, without any participation by Congress (No. 3). He issued an executive order in April 1952 directing the secretary of commerce to seize privately owned steel mills and operate them under government control, arguing, partly on the basis of his status as commander in chief, that averting a strike and continuing production of steel were essential for the war effort (No. 4). He did not consult with or inform Congress about his ordering of U.S. troops to Korea before announcing his decision to the American public (No. 5). And he cited a United Nations Security Council resolution as justification for sending U.S. forces to Korea (No. 6).[8]

Truman's actions established a precedent for presidents to ignore and bypass what had previously been understood and honored, more or less, as baseline constitutional requirements. Previous presidents had, at times, acted on their own authority. For example, Franklin D. Roosevelt made a destroyers-for-bases deal with Great Britain in 1940, and in the spring and summer of 1941 he sent American forces to Greenland and Iceland. He also ordered U.S. naval ships in the North Atlantic to "shoot on sight" any German and Italian submarines west of the twenty-sixth meridian.[9] Although Roosevelt ordered these actions without congressional authorization, historian Arthur M. Schlesinger Jr. has shown that, for the bases deal, the president did conduct "extensive and vigilant consultation—within the executive branch, between the executive and legislative branches, among leaders of both parties and with the press."[10] Schlesinger concedes that Roosevelt's prewar actions skirted the edge of the president's constitutional authority, but Schlesinger notes that FDR displayed "a lurking sensitivity to constitutional issues," that he "made no general claims to inherent presidential power," and that he "did not assert . . . that there was no need to consider Congress because his role as Commander in Chief gave him all the authority he needed." [11]

Thus the shift in constitutional approach from Roosevelt to Truman was significant, if not tectonic. Most important, it signaled a new interpretation of the commander in chief clause as a source of executive authority independent of Congress. Such power, once seized without effective challenge, is unlikely ever to be returned. Congress certainly has made little effort to remedy its loss of constitutional authority to the president. [12]

JUSTIFICATIONS FOR PRESIDENTIAL EXPANSIONISM

To understand how this changed interpretation of presidential authority was justified, one need look no further than a 1966 memo written in defense of the Vietnam War by State Department legal adviser Leonard Meeker. [13] Acknowledging that the president's authority to commit U.S. forces to Vietnam did not depend on constitutional sources alone, because Congress and the SEATO (Southeast Asia Treaty Organization) Treaty had supplemented that authority, Meeker nevertheless offered a sweeping, absolutist view of presidential power based on the commander in chief clause. "Under the Constitution," he wrote, "the President, in addition to being Chief Executive, is Commander in Chief of the Army and Navy. He holds the prime responsibility for the conduct of United States foreign relations. These duties carry very broad powers, including the power to deploy American forces abroad and commit them to military operations when the President deems such action necessary to maintain the security and defense of the United States." [14]

Meeker's argument is a blatant misrepresentation of what the framers intended the commander in chief clause to mean. The framers attached no substantive powers to that title, other than to direct the military once Congress had commanded the president to do so. Only to repel a sudden attack could the commander in chief initiate military action.

Meeker's counterargument is that "in 1787 the world was a far larger place, and the framers probably had in mind attacks upon the United States. In the twentieth century, the world has grown smaller. An attack on a country far from our shores can impinge directly on the nation's security. . . . The Constitution leaves to the president the judgment to determine whether the circumstances of a particular armed attack are so urgent and the potential consequences so threatening to the security of the United States that he should act without formally consulting Congress." [15] Even if Meeker's "small world theory" is accepted, it does not justify the transfer of constitutional power from Congress to the president. In fact, those who think the

Constitution's requirements have been superseded by the press of pragmatic contemporary considerations could begin the process of amending the Constitution to reflect the new realities. Any claim that the power to make war has now been effectively shifted to the president does not automatically make it so or justify it constitutionally.

CONGRESSIONAL EFFORTS TO REASSERT ITS AUTHORITY

Just how far presidents have strayed from the Constitution can be measured in the futile efforts by Congress from time to time to rein in rapacious executives and to reassert "first principles." Those efforts found a voice in the National Commitments Resolution of 1969, a nonbinding "sense of the Senate" resolution expressing that, henceforth, "a national commitment by the United States results only from the affirmative action taken by the executive and legislative branches of the United States Government by means of a treaty, statute or concurrent resolution of both Houses of Congress specifically providing for such commitment."[16] This first attempt by the Senate, at the height of the Vietnam War, to reassert its authority was buttressed by a report of the Committee on Foreign Relations that offered an extensive history and analysis of war making, identifying an unmistakable change after World War II that, by 1969, had reached "the point at which the real power to commit the country to war is now in the hands of the president. The trend which began in the early 20th century has been consummated and the intent of the framers of the Constitution as to the war power substantially negated."[17] The report explained that although the country still believed that Congress had the sole power to declare war, it was also

> widely believed, or at least conceded, that the President in his capacity as Commander in Chief had the authority to use the Armed Forces in any way he saw fit. Noting that the President has in fact exercised power over the Armed Forces we have come to assume that he is entitled to do so. The actual possession of a power has given rise to a belief in its constitutional legitimacy. The fact that Congress has acquiesced in, or at the very least has failed to challenge, the transfer of the war power from itself to the executive, is probably the most important single fact accounting for the speed and virtual completeness of the transfer.[18]

It took another four years after the Senate report and the National Commitments Resolution for Congress to organize itself sufficiently to pass, over President Richard Nixon's veto, the War Powers Resolution in 1973. That joint resolution, which has the force of law, imposed procedural requirements on presidents when they decided to send U.S. military forces into hostilities. Its lofty purpose was "to fulfill the intent of the framers of the Constitution of the

United States and insure that the collective judgment of both the Congress and the President will apply to the introduction of United States Armed Forces into hostilities."[19] Thus this resolution enacted into law the "commitment" that the Senate had urged in its report four years earlier. Today, however, after thirty years of experience with presidents refusing to comply strictly with its requirements, many scholars and commentators have concluded that this effort, though well meaning, has effected little, if any, change in presidential conduct. In short, the law has failed to accomplish its objectives.[20] If anything, it has simply added another set of requirements, in addition to the Constitution's, for presidents to ignore and violate.

In summary, presidents have grabbed Congress's war power for themselves; Congress has not been effective in reclaiming its lost power; and the courts have, at best, most often treated these issues as nonjusticiable, and, at worst, supported presidential usurpation of war powers.[21] The only serious effort to restrain a president's usurpation of Congress's war power was in the 1990 case of *Dellums v. Bush,* in which a federal district court refused to accept President George H. W. Bush's claim that the president alone had the authority to distinguish between military actions that constitute war, requiring congressional authorization, and those that are "only an offensive military attack," short of war, thereby needing no congressional approval. Judge Harold Greene called such a claim "far too sweeping to be accepted by the courts. If the Executive had the sole power to determine that any particular offensive military operation, no matter how vast, does not constitute war-making but only an offensive military attack, the congressional power to declare war will be at the mercy of a semantic decision by the Executive. Such an 'interpretation' would evade the plain language of the Constitution, and it cannot stand." If that was not enough to demonstrate the court's willingness to protect Congress's power, then a comment further into the opinion should suffice: "To put it another way: the Court is not prepared to read out of the Constitution the clause granting to Congress, and to it alone, the authority to declare war." Unfortunately, Judge Greene never decided the merits of the issue in that case, and so the decision stands as a rare announcement of judicial resolve but without any practical consequence flowing from it.

The distance that presidents have traveled from the Constitution in the last half-century to embrace the interpretation that they alone may decide on war is justified by some scholars on the grounds that the Constitution's allocation of war powers is an eighteenth-century anachronism that no longer makes sense in the twenty-first century.[22] The best answer to that claim is still that of the framers, whose reasons for separating the power to declare war from the power to conduct it, once declared, are just as valid and relevant today as they were in 1787. Those reasons were, in the words of scholar David Gray Adler, "a deep-seated fear of unilateral executive power and a commitment to collective decision-making in foreign affairs."[23] If the dangers of war in the twenty-first century are more consequential than ever before, that is all the more reason to ensure that the decision to enter a war is made by more than one person and with the benefit of the deliberative process that governs all of the important decisions the United States makes as a nation.

CON: Richard M. Pious

The Constitution is silent or ambiguous on many issues, and nowhere is this more of a problem than on the question of how war powers are to be exercised. The debates at the 1787 Constitutional Convention did not settle the issue. The framers had before them a proposal that gave Congress the power "to make war." Delegate Charles Pinckney proposed instead giving the power to the Senate, because it would be "more acquainted with foreign affairs" and smaller in size than the House of Representatives. Fellow South Carolinian Pierce Butler suggested vesting the war power in the president, "who will have all the requisite qualities, and will not make war but when the nation will support it." George Mason of Virginia spoke against "giving the power of war to the executive, because [the executive is] not safely to be trusted with it." Fellow Virginian James Madison and Elbridge Gerry of Massachusetts moved to insert "declare" instead of "make," thereby leaving the executive "the power to repel sudden attacks." That change was agreed to by seven states with two opposed and one absent. Delegates from all ten states present voted down a proposal by Butler to give the legislature "the power of peace, as they were to have that of war." The president was to be "Commander in Chief of the Army and Navy of the United States, and of the Militia of the several States, when called into the actual Service of the United States." George Washington of Virginia, Alexander Hamilton of New York, and Gouverneur Morris of Pennsylvania preferred to leave language incomplete or ambiguous, with presidential powers underdefined, because once in office they intended to exploit the silences and ambiguities of the Constitution in order to expand those powers.[1]

What can one conclude from the debates at the convention? Only that Congress has the power to declare war, and thus can turn a state of peace into a state of belligerency with another nation. But because presidents can repel invasion on their own authority, the power to "make" war or otherwise make use of the armed forces is not reserved to Congress alone but is a concurrent responsibility of the president and Congress. Beyond these principles nothing is clear. Some commentators argue that no language in the Constitution prevents the president from using force and making war and that many framers would have approved of presidential war making. Others argue that the intent of the framers was to have Congress participate in all decisions involving the use of force. Trying to parse meaning from the literal language of the constitutional text and the statements made by delegates in 1787 will not resolve the debate. A better way is to consider the precedents in American history: How have presidents exercised war powers without a congressional declaration of war? And how have Congress and the federal courts responded?

WAR POWERS: THE LIVING CONSTITUTION

Of the more than two hundred occasions on which the United States has committed armed forces abroad, Congress has declared war only in five: the War of 1812, the Mexican-American War in 1846, the Spanish-American War in 1898, World War I in 1917, and World War II in 1941. Of the early presidents, George Washington used forces without any congressional declaration to clear the Ohio Valley of Indians; John Adams ordered the navy into action under congressional prodding in an "undeclared" naval war against the French; and Thomas Jefferson used the navy and marine corps against pirates harassing American shipping in the Mediterranean Sea. Later presidents used the military to intervene on behalf of American settlers in Florida, Texas, California, and Hawaii. Once America became a world power, armed forces were used to defeat insurgents in the Philippines.

When presidents used force to topple regimes (Grenada in 1982, Iraq in 2003) or safeguard them from being toppled by others (South Korea in the 1950s and South Vietnam in the 1960s), no declaration of war was made by Congress. Since the start of the cold war in the 1950s, Congress has not declared war in any of the major hostilities that have seen the involvement of hundreds of thousands of U.S. troops. Presidents made the decision for peace or war, and Congress used its powers of appropriation, its power to draft or otherwise raise the armed forces, and its other war powers to back the executive, a pattern of behavior known to the courts as "joint concord."

Congress can even express its support retroactively. For example, at the beginning of the Civil War Abraham Lincoln did not call Congress into session (it was not scheduled to meet until December 1861), and he took many actions on his own prerogative, including raising military forces, calling state militias into federal service, sending funds from the Treasury to encourage western Virginia to secede from the Confederacy, and sending naval forces south to enforce federal law. Lincoln then called Congress into special session and informed it that the actions he had taken did not go beyond the scope of the war powers of the national government. This formulation begged the question of whether he had gone beyond the powers assigned to the executive by the Constitution. The congressional response was neither to repudiate his actions nor to impeach him for overreaching. Instead, Congress passed an appropriations act that retroactively legitimized all the actions he had taken in the war. In the *Prize Cases* (1863), the Supreme Court considered whether Lincoln's proclamation ordering a blockade of southern ports had been legal before Congress met and "ratified" it.[2] The Court ruled that no declaration of war was required in a civil conflict. The justices held that any decision to use force in a civil conflict could be made by the president and that federal courts would be governed by his decision. Finally, the Court observed that even if the president had erred in acting alone, the act passed by Congress ratifying his actions would "cure the defect."

Presidents Grover Cleveland and Theodore Roosevelt extended presidential war powers to include "international police powers." They argued that the president's duty to "take care that the laws be faithfully executed" extended to the treaty obligations of nations and the canons of international law. Harry S. Truman extended the police powers and fused the president's powers as commander in chief with the new U.S. obligation to enforce the United Nations Charter's provisions against aggression. Article 51 of the charter recognizes the right of self-defense against aggression and the right of collective security. Article 53 permits regional security pacts and organizations to repel aggression. When Truman sent troops to South Korea in the summer of 1950 to repel an attack from the North, the State Department claimed that a UN Security Council Resolution calling on nations to repel the aggression was an obligation to be met by the president without any need for a declaration of war by Congress. In taking these actions, Truman ignored the United Nations Participation Act of 1946, which requires congressional approval of U.S. collective security efforts under the UN. But instead of protesting, Congress acquiesced, though in this instance it was clear that Truman went beyond its intent and that of the framers.

Presidents also have argued that the North Atlantic Treaty Organization (NATO), Southeast Asia Treaty Organization (SEATO), and Organization of American States (OAS) collective security treaties are self-executing and give the president the right to use the armed forces to protect allies. By contrast, Congress interprets treaty provisions that every nation will act "in accordance with its constitutional processes" to mean that a declaration of war would be required. In consenting to these treaties, the Senate has "agreed to disagree" with the president's interpretation, leaving the president with a free hand to act.

During the cold war, Congress signaled support for presidential use of armed forces in two different ways. In the confrontations in 1955 with communist China in the Formosa Straits, in 1962 with the Soviet Union in the

Cuban missile crisis, and in 1964 with North Vietnam in the Gulf of Tonkin incident, Congress passed resolutions in which it would "approve" and "support" possible presidential military actions. In the two more recent conflicts with Iraq, the Persian Gulf War of 1991 and the Iraq War of 2003, Congress went much further, passing joint resolutions (with the force of law) that specifically authorized the president to use armed forces against Iraq. For all intents and purposes, these resolutions were the functional equivalent of declarations of war. Why, then, were they not declarations? Because Congress, in passing them, hoped to send a final signal to Iraq that it must agree to a diplomatic resolution of the crisis or else hostilities would ensue. If the intent of the framers was to require that the president obtain advance congressional consent to a decision to authorize hostilities, then in both conflicts with Iraq the president complied with that obligation.

WAR POWERS AND THE JUDICIARY

Through much of American history, the federal courts did not shy away from ruling on the merits of war powers cases and occasionally checking presidential prerogative. During and after the Vietnam War, however, the federal courts invoked a series of procedural hurdles in order to evade decisions on the substantive issues, thereby leaving the president with a free hand to take military actions without congressional assent.

In *Luftig v. McNamara* (1967), a draftee argued that the secretary of defense, Robert McNamara, had no legal authority to send him to Vietnam because Congress had not declared war.[3] The district court held that judges were precluded "from overseeing the conduct of foreign policy or the use and disposition of military power: these matters are plainly the exclusive province of Congress and the executive." However, in *Berk v. Laird* (1970), although the government argued that absent a declaration of war the president possessed all war powers, a federal appeals court rejected that claim, because it would reduce the congressional power to declare war to "an antique formality."[4] The court held that joint action by Congress and the executive was required. In *Orlando v. Laird* (1971), a court of appeals dealt with the question of whether there must be a declaration of war to satisfy the "joint concord" standard.[5] Orlando argued that the president had placed Congress in an impossible position, because once the war escalated, Congress could hardly refuse appropriations or draft legislation. The court disagreed, finding that "[t]he Congress and the executive have taken mutual and joint action" in prosecuting the Vietnam War from the very beginning. It pointed to the Gulf of Tonkin Resolution whose "broad language . . . clearly showed the state of mind of the Congress and its intention fully to implement and support the military and naval activities" of the president. In *Massachusetts v. Laird* (1971), an appeals court found that Congress had amply participated in the Vietnam War in the form of appropriations and selective service extensions.[6] Although the court held that the Constitution requires the "joint participation of Congress in determining the scale and duration of hostilities," it rejected the argument that a declaration of war was required to satisfy the joint concord standard, observing that no language in the Constitution says that Congress must declare war before supporting war. Most important, the court held that it would not decide which institution had what war power, but rather would accept the legality of war powers exercised by the national government when the president and Congress were held to be acting in joint concord.

Even after Congress repealed the Gulf of Tonkin Resolution (thereby ending joint concord in prosecuting the Vietnam War), a federal appeals court ruled in *Da Costa v. Laird* (1971) that the repeal did not change the fact that when the war began Congress had acquiesced in executive actions and had supported them.[7] "It was not the intent of Congress in passing the repeal amendment to bring all military operations in Vietnam to an abrupt halt," the court held. Instead, the court saw repeal as part of the process of Vietnamization of the war that had been started by the president, and it claimed that the war involved "mutual action by the legislative and executive branches." This claim, however, was quite a stretch, considering that the Nixon administration had opposed the repeal measure. Nevertheless, the court ruled that Congress and the president, not the courts, would decide how the war would wind down. Then it added a bit of dicta (language not needed for the decision), observing that "if the executive were now escalating the prolonged struggle instead of decreasing it, additional supporting action by the legislative branch over what is presently afforded might well be required." Yet in 1973, after the president escalated the war to put pressure on the North Vietnamese to negotiate an end to the war, the court did not find that the escalation required any "additional supporting action" by Congress. The court backed down from its earlier holding in *Da Costa* about escalation, and now it claimed that there was a "lack of discoverable and manageable judicial standards" and that "judges, deficient in military knowledge[,]" could not make decisions about whether a specific military operation constituted an escalation of the war.[8] By the end of the Vietnam conflict, the practical effect of judicial rulings on war powers cases was to provide the executive with great flexibility in the exercise of war powers.

THE FAILURE OF THE WAR POWERS RESOLUTION

In response to these court decisions, Congress passed in 1973 the War Powers Resolution (WPR) over President Nixon's veto. The WPR required the president to consult Congress in every possible instance before sending armed forces into either hostilities or a situation in which hostilities might be imminent; he was to report to Congress within forty-eight hours of doing so and every six months thereafter. It also required the president to withdraw forces if within sixty days he had not received from Congress a declaration of war, specific authorization, or an extension of the sixty-day period. He also was to withdraw forces if Congress, by concurrent resolution, required him to withdraw them. In such instances, he was given thirty days to execute the withdrawals.

Every president from Nixon to George W. Bush has denied that the WPR is constitutional. Moreover, they have sabotaged the resolution by failing to consult with Congress prior to the introduction of forces (they provide briefings instead) and by issuing one- or two-page "reports" that they say are consistent with the WPR but not in compliance with it. For example, in 1982 Ronald Reagan signed a measure Congress had passed extending his time period under the WPR, but in his signing statement he insisted that the legislature could not set conditions on his use of the armed forces. Congress, for its part, has turned a blind eye to case after case of presidential nonfeasance or misfeasance involving the WPR. In 1987, in the midst of a crisis with Iran over American-flagged Kuwaiti shipping in the Persian Gulf, Congress gave up entirely on trying to make the WPR a vehicle for joint decision making and instead used the more traditional authorization after the fact. During the crisis, 110 unhappy members of the U.S. House of Representatives contended that the Reagan administration had ignored the reporting requirements of the WPR by using U.S. naval vessels to escort the Kuwaiti tankers and engage in combat with Iranian mine-laying vessels. They then asked a federal court to rule that a report had been required months before. The judge not only refused to rule on the suit, but also observed that the very constitutionality of the WPR could not be assumed.

In both wars against Iraq, and in the intervening hostilities in the Balkans, the war powers of Presidents Clinton and both Bushes were left unscathed after judicial challenges. In *Dellums v. Bush* (1990), fifty-three members of the House and one senator sought a court order prohibiting George Bush from using armed forces for a war against Iraq in 1990.[9] In that case, Judge Harold Greene held that executive claims of complete war powers were too broad, denied that executive war powers could not be isolated from congressional powers, and further denied that harmonization of war powers was a political question, thereby abandoning two decades of contrary federal court doctrine. But having done so, he then used a new procedural dodge to avoid making a decision: the court could not rule because the case was not "ripe" for decision. "It would be both premature and presumptuous for the court to render a decision . . . when the Congress itself has provided no indication whether it deems such a declaration either necessary on the one hand or imprudent on the other." Greene would not take choices out of Congress's hands or use judicial injunctive relief absent a showing that it was what Congress itself required under the WPR. The intent of the WPR was that congressional inaction would lead within sixty days to the withdrawal of U.S. forces. But after the *Dellums* decision, it was clear that in the face of congressional inaction the courts would excuse themselves from enforcing the WPR, enabling the president to ignore it.

Even with this latitude, the only recent instances in which a president has engaged in war making without congressional support occurred under Bill Clinton. In 1994 he used war powers to threaten an invasion of Haiti and force out a ruling junta, in spite of the misgivings expressed in several nonbinding congressional resolutions that military operations should be authorized in advance and a subsequent resolution expressing the sense of the Senate that he should have consulted with Congress in advance of threatening force. Clinton relied on a resolution from the UN Security Council calling for regime change in Haiti—even though the Senate later passed a resolution saying that the UN resolution did not constitute authorization for the deployment of U.S. forces. In a second instance, in 1995 Clinton ordered the bombing of Serbian forces fighting in Bosnia without seeking or obtaining congressional authorization. Instead, he relied on NATO's establishment of a no-fly zone. He also did not seek advance congressional approval when he bombed Serbia in 1999 to end its war crimes in Kosovo. His counsel even argued that in the absence of a congressional prohibition, the WPR actually recognized the right of the president to use his own war powers—an argument that turned the intent of the law on its head.

In *Campbell v. Clinton* (1999), a district court concluded that the members of Congress who brought the case challenging the president's actions did not have standing.[10] Congress itself had sent contradictory messages. At first, it voted down a proposed declaration of war against Serbia. It also cast a tie vote in the House on authorizing air strikes, and so the measure failed to pass. But it then voted to fund the bombing and voted down a proposed funding cutoff. Because of this inconsistent congressional activity—part endorsement and part attempted check—the court held that "the President here did not claim to be acting pursuant to the defeated declaration of war or a statutory authorization, but instead 'pursuant to [his] constitutional authority to conduct U.S. foreign relations and as Commander-in-Chief and Chief Executive.' " Ironically, then, because Clinton relied on his own claim of war powers rather than on an action by Congress, the legislators were held to lack standing.

In conducting hostilities against Iraq, both Presidents Bush did not act contrary to the intent of the framers. The elder Bush secured congressional authorization, but he also indicated in a news conference that he reserved the right to act in defense of U.S. interests based on his own prerogatives. Similarly, the younger Bush claimed that a 1998 congressional resolution calling for "regime change" in Iraq could be combined with a 2002 resolution authorizing the use of force against Iraq as a form of "joint concord." In both wars, after receiving congressional authorization, the final decision to attack was made unilaterally by presidents without consulting with or reporting to Congress. And once the fighting began, Congress supported both presidents. In the second Iraq conflict, Congress, by overwhelming bipartisan votes, passed a resolution supporting the troops, and within three weeks it appropriated some $80 billion, in a clear demonstration of joint concord.

George W. Bush also claimed he had an international mandate to proceed against Iraq, but here he played fast and loose with the wording of a UN resolution warning Iraq of "serious consequences" if it did not allow inspections for weapons of mass destruction. After the resolution was passed, three of the five permanent members of the UN Security Council issued a statement saying that a further resolution authorizing the actual use of force would be required, but Bush disagreed. Later, when the administration failed to obtain an explicit Security Council authorization for the use of force, Bush asserted that the United States had the sovereign authority to use force to assure its own national security. Still later, the president pledged on the 2004 campaign trail that he would never ask the United Nations for a "permission slip" before using force.

The federal courts, citing passage of the prior congressional resolution, held once again that war powers involved a political question. In *Doe v. Bush* (2003), active duty service personnel, their parents, and some members of the House sought a preliminary injunction to prevent Bush from initiating war against Iraq.[11] They argued that, by passing the resolution, Congress had unconstitutionally delegated to the president its power to declare war. The court, however, declined to rule, claiming that the issue was nonjusticiable. It also held that there was evidence of joint concord, because Congress had called for regime change and had authorized hostilities.

CONCLUSION

Since the nation's earliest years, presidents have used the military on their own prerogative, making decisions to use force unilaterally and obtaining congressional support after the fact. For their part, since the start of the cold war the courts have been reluctant to rule on "boundary questions" between the president and Congress, preferring to find evidence of "joint concord." Any attempt to try to hold the president to an ambiguous (perhaps nonexistent) constitutional standard is ultimately to engage in fruitless speculation about whether a presidential use of force goes beyond the framers' intent. The real issue is not that presidents have made war without the consent of Congress—for the most part they have obtained that consent either before or after using the armed forces in major hostilities—but rather that Congress has failed to insist that presidents follow the collaborative mechanisms of the War Powers Resolution before making these decisions and that judicial decisions have left presidents free to do so.

In the final analysis, the issues in debates over presidential war making do not really involve legitimacy—such as whether the president followed proper procedures, or whether he made a decision that was lawful and constitutional—although they are often presented that way by critics. Criticisms of the president's war power usually stem from disagreements with a particular presidential action. These questions about the viability or wisdom of the policy, rather than attempts to parse original intent from limited debates and vague constitutional clauses, are the ones that really matter.

RESOLVED, the president has too much power in the selection of judges

PRO: David A. Yalof

CON: John Anthony Maltese

Few issues have engendered more controversy in Washington in recent years than the selection of federal judges. Republican president Ronald Reagan's nomination of Robert H. Bork to the Supreme Court in 1987 provoked a bitterly partisan debate between anti-Bork liberals and pro-Bork conservatives. In the end, the Democratic-controlled Senate voted Bork down. Reagan's Republican successor as president, George Bush, sparked an even fiercer firestorm when he nominated Clarence Thomas, a conservative, to the Court in 1991. Amid charges and countercharges about the Thomas's alleged sexual harassment of law professor and former employee Anita Hill, the Senate confirmed him by the narrowest majority of any Supreme Court nominee in history, 52–48. When Bill Clinton, a Democrat, became president in 1993 and the GOP took control of Congress in 1995, Republican members of the Senate Judiciary Committee defeated many of Clinton's appellate court nominations by refusing to send them to the full Senate for a vote. Although Republican George W. Bush has enjoyed a Republican Senate for most of his time as president, Democratic senators were able to defeat or delay several of his court of appeals nominees by threatening or launching filibusters. Because Republican senators were unable to come up with the three-fifths majority required under Senate rules to bring the nominations to a vote, the GOP threatened in 2005 to invoke the "nuclear option," forbidding filibusters on judicial nominees. Only a last-minute compromise by Senate moderates averted a showdown that threatened to bring Senate business to a virtual halt.

These controversies over judicial nominations have stemmed mainly from the bitter ideological partisanship that characterizes contemporary politics, with conservative Republicans and liberal Democrats fighting fiercely about a whole range of issues. Such "polarized politics" has been aggravated by the frequency of divided government, in which one party controls the presidency and the other controls Congress, as well as by the willingness of the federal courts to wade into controversial issues such as abortion, school prayer, and affirmative action. In such a climate, seats on the Supreme Court and the thirteen federal courts of appeals are prizes worth fighting about.

The roots of the fights over judgeships, however, extend deep into the Constitution. Although the framers gave federal judges life tenure in order to remove them from partisan politics once they were on the bench, they entrusted the process by which these judges are appointed to intensely political actors. Specifically, the framers mandated that the president "shall nominate, and by and with the Advice and Consent of the Senate, shall appoint" judges to the federal courts. In other words, the power of judicial selection is a shared power that can be exercised only if both branches cooperate. The Senate cannot "nominate" anyone to serve on a federal court. Nor can the president give a nominee the constitutional "Consent" necessary to make him or her a judge.

Does the president have too much power in the selection of federal judges? Although David A. Yalof says yes and John Anthony Maltese says no, both agree that much hinges on the meaning of the other crucial word in the Constitution's judicial appointments clause: "Advice." Specifically, did the framers want the president to seek advice from the Senate before making a judicial nomination, or did they intend to restrict the Senate's advisory role to the postnomination phase of the judicial selection process?

PRO: David A. Yalof

The late senator Strom Thurmond, a Republican from South Carolina, used to tell law school audiences a story that reveals just how far the theory of separation of powers sometimes strays from its actual practice. On October 23, 1987, the U.S. Senate rejected President Ronald Reagan's nomination of Judge Robert H. Bork to replace Lewis F. Powell Jr. on the Supreme Court. Within days of that defeat, the president's second choice for the post, Judge Douglas H. Ginsburg, withdrew his name from consideration amid allegations that he had used drugs while a Harvard Law School professor. By all accounts, Reagan, then a lame-duck president soon to be entering his final year in office, should have been at the nadir of his power to influence the appointment process. That is precisely the moment that Thurmond, then the ranking Republican on the Senate Judiciary Committee, chose to pay Reagan a visit at the Oval Office. As Thurmond tells it, he had wanted to convince the president to nominate his close friend, U.S. Court of Appeals Judge William Wilkins of South Carolina, to the high court. Thurmond told President Reagan that it might be a good idea to put a southerner on the Court—after all, Powell was a southerner, and his retirement had left the high court without a justice from that region of the country. But Reagan apparently had settled on his own third choice for Powell's seat, and even from this relatively weak political position he was not about to let Thurmond or any other senators share in the decision-making process. Thurmond even recalled Reagan's quick retort to his pleas for Wilkins: "You're from South Carolina and you want Willie Wilkins on the Court. But I'm from California, and the next Supreme Court Justice will be Anthony Kennedy of California." So much for senatorial advice and consent. With the help of Thurmond and other Senate Republicans, Kennedy was quickly confirmed and sworn in as the next associate justice just a few weeks later.[1]

In the modern appointment process, presidential arrogance is business as usual when selecting federal judges and Supreme Court justices. Presidents choose their high court nominees without giving most senators the privilege of even a cursory consultation beforehand. Even leading senators from the president's own party may discover the name of the president's nominee only a short time before everyone else. With its constitutional advice function a virtual dead letter, can the Senate fall back on its power to withhold consent for Supreme Court nominees? In theory, that power remains, but in practice it is only rarely exercised. For all the attention given to the nomination debacles of Bork, Ginsburg, Clarence Thomas, and, most recently, Harriet Miers, of those four only Bork was actually rejected by a vote of the Senate (Ginsburg and Miers withdrew, and Thomas was confirmed). In fact, since 1930 just three of forty-five Supreme Court nominees have been outright rejected in a Senate vote on the merits of the nomination.[2] That threesome does not even include Abe Fortas, whose ill-fated bid for chief justice in 1968 was technically filibustered by the Senate, thereby preventing a formal vote on the merits of his nomination.

Nor can senators find much consolation in the appointment process for the federal district and appeals courts, the venue in which senatorial advice has traditionally received its due. The era in which senators confidently instructed the White House whom to nominate for federal judgeships in their home states is long gone. Recent presidents have dominated the lower-court selection process, reducing senators from their own party to the status of well-respected advisers, on a par with important interest groups and other significant presidential constituents. Despite this shift in practice, Senate resistance to presidents' more objectionable nominees remains muted. Although Senate Democrats' recent resistance to President George W. Bush's lower-court appointments was unprecedented in one respect—the Senate minority leadership resorted to the filibuster time and time again to oppose ideologically extreme candidates—in raw numbers Democrats have stalled only ten of Bush's more than two hundred first-term judicial nominees.

How did the presidency come to enjoy such a stranglehold over judicial selections? Some of the chief executive's increased leverage in this area mirrors the growth of presidential power as a whole during the twentieth century. Yet there is something especially disconcerting about the growth in the president's power to appoint judges. In foreign affairs, the nation, arguably, must speak with a unified voice. But lively dialogue between the nominating institution (the president) and the advising and consenting institution (the Senate) hurts no one, save those nominees whose credentials are so thin that they stand little chance of surviving more intense forms of review.

THE FOUNDERS AND THE JUDICIAL APPOINTMENT PROCESS

Judicial appointments were a hotly debated subject at the Constitutional Convention in 1787. The initial efforts to vest the appointment authority in the executive were soundly defeated. A proposal by James Madison, delegate from Virginia, to give the president the power to appoint judges "unless disagreed to" by two-thirds of the Senate was rejected, because it would tip the balance too far toward the executive. Proposals to have the Senate make all appointments enjoyed the support of a majority of delegates for nearly two months, but that plan was eventually discarded. In the end, the convention settled on a shared arrangement between the two branches. The final scheme of presidential appointment with the Senate's advice and consent was eventually approved as a way to create a mutually dependent arrangement.

One noted scholar contends that by separating the act of nomination from the act of appointment (the Constitution says that the President "shall nominate, and by and with the Advice and Consent of the Senate, shall appoint . . ."), the framers meant to keep the Senate's advice and consent out of the nomination phase.[3] Such an interpretation would effectively merge the advice and consent functions into one: if the Senate must wait until after the president has submitted a nomination to advise, what difference is there between advising the president that a nominee will be rejected and actually rejecting the nominee with a formal vote? The framers would never have identified a separate advice function if they did not intend that function to have real influence in the nominating process.

The Constitution gives no specific criteria to guide the selection of justices, but this absence of criteria does not mean that the president was expected to have unlimited authority over the selection process. Consider the views of New York delegate Alexander Hamilton, perhaps the foremost advocate among the founders of a strong executive. In *Federalist* No. 77, Hamilton argued that Senate influence over presidential appointments was intended to provide a formidable check on the chief executive: "If by influencing the President be meant restraining him, this is precisely what must have been intended." At the same time, in *Federalist* No. 76 Hamilton assumed that the Senate would only rarely reject a president's nominees—after all, why would the Senate routinely reject candidates who emerge from a process in which the Senate offers significant assistance in the first place?[4]

In the early years of the Republic, the Senate quickly learned to practice what the founders preached. Although only one of President George Washington's nominees to the high court was rejected, that rejection was based on the Senate's *political* objections to the nominee, a clear rebuke to the notion that the Senate was intended to be merely a screening mechanism to ensure the minimal competence of judges. When, in 1795, Washington nominated John Rutledge of South Carolina to be chief justice, Rutledge's credentials were impressive, including previous service on the Supreme Court as an associate justice. But Rutledge had openly opposed ratification of the Jay Treaty with England, and he had urged Washington not to sign it. That stand put Rutledge squarely at odds with the Federalist majority in the Senate, which rejected his nomination 10–14. President Washington may have been disappointed by this turn of events, but he never openly challenged the Senate's power to reject his nominees on a political grounds. Because he had acted as president of the Constitutional Convention, Washington knew firsthand that the appointment authority had been granted to two branches rather than one.

THE ADVICE FUNCTION

For much of U.S. history, presidents have sought senators' advice on judicial appointments, and not just because the words of the Constitution encouraged them to do so. Involving senators at an early stage in the process was smart politics—it invested senators in the appointment process, thereby creating critical allies for the confirmation stage. Many senators were also knowledgeable Washington insiders, and most presidents valued their advice. Thomas Jefferson even relied on House and Senate members to scout out potential Supreme Court nominees. When Associate Justice Alfred Moore of North Carolina retired in 1804, Jefferson looked to two members of the South Carolina congressional delegation, Sen. Thomas Sumter and Rep. Wade Hampton, to help him find a replacement. Presidential–Senate dialogue over judicial nominees continued into the early twentieth century. For example, in 1902 Republican senator Henry Cabot Lodge of Massachusetts championed Oliver Wendell Holmes for a seat on the Supreme Court.

By contrast, presidents today rarely seek senatorial advice on Supreme Court vacancies. Modern presidents mobilize their administrations to identify and research prospective nominees behind the scenes, and senators learn about the shortlist of nominees only at the tail end of the process, after the president and his advisers have already performed most of the more critical vetting functions. On the rare occasion that the president publicly seeks advice, the process often entails meaningless consultations between presidential aides and senators about a decision that has already been made. For example, Chief of Staff Howard Baker insisted, even after Robert Bork became President Reagan's clear choice to fill a Court vacancy, that White House officials go through the charade of meeting with key senators and asking their advice about an artificial list of "potential nominees." Some observers believe that President Bill Clinton leaned heavily on senators for advice before making his two Supreme Court nominations: Stephen G. Breyer and Ruth Bader Ginsburg. In truth, however, in undertaking selection of nominees by trial balloon the Clinton White House floated names not only to senators but also to the public at large. In one instance, environmental groups were as influential as Senate Republicans in discouraging Clinton from nominating Interior Secretary Bruce Babbitt. Certainly, the Senate enjoyed no special privileges as an adviser in the process.

Even more dramatic changes have occurred in the lower-court appointment process, and once again senators have seen their opportunities to exert influence over such appointments sharply reduced. In the nineteenth century, such judgeships were mostly a matter of senatorial patronage. Well into the twentieth century, presidents continued to defer to senators—particularly those of the president's own party—on nominees to judgeships in their states.

Indeed, that practice continued up until the 1970s, when a president violated this norm by nominating his own candidate over the objections of the home state senator and risked seeing that nomination buried by the Senate Judiciary Committee. That was precisely the fate suffered by William Poff, President Gerald R. Ford's nominee for the federal district court in Virginia. Sen. William Scott of Virginia preferred another candidate, and he made his views known to the president. When Ford went ahead with Poff's nomination, the Senate Judiciary Committee, though run by the Democrats at the time, tabled the nomination in deference to their Senate colleague.[5]

No amount of deference to home state senators would keep the White House from exercising free rein over all the seats on the U.S. Court of Appeals for the D.C. Circuit, now widely recognized to be the second most powerful court in America. Meanwhile, in the other lower courts presidents are increasingly willing to disregard the preferences of home state senators. President Reagan, for example, insisted that Republican senators nominate three individuals for every judicial vacancy, and he required that those names meet his administration's stringent ideological criteria.[6] His successor in office, George Bush, continued this practice. At the end of the twentieth century, the rising use of "blue slips" by senators—a blue slip was in effect a veto over judicial appointments in a senator's state—allowed them to reassert some of their authority, but it did not result in a greater advisory role for the Senate.

In summary, today presidents control the choice of Supreme Court and D.C. Circuit Court nominees. For all other courts, senators play an active, if somewhat curtailed, role in the nominating process. The judicial appointment process now in place seems a far cry from the shared dialogue imagined by the framers.

THE CONSENT FUNCTION

Although senators' advisory function has been reduced substantially, the Senate can continue to exert considerable leverage by withholding consent for the president's judicial nominees. In practice, however, the Senate only rarely exercises that right. In his award-winning book *The Selling of Supreme Court Nominees,* my debate partner John Anthony Maltese speaks of the "increasingly contentious nature of recent confirmations."[7] Political scientist Mark Silverstein notes that in 1968 the politics of judicial confirmations underwent an abrupt transformation as "the presumption respecting presidential control was honored more in the breach than in the observance."[8] Yet what has the Senate gained in this supposedly new era of relative parity between the branches? As noted earlier, since 1930 only three Supreme Court nominees have been rejected outright by the Senate, and thirty-seven have been confirmed (four others withdrew before the Senate voted). Meanwhile, thirteen of the last sixteen nominees have been confirmed. Compared with those in the nineteenth century when one in four Supreme Court nominees was rejected, institutional relations in the modern era seems downright cooperative.

Changes in the confirmation procedures have contributed to Senate deference to the president. Nominees appeared at public confirmation hearings for the first time in 1925, but such appearances did not become routine until 1955.[9] Yet instead of clarifying matters for senators considering a possible challenge, public confirmation hearings have made evasion and obfuscation by nominees the norm. As Maltese notes, "Most nominees have refused to discuss cases with members of the Judiciary Committee."[10] Judge Antonin Scalia's refusal in 1986 even to comment on such a well-settled precedent as *Marbury v. Madison* made a near mockery of the proceedings. The exception was Robert Bork in 1987, and, by all accounts, his willingness to wrestle candidly with all the hot-button issues of the day contributed mightily to his undoing. Three years after the Bork fiasco, nominee David H. Souter deftly ducked pointed questions about his position on *Roe v. Wade*; in doing so, he denied potential conservative and liberal critics of his nomination any real ammunition with which to defeat him. Similarly, at his own hearings for chief justice in 2005 John Roberts refused to give one bit of ground to Democratic senators eager to learn of his specific views on whether *Roe v. Wade* should be reversed.

Another obstacle in the path of concerted Senate resistance to a president's judicial nominees has been the marked increase in partisan polarization. In the past, senators from the president's party would sometimes refuse to go along with a proposed Supreme Court nomination. For example, eight Senate Republicans opposed Robert Bork for the Supreme Court in 1987. Yet just four years later, the only Republican senator remaining from that octet to oppose the controversial nomination of Clarence Thomas was Sen. James M. Jeffords of Vermont, the same senator who bolted the Republican Party once and for all in 2001. Senators from the president's party have learned that in this current era of partisan polarization, the political cost of voting against the president's nominee can be very high. Consider the case of Democratic senator Zell Miller of Georgia, who became a pariah within his own party for consistently voting in favor of Republican president George W. Bush's policies and for supporting every one of Bush's lower-court nominees. By August 2004, Miller remained a Democrat in name only. He was even invited to deliver the keynote address to the Republican Party's national convention in New York City. By contrast, on the other side of the aisle moderate Republican senators such as Lincoln Chafee of Rhode Island and Olympia Snowe and Susan Collins of Maine have avoided the same fate, offering the president their steadfast support for nearly all of his most ideologically conservative nominees at the lower-court level. Because of the increased political costs of defection, it is a rare occasion indeed when senators choose to cross their own party leader in the White House.

Of course, senators from the president's own party recently *did* make themselves heard in the appointment process. In the fall of 2005 some of the more conservative Republican senators convinced President George W. Bush of the need to withdraw his second nominee for the high court, Harriet Miers. Miers, they felt, lacked a reliably conservative track record and was creating a serious split within the president's conservative base of support. But those senators pressing for her withdrawal may not have been acting from a position of strength. They feared that an up or down vote on Miers would have gone in her favor—most headcounts of the Senate at that time indicated that a pro-Miers alliance between Democrats and moderate Republicans would have provided more than enough votes to secure her confirmation. Even more telling was the degree to which key senators from President Bush's own party had been excluded from the decision-making process—how else can one explain their frustration with Miers' candidacy? Thus, although the president may occasionally confront resistance in the confirmation process, those occasional flare-ups should not be confused with what should be a truly deliberative appointment process.

To be sure, the Senate is likely to remain closely divided along partisan lines for the foreseeable future. If so, the filibuster (by which forty-one senators can deny a vote on any matter) becomes the principal means by which a Senate minority can erect a roadblock to the president's judicial nominees. But even if Senate Democrats continue to use the filibuster to block nominees, will the president's domination of the judicial selection process be significantly hindered? During his first term, President George W. Bush made 204 appointments to the federal judiciary. Of those nominees, Senate Democrats filibustered just ten. President Bush's record of successful appointments compares favorably with those of other recent presidents during the modern era: the elder president Bush appointed 187 lower-court judges during his term as president, and President Clinton made 366 judicial appointments in eight years. Even with the president and the Senate seemingly at loggerheads over the confirmation of federal judges, the wheels keep turning, and most nominees continue to be confirmed.

If anything, the use of extreme tactics such as the filibuster is an indication of just how desperate these times are for senators who wish to fight the president's judicial nominees. That each of these filibustered nominees would have been confirmed in a straight up-and-down vote by the Senate provides further evidence of Senate deference. In American politics today, presidents nominate judges for the federal judiciary, and, with very few exceptions, the Senate obediently confirms those choices.

CON: John Anthony Maltese

What exactly does Article II, Section 2, of the Constitution mean when it says that the president "shall nominate, and by and with the Advice and Consent of the Senate, shall appoint . . . Judges of the supreme court"? (By law, the same procedure is used for appointing lower federal court judges.) The Constitutional Convention of 1787 considered and ultimately rejected several different methods of judicial appointment: by Congress as a whole, by the Senate alone, and by the president alone. New York delegate Alexander Hamilton was among the most articulate defenders of the final constitutional language, and his explanation of that language in *Federalist* No. 76 is worth considering.[1]

First, Hamilton assumed that the Senate would rarely reject nominees put forth by the president. It is "not very probable," he wrote, that the Senate would often overrule the president's nomination. Only when there were "special and strong reasons for the refusal" would the Senate risk placing a "stigma" on a nominee through rejection and thereby call into question "the judgment of the chief magistrate."[2]

What might these "special and strong reasons" be? Could they include a nominee's failure to comply with a "litmus test" of how he or she should vote on particular issues? Anyone seeking to answer these questions must look at the precise wording of the Constitution and consider the intent of those who framed it.

The Constitution says that only the president has the power to *nominate*. As Hamilton wrote in *Federalist* No. 76, the president exercises "his judgment alone" in the act of nomination.[3] Even George Mason of Virginia, who opposed executive appointment of judges, conceded as much in a letter to fellow Virginian James Monroe: "There is some thing remarkable in the Arangement of the Words: 'He shall nominate.' This gives the President *alone* the Right of *Nomination*."[4]

Hamilton argued in *Federalist* No. 76 that the president's power to nominate meant that the "person ultimately appointed must be the object of his preference."[5] Why? Because "one man of discernment is better fitted to analyze and estimate the peculiar qualities adapted to particular offices, than a body of men of equal or perhaps even of superior discernment."[6] This is so, Hamilton said, because "a single well directed man . . . cannot be distracted and warped by that diversity of views, feelings, and interests, which frequently distract and warp the resolutions of a collective body."[7]

The Constitutional Convention ultimately rejected the legislative appointment of judges largely because the delegates feared that legislative appointments would be subject to intrigue and corrupted by factions. The Virginia Plan had originally proposed that Congress as a whole choose federal judges. When the convention debated that proposal on June 5, 1787, James Wilson of Pennsylvania objected. Experience among the states showed "the impropriety of such appointments in numerous bodies," he said. "Intrigue, partiality, and concealment were the necessary consequences. A principal reason for unity in the Executive was the officers might be appointed by a single, responsible person."[8]

On July 18, the convention considered appointment by the Senate alone. Nathaniel Gorham of Massachusetts argued that the Senate was still "too numerous, and too little personally responsible, to ensure a good choice."[9] He suggested a compromise: presidential appointment subject to the advice and consent of the Senate. James Madison of Virginia, who originally had been wary of executive appointment, conceded on July 21 that the executive would be more likely than any other branch "to select fit characters." He added that requiring Senate consent would check "any flagrant partiality or error" on the part of the president.[10] The phrase is revealing for the light it sheds on what "advice and consent" means, and just how much power it gives the Senate.

Some scholars have suggested that the word *advice* in the appointments clause gives the Senate broad power to advise the president on whom to nominate. But this view runs counter to Hamilton's position in *Federalist* No. 76. It suggests that the power to nominate is *not* one held solely by the president, but rather is a power shared with the Senate.[11] Such a view conforms neither to a strict reading of the advice and consent clause nor to the intent of the framers. As legal scholar John O. McGinnis has persuasively argued:

> The very grammar of the clause is telling: the act of nomination is separated from the act of appointment by a comma and a conjunction. Only the latter act is qualified by the phrase "advice and consent." Furthermore, it is not at all anomalous to use the word "advice" with respect to the action of the Senate in confirming an appointment. The Senate's consent is advisory because confirmation does not bind the President to commission and empower the confirmed nominee. Instead, after receiving the Senate's advice and consent, the President may deliberate again before appointing the nominee.[12]

In short, the Senate's proper role is to offer advice on the nominee presented by the president.

On what grounds should the Senate withhold its consent? When is a nominee "an unfit character" unworthy of confirmation? Hamilton, in *Federalist* No. 76, regards the Senate's power to withhold consent as primarily "a check upon the spirit of favoritism in the President" designed to prevent individuals from being appointed because of "family connection" or "personal attachment."[13] This statement corresponds with Madison's notion that the check be used to prevent "flagrant partiality or error." Some scholars have argued that the Constitutional Convention viewed Senate confirmation as a way of preventing the president from making too many appointments from large states.[14]

The failure of a nominee to pass a "litmus test" imposed by senators who want him or her to rule in cases in certain ways does not rise to the level of "special and strong reasons" for rejection. For one thing, this notion runs counter to the ideal of judicial independence, which the framers took great pains to protect. Moreover, it opens the door to the intrigue and faction that the framers sought to avoid. As noted earlier, Hamilton argued that because the president is best fitted to analyze the qualities necessary for each judgeship to be filled, the person appointed "must be the object of his preference." For senators to reject a nomination on the basis of a litmus test is to substitute improperly their preferences for those of the president.

Imposing such tests, however, is precisely what senators of both parties have done at all levels of the federal judicial appointment process in recent years. Not including the 2005 nomination of Samuel A. Alito Jr., Senate opposition led to the rejection or withdrawal of six out of twenty Supreme Court nominations from 1968 through 2005 (a failure rate of 30 percent).[15] If one omits the unsuccessful renominations of individuals already blocked by the Senate, the rate of failed Supreme Court nominations before 1968 was 17.1 percent (21 out of 123 nominations).[16] For many observers of the Court, the Senate's rejection of President Ronald Reagan's nomination of Robert H. Bork in 1987 was a watershed event. After an intensive fight against Bork led by a coalition of some three hundred liberal interest groups, the Democratic-controlled Senate rejected his nomination—not because of any improprieties or lack of qualifications, but because of how Bork might vote on the Court.

The Senate also now plays a more aggressive role in the lower federal court confirmation process. At that level, senators have resorted to procedural tactics to prevent the Senate Judiciary Committee from holding hearings on nominees, as well as to filibusters to keep the Senate from voting on them. Obstruction and delay have become common as senators from both political parties succumb to the powerful grip of interest groups eager to influence judicial decision making. In 1997, for example, the Free Congress Foundation (a coalition of more than 250 conservative pro-family, small business, victims' rights, and law enforcement organizations) pressured the Republican-controlled Senate to block many of Bill Clinton's lower federal court nominees. This group's Judicial Selection Monitoring Project claimed that Clinton's judicial appointees had "blazed an activist trail, creating an out-of-control judiciary," and urged that the Senate more closely scrutinize his nominees.[17] In a January 1997 letter to President Clinton and all one hundred U.S. senators, the project promised to "fight judicial activism with whatever tools and resources are legitimately at our disposal."[18] Two months later, House majority whip Tom DeLay, R-Texas, further escalated the rhetoric by suggesting that House Republicans should impeach liberal federal judges.[19]

Such pressure motivated Republican senators to use a procedural tactic called the "blue slip" to block hearings on nominees to federal courts in their states. This move resulted in a major slowdown in the confirmation of federal judges. By the end of 1997, one in ten seats on the federal judiciary was empty. President Clinton declared a "vacancy crisis," saying that the Senate's "failure to act on my nominations, or even give many of my nominees a hearing, represents the worst of partisan politics."[20] Although Republicans eased up on the stall tactics in 1998 after Chief Justice William H. Rehnquist criticized the delays in his 1997 year-end report to Congress, they revived their delaying tactics in 1999 in the hope of a Republican victory in the 2000 presidential election.[21] When Clinton left office in January 2001, forty-two of his judicial nominees remained unconfirmed (thirty-eight of them had never received a hearing). In Clinton's eight years as president, the Senate blocked 114 of his lower-court nominations and confirmed 366.[22] A look back reveals how much more aggressive the Senate had become. A Democratic Senate blocked none of Republican Richard Nixon's lower-court nominations and confirmed 224 during his five and a half years in office (1969–1974). In Ronald Reagan's eight years as president (1981–1989), the Senate blocked 43 lower-court nominees and confirmed 368.[23]

Senate obstruction of judicial nominees continued after George W. Bush took office in 2001. Like Clinton before him, President Bush declared a "vacancy crisis."[24] When Republicans regained control of the Senate after the 2002 midterm elections, Senate Judiciary Committee chair Orrin Hatch, R-Utah, altered the Senate rules to prevent Democrats from using blue slips to block hearings on President Bush's nominees.[25] This tactic spurred Democrats to filibuster nominees.

Is the filibuster an appropriate tool for senators to use to block a judicial nominee? It can be argued that it is not. The filibuster is not a power granted by the Constitution. As political scientists Sarah A. Binder and Steven S. Smith have noted, "Delegates to the convention did not write into the Constitution any procedural protections for Senate minorities."[26] The Senate's original rules are also instructive. These rules did not allow for a filibuster. Instead, they allowed for a simple majority to close debate. A senator would make a "motion for the previous question," and an up or down majority vote would follow. Not until an 1806 rules change eliminated "previous question motions" was a filibuster even possible. Even so, Binder and Smith point out, because previous question motions "had not been used as a means of limiting debate, its deletion could not have signaled a commitment to extended debate."[27] Lawyers Martin B. Gold and Dimple Gupta not only concur, but also argue that the 1806 rules change that opened up the possibility of filibusters was "a sheer oversight."[28] Indeed, no filibusters occurred in the Senate until the late 1830s. In 1917 the Senate enacted a cloture rule for ending debate by a two-thirds vote, and in 1975 the Senate changed the rule to a three-fifths vote.

The use of filibusters in the Senate has skyrocketed since the 1960s.[29] Using them to block judicial nominees is a relatively recent phenomenon. A coalition of progressive Republicans and Democrats considered filibustering against President Herbert Hoover's nomination of Charles Evans Hughes to the position of chief justice in 1930, but they decided not to take that path because they did not have the votes to sustain the filibuster.[30] In 1968 Republicans mounted a successful filibuster against President Lyndon B. Johnson's nomination of Abe Fortas to be chief justice (the nomination was withdrawn).[31] But only since 2002 has the practice become commonplace. Senate Democrats used the filibuster to block ten of President Bush's first-term appellate court nominees. In response, Republicans threatened to retaliate with the so-called nuclear option, a tactic that would prevent filibusters of judicial nominees.

What consequences attend the aggressive role taken by the Senate in the judicial appointment process? Arguably, it has contributed to a confirmation mess. Helped (and spurred) by interest groups, opposition party senators now look for ways to disqualify nominees who do not meet their approval. The result, as political scientist Stephen Carter puts it, is often a "bloodbath."[32] Public confirmation hearings and public relations campaigns are designed less to reveal nominees' knowledge and understanding of the law than to highlight their positions on policy issues and to expose embarrassing details of their past. Indeed, the confirmation gauntlet has become a political free-for-all. As the Twentieth Century Fund Task Force on Judicial Selection reported in 1988, the modern confirmation process has become "dangerously close to looking like the electoral process," with the use of "media campaigns, polling techniques, and political rhetoric that distract attention from, and sometimes completely distort, the legal qualifications of the nominee." The task force warned that "choosing candidates for anything other than their legal qualifications damages the public's perception of the institutional prestige of the judiciary and calls into question the high ideal of judicial independence."[33] The prospect of enduring the gauntlet may also discourage potential nominees from engaging in public service.

In light of this recent history, it is hard to conclude that the president has too much power in the selection of judges. If anything, one could argue that the pendulum has swung in the direction of the *Senate* exercising too much power. Both Presidents Bill Clinton and George W. Bush declared a "vacancy crisis" because they believed senators were misusing their power by obstructing the confirmation process for partisan and ideological reasons. That sounds a lot like what some of the framers sought to avoid: a process corrupted by factions and subject to intrigue.

RESOLVED, a broad executive privilege is essential to the successful functioning of the presidency

PRO: Mark J. Rozell
CON: David Gray Adler

The framers of the Constitution created what political scientist Richard E. Neustadt has called a system of "separated institutions sharing powers"—that is, a system in which the president and Congress are distinct branches of government but share in the exercise of nearly all the powers of the federal government. A fault line runs through the framers' plan, however. What is supposed to happen when Congress or a federal court requests information from the president that the president does not want to disclose? "Separated institutions" seems to imply that the president has the authority to decide what to turn over and what to keep within the executive branch. Indeed, that is the reasoning that sustains the constitutional doctrine of executive privilege. But "sharing powers" seems to imply something different. If the branches must participate jointly in the exercise of the powers of the federal government, then presumably Congress and the courts are entitled to see any executive document they need to exercise their share of power. Cast this way, executive privilege seems a more dubious constitutional doctrine. And the Constitution itself is silent on the matter.

Throughout most of American history, controversies about what executive information Congress and the courts are entitled to see and what the president is entitled to keep from them have been settled through the political process. Some combination of which branch cared more in a particular case and which occupied the political high ground usually determined the outcome of each dispute. But the Watergate crisis that dominated the second term of President

Richard Nixon lent itself to no such solution, especially when it turned out that the president had installed a voice-activated audio-taping system in the White House that probably had recorded conversations in which Nixon and his aides either had (their critics' version) or had not (their own version) plotted criminal activities.

Not surprisingly, the Senate, the House of Representatives, and the federal district court in Washington that was trying a Watergate-related criminal case all insisted that Nixon turn over the tapes. Nixon refused to do so, invoking the doctrine of executive privilege. In 1974 the Supreme Court stepped in, ruling unanimously in the case of *United States v. Nixon* that the president must obey the district court's subpoena. "[A]bsent a claim of need to protect military, diplomatic or sensitive national security secrets," wrote Chief Justice Warren E. Burger, no presidential claim of executive privilege could prevail over "the fundamental demands of due process of law in the fair administration of criminal justice."[1] But that ruling did not mean the doctrine of executive privilege was invalid. Indeed, Burger continued, some form of executive privilege was "fundamental to the operation of government and inextricably rooted in the separation of powers under the Constitution." Thus, in the course of rejecting Nixon's claim of executive privilege in that particular case, the Court ruled for the first time that executive privilege had solid constitutional roots.

United States v. Nixon hardly settled all the disputes about executive privilege. Left unresolved were the extent of Congress's right to information that the president refused to disclose and the extent of the president's authority to use claims of national security to deny information even to the courts. Because so much about executive privilege is still uncertain, ample room for debate remains between scholars such as Mark J. Rozell, who defends the doctrine, and David Gray Adler, who opposes it.

PRO: Mark J. Rozell

Controversies over executive privilege date back to the earliest years of the Republic. Although the phrase "executive privilege" was not a part of the nation's common language until the 1950s, almost every president has exercised some form of this presidential power.

Executive privilege is controversial because it is nowhere mentioned in the Constitution. That fact has led some observers to suggest that executive privilege does not exist and that the congressional power of inquiry is absolute. This view is mistaken. Executive privilege is an implied presidential power and is sometimes needed for the proper functioning of the executive branch. Presidents and their staffs must be able to deliberate without fear that their every utterance may be made public.

Granted, the power of executive privilege is not absolute. Like other constitutionally based powers, it is subject to a balancing test. Presidents and their advisers may require confidentiality, but Congress must have access to information from the executive branch to carry out its investigative function. Therefore, any claim of executive privilege must be weighed against Congress's legitimate need for information to carry out its own constitutional role. Yet the power of inquiry is also not absolute, whether it is wielded by Congress or by prosecutors.

Not all presidents have exercised executive privilege judiciously. Some have used it to cover up embarrassing or politically inconvenient information, or even outright wrongdoing. As it is with all other grants of authority, the power to do good things is also the power to do bad things. The only way to avoid the latter is to strip away the authority altogether and thereby eliminate the ability to do the former. Eliminating executive privilege would hamper the ability of presidents to discharge their constitutional duties effectively and to protect the public interest.

THE NEED FOR CANDID ADVICE

The constitutional duties of presidents require that they be able to consult with advisers without fear that the advice will be made public. If officers of the executive branch believe their confidential advice could be disclosed, the quality of that advice could be seriously damaged. Advisers cannot be completely honest and frank in their discussions if they know that their every word might be disclosed to partisan opponents or to the public. In *United States v. Nixon* (1974), the Supreme Court recognized that the need for candid exchanges is an important basis for executive privilege:

> The valid need for protection of communications between high govern-
> ment officials and those who advise and assist them in the performance of
> their manifold duties . . . is too plain to require further discussion.
> Human experience teaches that those who expect public dissemination of
> their remarks may well temper candor with a concern for appearances
> and for their own interests to the detriment of the decision-making
> process. . . . The confidentiality of presidential communications . . . has
> constitutional underpinnings. . . . The privilege is fundamental to the
> operation of government and inextricably rooted in the separation of
> powers under the Constitution.[1]

In 1979 the Court reiterated its support of executive privilege based on the
need for a candid exchange of opinions among advisers. "Documents shielded
by executive privilege," the Court explained, "remain privileged even after the
decision to which they pertain may have been effected, since disclosure at any
time could inhibit the free flow of advice, including analysis, reports and
expression of opinions."[2]

Although Congress needs access to information from the executive branch
to carry out its oversight and investigative duties, it does not follow that
Congress must have full access to the details of every executive branch communication. Congressional inquiry, like executive privilege, has limits. That is
not to suggest that presidents can claim the need for candid advice to restrict
any and all information. The president must demonstrate a need for secrecy in
order to trump Congress's power of inquiry.

LIMITS ON CONGRESSIONAL INQUIRY

Congress's power of inquiry, though broad, is not unlimited.[3] A distinction must
be drawn between sources of information generally and those necessary to
Congress's ability to perform its legislative and investigative functions.[4] There is
a strong presumption of validity to a congressional request for information relevant to these investigative functions. The presumption weakens in the case of a
congressional "fishing expedition"—a broad, sweeping quest for any and all
executive branch information that might be of interest to Congress for one reason or another. Indeed, Congress itself has recognized that there are limits on its
power of inquiry. For example, in 1879 the House Judiciary Committee issued a
report stating that neither the legislative nor the executive branch had compul-
sory power over the records of the other. Congress gave the executive branch the
statutory authority to withhold information when it enacted the "sources and
methods proviso" of the 1947 National Security Act, the implementation provision of the 1949 CIA Act, and the 1966 Freedom of Information Act.

Nevertheless, critics of executive privilege argue that Congress has an
absolute, unlimited power to compel disclosure of all executive branch infor-

mation. Rep. John Dingell, D-Mich., for example, said that members of Congress "have the power under the law to receive each and every item in the hands of the government."[5] But this expansive view of congressional inquiry is as wrong as the belief that the president has the unlimited power to withhold all information from Congress. The legitimacy of the congressional power of inquiry does not confer an absolute and unlimited right to all information. The debates at the 1787 Constitutional Convention and at the subsequent ratifying conventions provide little evidence that the framers intended to confer such authority on Congress. There are inherent constitutional limits on the powers of the respective governmental branches. The common standard for legislative inquiry is whether the requested information is vital to the Congress's lawmaking and oversight functions.

THE OTHER BRANCHES AND CONFIDENTIALITY

Executive privilege can also be defended on the basis of accepted practices of secrecy in the other branches of government. In the legislative branch, members of Congress receive candid, confidential advice from committee staff and legislative assistants.[6] Meanwhile, congressional committees meet on occasion in closed session to mark up legislation. Congress is not obligated to disclose information to another branch. A court subpoena will not be honored except by a vote of the legislative chamber concerned. Members of Congress enjoy a constitutional form of privilege that absolves them from having to account for certain official behavior, particularly speech, anywhere but in Congress. But as with the executive, this protection does not extend into the realm of criminal conduct.

Secrecy is found as well in the judicial branch. It is difficult to imagine more secretive deliberations than those that take place in Supreme Court conferences. Court observer David M. O'Brien refers to secrecy as one of the "basic institutional norms" of the Supreme Court. "Isolation from the Capitol and the close proximity of the justices' chambers within the Court promote secrecy, to a degree that is remarkable. . . . The norm of secrecy conditions the employment of the justices' staff and has become more important as the number of employees increases."[7] Members of the judiciary claim immunity from having to respond to congressional subpoenas. The norm of judicial privilege also protects judges from having to testify about their professional conduct.

It is thus inconceivable that secrecy, so common to the legislative and judicial branches, would be uniquely excluded from the executive.[8] Indeed, the executive branch regularly engages in activities that are secret in nature. George C. Calhoun explains that the executive branch "presents . . . matters to grand juries; assembles confidential investigative files in criminal matters; compiles files containing personal information involving such things as census, tax, and veterans information; and health, education and welfare benefits to name a few. All of these activities must, of necessity, generate a considerable amount of confidential information. And personnel in the executive branch . . . necessarily prepare many more confidential memoranda. Finally, they produce a considerable amount of classified information as a result of the activities of the intelligence community."[9]

Legislative, judicial, and executive branch secrecy serves a common purpose: to arrive at policy decisions more prudent than those that would be made through an open process. And in each case, the end result is subject to scrutiny. Indeed, accountability is built into secretive decision-making processes, because elected public officials must justify the end result at some point.

GIVING EXECUTIVE PRIVILEGE ITS DUE

The dilemma of executive privilege is how to permit governmental secrecy while maintaining accountability. On the surface, the dilemma is a difficult one to resolve: how can democratically elected leaders be held accountable when they are able to deliberate in secret or to make secretive decisions?

The post-Watergate period witnessed a breakdown in the proper exercise of executive privilege. Because of former president Richard Nixon's abuses, Presidents Gerald R. Ford and Jimmy Carter avoided using executive privilege. Ford and Carter still sought to preserve presidential secrecy, but they relied on other constitutional and statutory means to achieve that goal. President Ronald Reagan tried to restore executive privilege as a presidential prerogative, but he ultimately failed when congressional committees threatened administration officials with contempt citations and adopted other retaliatory actions to compel disclosure. President George Bush, like Ford and Carter before him, avoided executive privilege whenever possible and used other strategies to preserve secrecy. President Bill Clinton exercised executive privilege more often than all of the other post-Watergate presidents combined, but often improperly, such as in the investigation into his sexual relationship with White House intern Monica Lewinsky. President George W. Bush has exercised the privilege more sparingly than his predecessor, but he also has exercised this power in some questionable circumstances, such as his attempt to deny Congress access to decades-old Justice Department documents.[10]

Thus in the post-Watergate era either presidents have avoided uttering the words "executive privilege" and have protected secrecy through other sources of authority (Ford, Carter, G. Bush), or they have tried to restore executive privilege and failed (Reagan, Clinton, G. W. Bush). Clinton's aggressive use of executive privilege in the Lewinsky scandal served to revive the national debate over this presidential power—a debate that continued into the Bush years. It is therefore an appropriate time to discuss how to restore a sense of balance to the executive privilege debate.

First, it needs to be recognized that executive privilege is a legitimate constitutional power—not a "constitutional myth." Consequently, presidents should not be devising schemes for achieving the ends of executive privilege while avoiding any mention of this principle. Furthermore, Congress (and the courts) must recognize that the executive branch—like the legislative and judicial branches—has a legitimate need to deliberate in secret and that every assertion of executive privilege is not a devious attempt to conceal wrongdoing.

Second, executive privilege is not an unlimited, unfettered presidential power. It should be exercised rarely and only for the most compelling reasons. Congress has the right—and often the duty—to challenge presidential assertions of executive privilege.

Third, there are no clear, precise constitutional boundaries that determine, a priori, whether any particular claim of executive privilege is legitimate. The resolution to the dilemma of executive privilege is found in the political ebb and flow of the separation of powers system. Indeed, there is no need for any precise definition of the constitutional boundaries surrounding executive privilege. Such a power cannot be subject to precise definition, because it is impossible to determine in advance all of the circumstances under which presidents may have to exercise that power. The separation of powers created by the framers provides the appropriate resolution of the dilemma of executive privilege and democratic accountability.

Congress already has the institutional capability to challenge claims of executive privilege by means other than eliminating the right to withhold information or attaching statutory restrictions on the exercise of that power. For example, if members of Congress are not satisfied with the response to their demands for information, they have the option of retaliating by withholding support for the president's agenda or for the president's executive branch nominees. In one famous case during the Nixon years, a Senate committee threatened not to confirm a prominent presidential nomination until a separate access to information dispute had been resolved. That action resulted in President Nixon ceding to the senators' demands. If information can be withheld only for the most compelling reasons, it is not unreasonable for Congress to try to force the president's hand by making him weigh the importance of withholding the information against that of moving forward a nomination or piece of legislation. Presumably, information being withheld for purposes of vital national security or constitutional concerns would take precedence over pending legislation or a presidential appointment. If not, then there appears to be little justification in the first place for withholding the information.

Congress possesses many other means by which it can compel presidential compliance with requests for information. One of those is the control Congress maintains over the government's purse strings, which means that it holds formidable power over the executive branch. In addition, Congress often relies on the subpoena power and the contempt of Congress charge to compel release of withheld information. It is not merely the exercise of these powers that matters, but the threat that Congress may resort to such powers. Congress has successfully elicited information from the executive branch using both powers. During the Reagan years, for example, in several executive privilege disputes Congress prevailed and received all the information it had requested from the administration—but only after it subpoenaed documents and threatened to hold certain administration officials in contempt. The Reagan White House simply decided it was not worth the political cost to continue such battles with Congress. In these cases, the system worked as it is supposed to. Had the information in dispute been critical to national security or preserving White House candor, certainly Reagan would have taken a stronger stand to protect the documents.

In the extreme case, Congress also has the power of impeachment—the ultimate weapon with which to threaten the executive. Clearly, this congressional power cannot be routinely exercised as a means of compelling disclosure of information, and thus it will not constitute a real threat in commonplace information disputes. Nevertheless, when a scandal emerges of Watergate-like proportions and in which all other remedies have failed, Congress can threaten to exercise its ultimate power over the president. In fact, for a time in 1998 Congress considered an impeachment article against President Clinton for abuses of presidential powers, including executive privilege. Congress ultimately dropped that particular article.

In the vast majority of cases—and history verifies this point—it can be expected that the president will comply with requests for information rather than withstand retaliation from Congress. Presidential history is replete with examples of chief executives who tried to invoke privilege or threatened to do so, only to back down in the face of congressional challenges. If members of Congress believe that the executive privilege power is too formidable, the answer resides not in crippling presidential authority, but in exercising to full effect the vast array of powers already at Congress's disposal.

CON: David Gray Adler

Executive privilege—the claim that a president has the right to withhold information from Congress and the courts—has become a principal tool in the promotion of executive secrecy and deception. Executive secrecy represents a continual threat to the values and principles of the Republic. Some of the nation's darkest moments have stemmed from a presidential penchant for secrecy: the quagmire of Vietnam, the suppression of the *Pentagon Papers,* Watergate, the Iran-contra scandal, and President George W. Bush's obscurantism over the rationale for the invasion of Iraq.

The pernicious effects of executive secrecy have not deterred advocates of executive privilege from asserting its central importance to the president's performance of his constitutional responsibilities, particularly in matters of national security and foreign affairs. Yet advocates of executive privilege have been unable to document instances in which resort to executive privilege has served the interests of the nation. Nor have they been able to document any national disasters that have resulted from executive transmission of information to Congress.

Defenders of executive privilege have urged legal justifications as well, yet there is no mention of executive privilege in the Constitution. Like Topsy in *Uncle Tom's Cabin,* executive privilege "never was born. It just growed like cabbage and corn." Even if, for the sake of argument, one were to concede the occasional utility of a claim of executive privilege, that would not establish its constitutionality. As Chief Justice John Marshall wrote in *McCulloch v. Maryland,* "The peculiar circumstances of the moment may render a measure more or less wise, but cannot render it more or less constitutional."[1]

There are a good many reasons to doubt both the constitutionality and the utility of executive privilege. When the concept of a constitutionally based executive privilege was created by the judiciary in *United States v. Nixon* (1974), it was said to be grounded in the separation of powers.[2] Proponents of executive privilege have also sought its justification in historical precedents. In truth, both of these efforts to establish the legality of executive privilege rest on flimsy scaffolding. Moreover, whatever the legality of executive privilege it is not essential to the success of the presidency and, in fact, poses serious harms to the political system.

CONSTITUTIONAL CONSIDERATIONS

Questions of presidential authority properly begin with constitutional analysis. Where in the Constitution—in its express provisions or implied derivations—is provision made for executive privilege? Moreover, which of the president's constitutional assignments require resort to claims of executive privilege?

The framers of the Constitution made no provision for executive privilege, which is not surprising because of the framers' deep-seated fear of executive power. As the historian Charles Warren has pointed out, "Fear of a return of Executive authority like that exercised by the Royal Governors or by the King had been ever present in the states from the beginning of the Revolution."[3] The founders assumed, as James Iredell stated at the North Carolina ratification convention, that "nothing is more fallible than human judgment."[4] And so it was a cardinal principle of republicanism that the conjoined wisdom of the many was superior to the judgment of one. Accordingly, the founders embraced the doctrine of checks and balances as a check on executive unilateralism. In foreign affairs, too, the founders insisted on a structure of shared powers. For, as even Alexander Hamilton agreed, "The history of human conduct does not warrant that exalted opinion of human virtue which would make it wise in a nation to commit interests of so delicate and momentous a kind, as those which concerns its intercourse with the rest of the world, to the sole disposal of a magistrate created and circumstanced as would be a President of the United States."[5]

The framers showed no sympathy for the notion of executive privilege. Speaking at the Pennsylvania ratifying convention, James Wilson, the delegate from Pennsylvania who was second in importance only to James Madison of Virginia as an architect of the Constitution, defended the Constitutional Convention's decision to establish a single presidency rather than a plural presidency. "Executive power," he explained, "is better to be trusted when it has no screen." Wilson noted the visibility and accountability of the president: "he cannot act improperly, and hide either his negligence or inattention," and although he possesses sufficient power, "not a *single privilege* is annexed to his character; far from being above the laws, he is amenable to them in his private character as a citizen, and in his public character by impeachment."[6] The president was to be bound by the strictures of the Constitution, made amenable to the laws and the judicial process, and barred from hiding his activities. The framers' understanding, as Madison put it, that the executive power should be "confined and defined" affords no ground for the view that executive privilege was regarded as an attribute of executive power that might be advanced to conceal the president's "negligence or inattention."[7]

The delegates' refusal to grant the president the authority to conceal information from Congress reflected more than just a generalized distrust of executive power. That decision also reflected the framers' belief that Congress, like the British Parliament, would need on occasion to pursue investigations as a prelude to impeachment. Wilson was one of many delegates to trumpet the role of the House of Commons as the "Grand Inquest of the Nation," which, he declared, has "checked the progress of arbitrary power. . . . The proudest ministers of the proudest monarchs . . . have appeared at the bar of the house to give an account of their conduct."[8] In addition, the framers acted out of a belief that the powers vested in Congress—including its general oversight authority to supervise the enforcement of its laws and the implementation of its appropriations, as well as its broad informing function—required legislative access to information possessed by the executive.

The lone provision of the Constitution that addresses secrecy vests in Congress, not the president, the authority to conceal information from the public. Article I, Section 5, requires both houses of Congress to keep and publish journals, except "such parts as may in their judgment require secrecy." This provision proved divisive in the Constitutional Convention and in the state ratifying conventions. Wilson was one of those who objected. "The people," he insisted, "have a right to know what their Agents are doing or have done, and it should not lie in the option of the Legislature to conceal their proceedings." The framers preferred publicity over secrecy, and they understood that information and knowledge were critical to the preservation of liberty and the enterprise of self-governance.[9]

In summary, neither the Constitutional Convention debates—in which the idea of executive privilege was never discussed—nor the text of the Constitution supports the notion that the founders intended to bestow upon the president the power to conceal information from Congress. Nor at the time of the framing was there either an inherent or implied executive power to conceal information from legislative inquiry. The framers knew how to grant power, confer immunities, and create exceptions to power, but there is no evidence to support the contention that they ascribed to the president an implied power to undercut the investigatory power of Congress.[10]

In *United States v. Nixon,* the Supreme Court ignored the text and the architecture of the Constitution in creating the doctrine of a constitutionally based executive privilege. The Court, in an opinion written by Chief Justice Warren E. Burger, held that "a presumptive privilege for confidential communications . . . is fundamental to the operation of government and inextricably rooted in the separation of powers" and that "to the extent this interest relates to the effective discharge of a President's powers, it is constitutionally based."[11] The Court's employment of a mere ipse dixit served to elevate executive privilege to the constitutional level for the first time. Before that ruling, executive privilege had been known only as an "evidentiary" or "presumptive" privilege—that is, one similar to the lawyer–client or doctor–patient relationship that must yield to the showing of a greater public need.

The Court's effort to ground executive privilege in the separation of powers is unpersuasive. Separation of powers does not create or grant power; rather, it constitutes a rough division of authority that serves to preserve the Constitution's enumeration of powers against acts of usurpation. The Court's claim that executive privilege is "inextricably rooted in the separation of powers" would have astonished Chief Justice Marshall, who faced the question of a presidential privilege to withhold information from the courts in 1807 in the treason trial of Aaron Burr.[12] Burr had requested from President Thomas Jefferson a letter written to him by Gen. James Wilkinson. Jefferson's attorney, George Hay, offered to submit the letter to Marshall, "excepting such parts thereof as are, in my opinion, not material for the purposes of justice, for the defense of the accused, or pertinent to the issue. . . . The accuracy of this opinion, I am willing to refer to the judgment of the Court, by submitting the original letter for its inspection."[13] When Jefferson submitted the letter, with certain deletions, he did not assert a right to withhold information from the court; indeed, he made no challenge to the authority of the court to demand from the president materials relevant to the trial.

Marshall said nothing at all about an executive privilege "rooted" in the separation of powers. The chief justice approached the question of a presidential power to withhold information as an evidentiary privilege, not as a constitutional power. To acknowledge a constitutionally based privilege would acknowledge the president's authority to draw the line and determine issues of disclosure. But Marshall made it clear that he, not the president, would determine the measure of a president's authority to withhold material from the Court.

No historical materials, English or American, would have given the framers an understanding of executive power that included the authority to conceal information from a legislative inquiry. The framers largely drew their understanding of separation of powers from Baron de Montesquieu, who found no grounds in separation of powers for an executive to resist a legislative inquiry. The legislature, Montesquieu wrote, "has a right, and ought to have the means, of examining in what manner its laws have been executed." That right is an attribute of the English system, unlike others, he noted, in which government officers give "no account of their administration."[14] In short, for the framers the separation of powers did not imply an executive right to withhold information from the legislature. On the contrary, it entailed a strong belief that the legislature had a right to demand from the executive the information it deemed relevant to its inquiries.

The effort to ground executive privilege in the original understanding of separation of powers fails to withstand historical scrutiny. The case for executive privilege fares no better when early precedents are considered.

PRECEDENTS

Political scientist Mark J. Rozell has contended that "President George Washington's actions established precedents for the exercise of what is now known as executive privilege."[15] This contention rests on the slender reed of

Washington's response to a House investigation in 1792 into the disastrous military campaign of Gen. Arthur St. Clair against the Indians. The House had appointed a committee to investigate the "causes of the failure" of the campaign and had vested in it the authority to call for persons and papers to assist its investigation. For his part, Washington recognized the authority of Congress to conduct an inquiry into the conduct of an executive officer, which reflected the historic practice of parliamentary inquiries into executive actions. As president, he cooperated completely.

The assertion that Washington claimed executive privilege is drawn not so much from anything he said or did, but rests, rather, on an excerpt from Secretary of State Jefferson's notes of a cabinet meeting. Jefferson wrote that the cabinet had agreed that the "house was an inquest, and therefore might institute inquiries," but determined that the president had discretion to refuse papers, "the disclosure of which would injure the public."[16] There is no reason to doubt the accuracy of Jefferson's notes, but little precedential value can be gleaned from this episode. First, Washington complied with the committee's demand and supplied all materials and documents relevant to the failed expedition. He offered no separation of powers objection. Second, there is no evidence that Jefferson's notes were presented to Congress or filed with the government. In short, they formed no part of the official record; there was no assertion to Congress of an executive privilege and no statement or declaration of an executive power to withhold information from Congress. Finally, the incident's precedential value is vitiated by the fact that neither Washington nor Jefferson ever invoked the St. Clair "precedent" in subsequent episodes that allegedly involved their respective claims to executive privilege.

The early years of the Republic reflect widespread understanding of Congress's right to demand information relevant to the exercise of its constitutional powers and responsibilities. President Washington freely supplied information to Congress pursuant to investigations of the St. Clair disaster and accusations of impropriety brought against Secretary of the Treasury Alexander Hamilton.[17] He refused demands from the House for information relative to the Jay Treaty, but not for reasons of executive privilege. Rather, he withheld the requested materials on grounds that the House has no part of the treaty power.[18] During Washington's tenure, the question was not executive concealment from Congress, but disclosure to the public. As a consequence, as political scientist Daniel N. Hoffman has shown, information was supplied to Congress, "some on a public and some on a confidential basis."[19] On some occasions, Congress disclosed information to the public; on others, Congress persuaded the executive to disclose information to the public. It was able to do so because Article I, Section 5, of the Constitution grants to Congress the exclusive authority to withhold information from the citizenry. At all events, what emerged from this early period was not a record of constitutionally based claims to executive privilege, but rather an institutional practice of comity between the president and Congress.[20]

EXECUTIVE PRIVILEGE AND A SUCCESSFUL PRESIDENCY

In *United States v. Nixon,* the Court declared that executive privilege is "constitutionally based" if it "relates to the effective discharge of a President's powers." This test begs the question: which of the president's constitutional powers requires resort to concealment of information from Congress in the pursuit of a successful presidency? None. The primary purpose animating the invention of the presidency was to create an executive to enforce the laws and policies of Congress.[21] And although the "Imperial Presidency" has soared beyond the constitutional design, it remains true that the constitutional powers and roles assigned to the president do not require the use of executive privilege.[22] The president's constitutional duty to faithfully execute the laws requires no resort to executive privilege; indeed, it was President Nixon's resort to executive privilege that obscured his failure to faithfully enforce the laws. Moreover, the exercise of the pardon and veto powers are subject to close scrutiny and demand accountability and explanation—hardly criteria for concealment. The appointment power—a shared power, it bears reminding—cannot be carried out unless the president and the Senate cooperate, a dynamic that precludes the claim of executive privilege. In none of these areas do presidents need executive privilege to successfully carry out their constitutional duties.

The argument for executive privilege in foreign policy and national security, a favorite among extollers of a strong presidency, shatters upon close analysis. The argument assumes that executive unilateralism in foreign affairs and war making is constitutionally based. It is not. The constitutional governance of American foreign policy reflects the framers' commitment to collective decision making and their fear of executive unilateralism. As a consequence, the Constitution grants to Congress the lion's share of the nation's foreign policy powers; the president's powers pale in comparison, and they require no resort to an executive privilege.[23] The president is commander in chief of the nation's armed forces, but in this role the president is accountable to Congress and thus possesses no authority to withhold information from it. The president is assigned the duty of receiving ambassadors from other countries, but the framers viewed the performance of this duty as a routine, administrative function, exercised in most other countries by a ceremonial head of state. The lack of discretionary or policy-making authority in this duty precludes any presidential need to conceal information from Congress.[24] Finally, in partnership with the Senate the president appoints ambassadors and makes treaties. Because neither power can be effectuated without the consent of both parties, the claim of privilege would defy not only the text and structure of the Constitution, but also the values, policy concerns, and logic that undergird the partnership.

Nothing in the creation of the commander in chief clause justifies presidential concealment of information from Congress. The war clause vests in Congress the sole and exclusive authority to initiate military hostilities, large or small, on behalf of the American people.[25] In his role as commander in chief, the president conducts war, as Hamilton explained at the Constitutional Convention, "once war is authorized or begun."[26] In the capacity of "first General or Admiral," the president conducts the military campaign, but the president remains accountable to congressional supervision. As Madison explained, Congress has the sole authority to determine whether "a war ought to be commenced, continued or concluded."[27] As a consequence, Congress is entitled to complete information about the status of military activities, a need that prohibits resort to executive concealments. At bottom, no theory of executive privilege can be adduced to subvert the express grant of the war power to Congress.[28]

It is folly as well to assert a presidential privilege to conceal information from the Senate in matters relevant to treaty making, because the Constitution conceives the treaty power as the joint province of the president and the Senate.[29] Under the Constitution, treaties require the advice and consent of the Senate, an arrangement that urges consultation and cooperation and renders concealment unwise and inefficacious. In *Federalist* No. 64, John Jay of New York conveyed his understanding that negotiations with those who desired to "rely on the secrecy of the President" might arise, but he emphasized that such secrecy applied to "those preparatory and auxiliary measures which are not otherwise important in a national view, than as they tend to facilitate the attainment of the objects of the negotiations."[30] The president may "initiate" the negotiations, which require secrecy, but the framers anticipated that the Senate would, consistent with the meaning of "advise," participate equally with the president throughout the negotiation of treaties.[31]

In summary, the constitutional design for foreign affairs provides no basis for the assertion of a presidential power to withhold information from Congress. Rather, the Constitution reflects the understanding that Congress possesses in the realm of foreign policy the same interests, powers, and responsibilities that it has in domestic matters: an informing function, an interest in knowing how its laws and policies have been executed, a responsibility to determine that its appropriations have been effectuated, as well as a general oversight function and the power of inquiry, as prelude to impeachment.

CONCLUSION

Little or no evidence exists to suggest that resort to executive privilege has served the national interest. Of course, the president's interests may differ from the nation's. In that event, executive concealment may be a viable option, as it was for Richard Nixon, but it is unlikely to be worthy of emulation and likely to inflict harm on the Republic. Mark Rozell has suggested that the competitive political process will provide a sufficient safeguard against the abuse of executive privilege. That is doubtful. American history has richly affirmed the framers' understanding that the integrity of government officials will not afford a sufficient bulwark against the abuse of power. That is why the founders wrote a constitution, and it is safe to say that trust in government officials was not an animating force behind the Constitutional Convention. Convention delegates did not fail to address the issue of secrecy; rather, they chose not to clothe the president with authority to withhold information from Congress. Nothing in law or history suggested to them the wisdom of an executive power to conceal information from Congress. Nothing since—either in law or in history—has offered persuasive evidence that the framers were mistaken.

RESOLVED, a president's cabinet members should have a larger role in the formation of public policy

PRO: Andrew Rudalevige
CON: Matthew J. Dickinson

The term *cabinet* reveals the nation's British roots. Advisers to the king were designated the "Cabinet Council" as far back as the 1620s. What began in Great Britain as an advisory institution evolved in the late eighteenth and nineteenth centuries into the modern British cabinet, a collective body that fuses legislative and executive powers and personnel. Each member of the cabinet is also a member of Parliament. Selected by the prime minister, the cabinet is accountable to Parliament for its policies. Each cabinet member takes individual responsibility for the acts of his or her department and shares a collective responsibility with the other cabinet members for government actions of great importance. That, at least, is the theory of "cabinet government."

Americans adopted the British terminology of the *cabinet,* but by separating the executive from the legislature (specifically by forbidding members of Congress to hold executive office simultaneously) the framers ensured that the United States would not follow the British model of cabinet government. What the American cabinet did resemble was the older British model of advisory councils. Every colonial government and nearly all of the new state constitutions adopted after the American Revolution included provisions for a council to advise the governor. Under most of these early constitutions, the governor could not act without first receiving advice from the council. In Virginia, for example, the executive council, which was selected by the legislature, was required to keep a written and signed record of its advice, which the legislature could ask to see whenever it wished. The framers of the U.S. Constitution rejected calls for an executive council—though they did grant to the Senate a number of advise and consent functions that state constitutions often lodged in councils—because they feared such a council would either weaken the president or enable the president to escape accountability. A president without a council would be both firmer and less devious.

Yet the framers still wanted the president to receive advice and assistance from the heads of the executive departments. They understood that the president could not manage the entire federal government. Indeed, as government has grown the president's need for help has increased dramatically. But the question debated in the essays in this chapter is not whether the president needs help. Rather, the question is where that help should come from. Should it come mostly from cabinet members, or should it come from White House staff members who, arguably, are more in touch with the president's preferences and more attuned to the president's political needs?

White House aides repeatedly voice concerns that department heads "go native"—that is, that department heads begin to see the world from the point of view of the departments they are overseeing rather than from the point of view of the president who selected them. Department heads, by contrast, complain about being frozen out by White House aides half their age and with a fraction of their experience and accomplishments. In *Locked in the Cabinet,* Robert B. Reich, who served as secretary of labor in the Clinton administration, voices the familiar lament of the department head.[1] When told by his secretary that a White House staffer has called to tell him that he needs to go to Cleveland, Reich explodes that "some twerp in the White House who has no clue what I'm doing in this job" cannot order him around. After resigning himself to his fate, Reich impotently implores his secretary, "Next time when the White House gives me an order, find out how old he is. If he's under thirty don't talk to me unless you've checked with someone higher up."

Reich, however, has no trouble understanding why a president would not want to meet with his cabinet as a body. Seated around a massive table at "the first cabinet meeting in months," Reich reports that "we sit stiffly while [the president] talks about current events as if he were speaking to a group of visiting diplomats. . . . It suddenly strikes me that there's absolutely no reason for him—for any president—to meet with the entire cabinet. Cabinet officers have nothing in common except the first word in our titles." To relieve the boredom of the meeting, Reich scratches out "a list of the *real* cabinet":

SECRETARY OF THE INTERIOR—Secretary of the West (mining and timber companies, cattle ranchers, environmentalists)

SECRETARY OF THE TREASURY—Secretary of Wall Street (bond traders, investments, institutional investors, money managers, the very rich)

SECRETARY OF HUD [HOUSING AND URBAN DEVELOPMENT]—
Secretary of Big Cities (mayors, developers, downtown realtors, minority
entrepreneurs, the very poor)

SECRETARY OF AGRICULTURE—Secretary of Small Towns (farmers,
small-town mayors, rural electrical cooperatives, highway contractors,
local chambers of commerce)

SECRETARY OF COMMERCE—Secretary of Corporate America (Fortune
500 companies, conglomerates, top exporters and importers, large trade
associations)

SECRETARY OF LABOR—Secretary of Blue-Collar America (industrial
unions, building trades, unorganized low-wage workers, the shrinking
middle class, the working poor) . . .

The Secretary of Energy is really the Secretary of Mountains and Deserts,
especially oil and gas production and nuclear wastes. The Secretary of
Transportation is the Secretary of Disastrous Crashes. . . .

And so the list goes on. "No wonder we rarely meet," Reich concludes.

It is easy to poke fun at the parochial attentions of American cabinet members, and even easier to understand the appeal of a view that holds that cabinet members should be responsive to the preferences of the only executive official who is elected by the people. But it is worth remembering, too, that
agencies and departments are the sources not just of political pressures from
interest groups but also of enormous expertise and experience. If the aim is to
create good public policy, then presidents should perhaps pay closer attention
to the advice coming from the departments, both for their own good and for the
good of the country. At stake in the debate between Andrew Rudalevige and
Matthew J. Dickinson is not just the role of cabinet members, but also the
proper place of expertise and responsiveness in the political system.

PRO: Andrew Rudalevige

W hen George W. Bush was elected president in 2000, the *New York Times* reported in an article headlined "Bush's Selections Signal a Widening of Cabinet's Role" that he intended "to run a government by cabinet, delegating more authority than usual to seasoned executives."[1] Twenty years earlier, Ronald Reagan had put it this way: if elected, he said, "the Cabinet would be my inner circle of advisers, . . . almost like the board of directors."[2] Most presidents have made similar pledges at the altar of "cabinet government."

Not surprisingly, then, people tend to think of the Cabinet Room in the White House as a corporate boardroom where the president huddles with the best and brightest in the land to devise governing strategies. Such a model does (more or less) describe the cabinet's role in many parliamentary systems. For example, in the British cabinet the prime minister is what that title suggests: first among equals but not his or her ministers' superior. The PM, like them, is elected from a single constituency and then elevated to office by a majority vote of the majority party. The cabinet's approval is needed to move forward on the PM's major policy initiatives.

All very nice—but when judged on those terms, the American cabinet is a failure. Indeed, constitutional imperatives mean that on those terms the cabinet *must* be a failure. The framers created a single president with some trepidation but for good reason: the buck must stop somewhere if decisions are to be made with responsibility and dispatch, and only the president is held accountable by the electorate for the decisions he makes. One cannot expect collective action in the absence of collective responsibility. Worse, presidents fear correctly that cabinet secretaries have divided loyalties, courting both Congress's favor and that of the constituencies their departments serve.

The American cabinet, then, brings together too many people, with too many vested interests, to serve as the comprehensive sounding board for decision making that presidential promises of cabinet government imply. Such promises are therefore broken as often as they are made. Richard Nixon's comment in doing so was more colorful than most but otherwise typical. "Screw the Cabinet," he told a staffer. "I'm sick of the whole bunch . . . to hell with them. That's all there is to it."[3]

But that's *not* all there is to it. The role of cabinet members in policy formation is easy to discount only if the standard is parliamentary-style collective governance. It is true that cabinet government, in the British sense, will not emerge in Washington. But that does not rule out cabinet government, American-style.

Why should presidents rely more on their cabinets? The short answer is that presidents need good advice. In evading their cabinets, presidents have built up massive White House staffs that create new bureaucratic difficulties and cocoon their bosses in delusions of grandeur. They have moved responsibility for formulating and implementing policy to staffers who are long on enthusiasm but short on expertise. Properly leveraging the virtues of the cabinet and its members is a management challenge, but, in a complex world, it is indispensable to sound governance.

"THE GREAT BUSINESS OF THE STATE"

"The impossibility that one man should be able to perform all the great business of the state," wrote George Washington, "I take to have been the reason for instituting the great departments." What was true in 1789 is truer now, when instead of three departments there are fifteen, employing four million civilian and military personnel. Nearly twelve hundred programs are funded by a federal budget that now surpasses $2.5 trillion annually.[4]

Presidents are expected to lead this mass of people and policy. They must formulate a programmatic agenda, sell it to Congress, and then implement it effectively. In each of these areas, the members of the cabinet can, and should, play a valuable role.

Formulation

Since Franklin D. Roosevelt's famous "hundred days" in 1933, and more systematically since the late 1940s, presidents have presented Congress with an annual legislative program to address the problems facing the nation.[5] Between 1949 and 2002, the result was more than three thousand messages to Congress, comprising more than seven thousand specific proposals.[6]

These proposals have to come from somewhere. One source is the president's staff in the Executive Office of the President (EOP). However, even though EOP's resources have expanded over time, the departments and agencies still retain a key role in incubating policy and translating ideas into legislative language. In 1971 one author concluded that although "in the public mind, line bureaucrats appear to have been eclipsed as legislative innovators by presidential task forces and other outsiders . . . in the business of elevating ideas as serious proposals and issues, bureaus remain well situated and prolific."[7] That conclusion still holds: from 1949 to 1996 about half of all presidential legislative initiatives were created using a "mixed" strategy that relied on the joint efforts of the EOP and departmental staff in some combination.[8]

The reason presidents continue to rely on the departments is clear: the departments' institutional memory and substantive expertise are hard to duplicate. Presidents need to know what the likely effects of a given policy option will be, but, by necessity, presidential staffers are generalists. There is simply not enough room on the president's domestic policy staff for separate experts on, say, soybeans, sorghum, and sugar. Yet the Department of Agriculture (with more than 100,000 employees) can provide them. Former attorney general and undersecretary of state Nicholas Katzenbach warned of "the danger" of advice that comes to the president "from extremely able people with good judgment, who are just badly informed" about "terribly complex" issues.[9] Government policy issues *are* complex, and they have grown ever more intertwined, their consequences relevant not just to domestic politics but, through globalization, to international economics as well. Expertise is a valuable commodity. Presidents should draw on it.

Communication

Once the executive branch develops a policy, legislators must be convinced of its merits. Members of Congress, like the president, need information about the proposals they must consider. Legislative committees exist, at least in part, to analyze the likely outcomes of various policy options for the membership as a whole.

Committees, in turn, have tight links to the executive branch agencies handling the same substantive matters. Through a variety of mechanisms, such as investigative oversight hearings and budget authorizations, committees keep close tabs on their executive counterparts. Presidents' centralized staffs are well connected to the legislative leadership, but at the committee level connections come largely through the departments rather than the White House or the president's Office of Management and Budget (OMB). To the committees, as one congressional staffer put it, OMB "is essentially this very mysterious organization. . . . The communication channels just don't cross there."[10]

Thus another reason to rely on the cabinet departments in policy development is to ensure they can be effective advocates of the president's agenda on Capitol Hill. "The function of the Bush cabinet," a White House staffer claimed after the 2004 election, "is to provide a chorus of support for White House policies and technical expertise for implementing them."[11] But secretaries who are cut off from the policy formulation process make poor salespeople; their chorus is off-key. Indeed, they may even discreetly use their contacts with legislators and congressional staff to undercut White House proposals.

Conversely, departments can also serve as credible sources of information for uncertain legislators. Arguments or evidence offered by presidential staffers are often discounted on Capitol Hill because of their pronounced tendency to support the president's point of view. Departments, by contrast, are thought more likely to provide analysis that is untainted by what one Republican congressional aide recently called "drinking the [White House] Kool-Aid."[12]

As a result, proposals produced by formulation strategies that exclude the relevant cabinet departments tend to do worse in Congress. One study found that, controlling for other variables known to affect such success—notably the strength of the president's party in Congress—a proposal created entirely in the EOP was about sixteen percentage points less likely to gain legislative approval than a proposal created entirely in a department.[13] This finding does not mean that cabinet departments should be the sole arenas of policy formulation. But creative management of the working groups that meld the departmental and White House staffs can help presidents to ensure that policy initiatives will meet their substantive preferences and political needs without being dead on arrival on Capitol Hill.

Implementation

Expertise also plays a big role in the implementation of policies. By definition, executive orders require executive follow-through. On the legislative side, when a provision in a law is vague or silent on a particular matter, its substance is determined by the executive regulations issued in its name. The education reforms passed in 2002, for example, increased the number of standardized tests required of elementary school students, but it did not specify exactly what those tests should measure or how hard it should be for pupils to prove their proficiency. U.S. Department of Education regulations, and departmental reviews of individual state proposals, did that. Indeed, bureaucrats define in practice everything from the level of pollutants allowed to enter the environment, to how strictly immigration laws are enforced, to how occupied countries are reconstructed. At times, implementation may move policies in directions lawmakers did not contemplate. Regular perusal of the *Federal Register* is a sure cure for insomnia, which makes it an ideal forum for the stealthy redirection of government priorities. This practice is policy formation as well.

Presidents have long recognized the value of controlling bureaucratic behavior. For example, President George Bush's long résumé of government service in Washington convinced him in 1989 to place his closest advisers not on the White House staff but in the executive departments, thereby creating a "cabinet of managers" with wide experience in government.[14] His son George W. Bush moved several longtime staffers from the West Wing to the departments in preparation for his second term in 2005. Most notably, Condoleezza Rice, Alberto Gonzales, and Margaret Spellings became the secretary of state, attorney general, and secretary of education, respectively. As cabinet members, they hoped to institutionalize the Bush legacy in the bureaucracy through their implementation of the first-term policy priorities.

Vesting cabinet secretaries with a role in policy direction can also be useful to presidents by allowing the secretaries to serve as "presidential lightning rods."[15] As the analogy suggests, department heads can draw unwanted energies away from the White House and onto themselves—whether that energy runs safely to ground, or consumes the secretary in flames, depends on many factors. During the 1950s, Eisenhower's agriculture secretary, Ezra Taft Benson, deflected criticism of the administration's opposition to farm price supports away from the president and onto himself. More recently, Attorney General John Ashcroft happily shielded George W. Bush from the criticism of civil libertarians upset with the administration's zealous implementation of the USA PATRIOT Act after the terrorist attacks of September 11, 2001, on the United States.

THE "COUNTER-BUREAUCRACY" AND "CREATIVE CONFRONTATIONS"

One result of centralizing resources for policy formulation in the EOP has been the creation of a large and functionally specialized hierarchy within the president's personal staff. In the 1930s, Franklin Roosevelt's request for a half-dozen additional personal aides met with suspicion. However, in the 2006 budget George W. Bush sought funding for more than 900 White House Office personnel (including those working for the National Security Council [NSC], the Council of Economic Advisers, the Office of Policy Development, and the vice president's policy staff), plus almost 500 in OMB, 120 in the drug czar's office, 40 in the Office of Science and Technology Policy, and two dozen in the Council for Environmental Quality. Scholar (and Nixon staffer) Richard P. Nathan has used the term *counter-bureaucracy* to describe this growth.[16]

Many of these staffers are needed for coordination of and leverage over the wider workings of the executive branch. Nevertheless, Nathan concludes that as "the White House staff grew, its general caliber declined." More broadly, two major problems for policy formulation have arisen with the creation of a White House–centered executive staff: the managerial difficulties it presents and the advisory diversity it curtails.

As for the first problem—managerial difficulties—it is ironic that the organizational dilemmas that arise in managing the departmental bureaucracy are replicated in the counter-bureaucracy originally designed to mitigate those dilemmas. The bigger the White House staff, the less able is the president to manage it. Presidents can no longer serve as their own chiefs of staff—and recent chiefs have had multiple deputies of their own, one of whom is usually given the task of simple administrative management. As management problems consume the White House, the "real" bureaucracy gets more freedom of action, not less.[17]

Furthermore, the larger the president's staff, the more likely problems are to enter the White House that do not belong there; presidents' personal aides (even those with whom he has few personal dealings) make unconvincing lightning rods. As Richard E. Neustadt pointed out while discussing Ronald Reagan's Iran-contra crisis, which was fomented by overactive and undersupervised NSC staff, "the White House is a national shrine" and the president its "priestly guardian, custodian, precisely of that shrine. There is no likelihood that anything occurring there, or immediately adjacent and identified with 'there,' can publicly be separated from him."[18]

The president is thusly, and rightly, held responsible for what his staffers do. At the same time, he may find it difficult to control what they do in his name. As Ted Sorensen, White House counsel to President John F. Kennedy, warned, "More important than who gets a White House parking permit or who eats in the White House mess is who is able to invoke the president's name, who is using the president's telephone, and who is using the president's stationery. That's serious. If you have hundreds of people doing that, there is no way you can keep out of mischief."[19] And mischief has often resulted.

Relying solely on White House advice in the policy formation process poses a second problem as well. Members of the president's personal staff are just that—assistants devoted to the person of the president, to what they think are his interests, and to his triumph over the contending political forces unleashed by the American system of checks and balances. As Clinton aide George Stephanopoulos put it, "Doing the president's bidding was my reason for being; his favor was my fuel."[20] White House staff transgressions rarely stem from a desire to sabotage the president, but rather from an overeagerness to help him. The departments quickly become the enemy, to be circumvented.

However, insulating the president from direct access by cabinet members serves to wall off the concerns of much of the political system. That is a tempting prospect to overburdened chief executives. But it tends to distort their view of policies, and polity. Presidents live in a bubble. They need to hear a variety of voices informed by a wide range of perspectives. Staffers filter information to the point of suffocating presidential choices. Bursting the bubble to include cabinet advice is one way to let them breathe.

To be sure, cabinet members represent their departments—if they do not, they will fail as effective administrators. But the links thus forged to constituencies outside the White House should be exploited, not evaded. A cabinet member's advice may be self-interested, but American government is built on the premise that clashing self-interests will add up to the public interest. Regular discussions with cabinet members give the president the chance to learn from what political scientist Thomas E. Cronin has called the "creative confrontations that should be continuous in a democratic political system."[21] Presidents who realize that they are not the government may also realize that their cabinet provides a window to the workings of the wider world.

The point is not to lecture presidents not to "play politics" when making a decision, but rather that politics properly includes a decision's real-world consequences and technical merits. Presidents not consciously seeking diversity in their advisory structures court "groupthink." President George W. Bush indicated that he understood the problem, noting in early 2005 that "they walk in here and they get just overwhelmed by the Oval Office and the whole atmosphere and the great beauty of this place, and they say, 'Man, you're looking good, Mr. President.' So I need people walking in here saying, 'You're not looking so good.'"[22] The wider the advisory net is cast, the more likely that the emperor's wardrobe will receive the scrutiny it deserves.

CABINET GOVERNMENT, AMERICAN STYLE

But Bush, like other presidents, has rarely used the cabinet in this way. Indeed, his first Treasury secretary, Paul O'Neill, described cabinet meetings as literally "scripted," with participants assigned the sequence and substance of their comments in advance. More promisingly, Bush said that in the second term he would require cabinet members to spend at least part of each workweek at the White House, both to receive marching orders and (one hopes) to give advice.[23]

Such a strategy helps to address the fact that the weaknesses of the collective cabinet, noted at the outset, have not diminished; if anything, with the growth of cabinet membership, they have grown. A smaller cabinet made up of consolidated departments would help, serving both to shrink meeting sizes and to give each department more leverage against interest group demands. But Congress has resisted such plans in the past.

Still, plenary meetings of the cabinet are less important than finding regular methods to involve department heads in policy partnership, using the strengths of each part of the president's team. The great value of the EOP staff is its ability to see issues from the president's vantage point and to pull together the many issues that bridge departmental jurisdictions.[24] But this sort of White House leadership does not have to preclude the use of departmental expertise. One model was provided by Dwight Eisenhower, who appointed multiple White House staffers to coordinate policy areas from foreign aid to transportation but did not give them their own supporting staff. Another is the

Economic Policy Board (EPB) under Gerald R. Ford or the similar cabinet council model of Ronald Reagan's first term, which encompassed six groups led by a small White House staff but representing the departments concerned with economic affairs, human resources, legal policy, the environment, management and administration, and commerce and trade. These councils served as conduits of information between the departments and the White House, as well as coordinators of policy development. When needed, they were also clerks who kept track of promises the departments preferred to forget and catalysts for administrative action of all stripes.[25]

Cabinet councils can serve as a template for issue-specific groups or for a wider "Presidential Executive Cabinet."[26] Where they have worked, they have given presidents a chance to consider a wide range of issues and options in a timely fashion. And when they have worked, it has been because presidents took them seriously. The EPB met more than 250 times a year and met with the president nearly once a week.[27] Presidents must use one of their most valuable assets—their time—if such structures are to be anything more than a forum for endless meetings to little purpose.

If used properly, the institutional resources of the wider government will help presidents to make better decisions. And, in the end, the irony is that presidents can enhance the constitutional authority that is solely theirs by delegating responsibility.[28] Good administration can be good politics. Presidents should be urged to put that proposition to the test.

CON: Matthew J. Dickinson

It may not be true, as Charles G. Dawes, vice president in the Coolidge administration, once famously observed, that "members of the Cabinet are a president's natural enemies." But neither can they be considered his (someday her) natural allies.[1] In a system of "separate institutions sharing powers," cabinet secretaries do not swear political fealty to the president alone; they also must pay homage to Congress, executive branch officials, interest groups, and the courts.[2] Indeed, "cabinet government," in which the president governs with the collective assistance of the secretaries who head the major executive branch departments, has always been more myth than reality. This is especially true today for four reasons. First, the number of departments with cabinet status—fifteen—and the more than one thousand federal programs in place that often cut across departmental jurisdictions blur the lines of cabinet responsibility.[3] This expanse makes full cabinet meetings ill-suited to policy formulation, particularly because cabinet secretaries are at least as responsive to Congress, which has created these federal programs, as they are to the president.[4] Second, more than eighty federal agencies, many of them exercising important regulatory powers, do not fall within the jurisdiction of any cabinet-level department, thereby further reducing the usefulness of the president's cabinet for formulating public policy.[5] Third, federal civil service protection reduces the president's control of policy at the lower and mid-departmental levels. And, fourth, a longer and increasingly contentious Senate confirmation process has made it more difficult to fill cabinet positions with able people and to develop a unified cabinet.

Taken individually or as a group, then, cabinet secretaries should not be expected to play a larger role in policy formulation. This is not to say that cabinet secretaries should have no policy role whatsoever. But their effectiveness will depend on how well they are integrated into a policy formulation process that is controlled by the White House staff, not the cabinet. Because the president's personal aides are more likely to share the president's broad political vantage point, they are better positioned to ensure that policies address the general public interest rather than the more parochial interests of the cabinet departments. In the words of a former Nixon White House aide, "We over here in the Executive Office of the President only have one constituent—the President. . . . But over in the . . . departments and agencies . . . they not only have the president as a constituent but they also have Congress, the civil servants, outside pressure groups, etc."[6]

This line of reasoning may seem to belie the words of recent presidents who took office promising to restore a semblance of "cabinet government."[7] Media accounts also repeatedly emphasize the importance of a president's cabinet selections, particularly at the beginning of the first presidential term. But the media typically focus on cabinet members' race, gender, and other ascriptive characteristics, an implicit acknowledgment that cabinet secretaries are selected today more for how they look and what they represent than for their policy expertise. And presidents, despite their professed love of cabinet government, soon find that cabinet meetings are better suited for team building and devotional exercises than as a mechanism for policy development or debate.

Indeed, the term *cabinet government* is a misnomer in the American political context; it more accurately describes Westminster or parliamentary systems. In the Westminster system, the heads of the major government ministries exercise executive authority as a group, with the prime minister serving as first among equals. These cabinet ministers are usually members of, and derive their authority from, the majority party or ruling coalition within the legislative assembly. In a parliamentary form of government, then, the cabinet is the government: it is appointed by the ruling party; it exercises executive powers on its behalf; and it is collectively removed when it "falls" because of an electoral defeat or a legislative vote of no confidence.

By contrast, in the United States the president's "cabinet," composed primarily of the secretaries heading executive departments, is a creature of custom that exercises no formal authority. It has no basis in constitutional or statutory law and cannot be considered a government in any sense of the word. Although Article II of the Constitution specifies that presidents "may require the Opinion . . . of the principal Officer in each of the executive Departments," nowhere does it mention a presidential cabinet. In fact, the framers specifically rejected creating either a plural executive or an official "privy council" to advise the president, because they feared that such a body would obscure executive accountability.[8] As Alexander Hamilton wrote in *Federalist* No. 70, "A council to a magistrate, who is himself responsible for what he does, are generally nothing better than a clog upon his good intentions, are often the instruments and accomplices of his bad, and are almost always a cloak to his faults."[9] In order to vest executive authority in a single individual, then, the framers created a unitary presidency unencumbered by any cabinet-like governing council.

Despite the framers' intent, a presidential cabinet developed early in George Washington's administration. Traditionally, a "cabinet secretary" was responsible for overseeing documents that were kept under lock and key in a wooden cabinet.[10] That term was soon used to describe the secretaries of the three major executive departments (State, Treasury, and War) and the attorney general, whom Washington relied on as his main advisers, both singly and as a group.[11] The phrase "president's cabinet" was most likely coined in 1793, when Washington met almost daily with his departmental secretaries to hear them debate the issue of American neutrality in the war between France and Great Britain.[12]

The neutrality debate among Washington's advisers not only established the "cabinet" label, but also revealed the cabinet's limits as a source of policy advice. Washington's two main cabinet secretaries, Secretary of the Treasury Alexander Hamilton and Secretary of State Thomas Jefferson, clashed about the president's constitutional authority to unilaterally declare U.S. neutrality.[13] Their debate echoed differences between the two across a range of issues, including whether to create a national bank and whether to send federal subsidies to the states for capital improvements. As a result, Washington's efforts to rely on his cabinet as a source of policy advice were stymied until Jefferson finally resigned his post in 1794, a move that precipitated the creation of the two-party system.

The divisions in Washington's cabinet did not stem solely from its members' ideological and personal differences. Instead, as the next section makes clear, they presaged the limitations of cabinet government in the American political system more generally.

THE LIMITATIONS OF CABINET GOVERNMENT

For one thing, the cabinet is not truly presidential. Under the Constitution, departmental secretaries must be at least as responsive to Congress as to the president. It is Congress that creates departments and appropriates monies to fund them. Moreover, although the president nominates cabinet and subcabinet officials, their appointment requires majority approval of the Senate. The president's authority to fire these appointees was not firmly established until a 1926 Supreme Court ruling.[14]

Because cabinet members are not just responsible to the president, they tend to not view policy from the president's vantage point. In Richard E. Neustadt's words, "Their personal attachment to the president is all too often overwhelmed by duty to other masters."[15] Recognizing this, presidents have sought to diminish the influence of these other masters by choosing cabinet secretaries on the basis of their loyalty rather than their policy expertise. In this vein, Washington abandoned his initial effort to build a cabinet containing diverse views, and instead replaced Jefferson as a secretary of state with his former aide-de-camp and current attorney general Edmund Randolph, who more closely shared the president's political preferences.[16]

Although most presidents have followed Washington's lead and sought political compatibility when nominating cabinet secretaries, that strategy is not a foolproof means of ensuring cabinet unity. Two hundred and ten years after Washington replaced Jefferson with Randolph, George W. Bush began his second term by replacing Secretary of State Colin Powell with his former national security adviser, Condoleezza Rice, and for much the same reason: he wanted a more unified cabinet. Why do presidents so often find their initial cabinet appointments unsatisfactory? For starters, presidents cannot always choose whomever they want for cabinet posts; these positions sometimes must be used as consolation prizes to party rivals or as ways to pay off political debts to key constituencies, to maintain geographical "balance" among party supporters, or to satisfy representational claims related to race, ethnicity, or gender. In recent years, as the range of government tasks has expanded and as the cabinet departments have grown in size, a candidate's managerial expertise has become another factor to consider.[17] And even the most politically loyal appointees are susceptible to the centrifugal forces created by the constitutional provisions outlining Congress's role in the creation, funding, and staffing of the executive departments. As the recent memoirs of several disillusioned cabinet members reveal, these forces invariably fray, and often break, the most loyal cabinet member's ties to the president and to other cabinet members.[18] In Richard F. Fenno's words, "In the day-to-day work of the Cabinet member, each man fends for himself without much consideration for Cabinet unity."[19]

These tendencies have only grown stronger in the modern presidential era as the federal government takes on new responsibilities. During the eighteenth and early nineteenth centuries, cabinet posts were fewer in number and often served as steppingstones to the presidency. Cabinet secretaries operated more nearly in the president's orbit, and they had a greater appreciation of the president's perspective. But the expansion in the number of "outer cabinet"–level departments weakened these ties.[20] The outer cabinet consists of departments devoted primarily to nurturing a particular constituency (Agriculture, Labor, Commerce, Interior, Education, and Veterans Affairs), or to overseeing domestic policy sectors (Transportation, Energy, Health and Human Services, Housing and Urban Development, and Homeland Security). The secretaries of these departments are less likely to meet with the president than are the "inner cabinet" secretaries of state, Treasury, and defense, as well as the attorney general, in part because they are viewed as more beholden to outside constituencies and interest groups. They also typically stay in office a shorter time; the average tenure for the outer cabinet secretaries is about fifty months, or about nine months less than those heading the inner cabinet departments.[21] At the same time, many government programs do not fall squarely within the jurisdiction of any single cabinet department. This overlap makes it more difficult for presidents to hold any cabinet secretary responsible for a program's success or failure.

A second limitation of cabinet government is Congress's penchant, beginning in the late nineteenth century, for creating so-called independent agencies, many headed by multimember commissions and exercising regulatory functions. As noted earlier, there are more than eighty such agencies, including the Federal Trade Commission, Federal Communications Commission, Food and Drug Administration, National Labor Relations Board, and Securities and Exchange Commission.[22] None of these agencies is controlled by the president or the cabinet secretaries. Moreover, the courts have ruled that because these agencies exercise quasi-judicial functions and the agency heads serve fixed terms of office, these officials cannot be removed by the president. In the 1930s, Franklin D. Roosevelt tried to bring the independent agencies more firmly under presidential control by moving them into the executive departments, but Congress rebuffed him, and no president has tried to do so since. As a result, officials who do not report directly to the president exercise much of the executive branch's regulatory powers.

The existence of civil service protection for government employees is the third limitation of cabinet government. When Andrew Jackson took office in

1829, he replaced the roughly two thousand executive branch bureaucrats with appointees who shared his political interests. Political patronage of this type gave department secretaries some leverage to exercise administrative control on the president's behalf. However, the "spoils" system was gradually replaced with federal civil service protection, beginning in 1883 with passage of the Pendleton Act. The result is that federal employees are hired through competitive examinations and cannot be removed without just cause. Because this change eliminated an important source of presidential control at the lower and mid-departmental levels, presidents must try to guide policy development within departments from the top down by relying on senior-level appointees. For example, in 2001 George W. Bush was allowed to appoint—subject to Senate confirmation—15 secretaries, 24 deputy secretaries, and more than 275 assistant secretaries within the departments.[23]

Although these numbers have increased significantly since Roosevelt's presidency, the "thickening" of political appointees at the upper departmental levels has not been matched by a commensurate increase in presidents' policy control.[24] Instead, by some accounts it has had the opposite effect: the lengthening of the chain of command has cut the president off from direct communication with those officials who are most knowledgeable about policy details. Modern cabinet secretaries face a Hobson's choice. To exercise influence, they must cater to the interests of the permanent government, but in so doing they are likely to lose the support of the president who appointed them. Conversely, the more a departmental secretary relies on political ties to the president for influence, the less power he or she will wield within the cabinet department.[25]

The fourth limitation to cabinet government is linked to the appointment process, which has become much more politicized in recent years because of the greater involvement of interest groups and the greater scrutiny of nominees' backgrounds. The average time between nomination and confirmation during John F. Kennedy's presidency was roughly 2.4 months; by Clinton's presidency it extended to more than eight months. This more grueling confirmation process has meant both a decrease in the number of qualified individuals willing to be appointed and an increase in the number of vacancies in important departmental posts. Six months into George W. Bush's first term, for example, barely a quarter of the presidential appointees who would later be involved in the "war on terrorism" had been either nominated or confirmed; on September 11, 2001, the share of filled posts was still well below half.[26]

PRESIDENTIAL ALTERNATIVES TO CABINET GOVERNMENT

Because presidents faced such obstacles, it is no wonder that Dwight D. Eisenhower was the last president to attempt to govern from behind even the façade of cabinet government. He met regularly with his departmental secretaries as a group, but primarily to inform them of his decisions and to foster a sense of collegiality; cabinet meetings generally were not used to debate policy details. Kennedy did not make even this superficial bow to cabinet government, reportedly remarking, "Cabinet meetings are simply useless. . . . I don't know how presidents functioned with them or relied upon them in the past."[27]

Instead of the cabinet, modern presidents increasingly rely on advisers in the Executive Office of the President (EOP), particularly the White House staff, for advice and support.[28] Franklin Roosevelt formally established the EOP in 1939 to provide the requisite staff to better coordinate policy formulation.[29] Under Roosevelt's plan, policy still emanated from, and was implemented by, the cabinet departments. But managing budgeting, personnel, and policy planning through his own staff helped Roosevelt to ensure that policy reflected a presidential perspective. His successors have gone one step further by gradually centralizing policy development within the White House. Because the White House staff does not require Senate confirmation and cannot be compelled to testify before Congress, it is more responsive to the president's political and policy interests, unlike cabinet members whose loyalty is often torn between competing power centers.

Even as presidents have built up the White House staff, they have broken the full cabinet into smaller, more manageable issue-specific councils—a limited policy role for which the modern cabinet is far better suited. The first such council was actually established by Congress as part of the 1947 National Security Act, which Harry S. Truman reluctantly signed into law as the price for unifying the separate military services into one Department of Defense. The act created the National Security Council (NSC), which was composed initially of the president and the secretaries of state, defense, army, navy, and air force.[30] Ironically, by establishing the NSC Congress hoped to constrain presidential policy making in foreign affairs by forcing the president to consult with the primary cabinet and military officers. But Truman's successors turned Congress's intent upside down. Instead of relying on the NSC for foreign policy advice, presidents have gradually developed the NSC staff into a personal foreign policy staff, headed by a national security adviser who reports directly to the president.

The NSC established the precedent for the creation of additional councils dealing with domestic, economic, and, most recently, homeland security policy.[31] Although each of these councils is composed of the relevant cabinet secretaries, they are headed by an assistant to the president and supported by a White House staff. Presidents rely on these councils to integrate cabinet members into the policy process, but without sacrificing administrative control. Through these means, the White House staff, and not the cabinet, takes the lead in policy formulation. The result is a policy process oriented toward the national interest, because White House aides are not subject to the narrow countervailing pressures that buffet cabinet secretaries.

At the same time, issue-based cabinet councils allow departmental secretaries and subcabinet officials to play a useful role. They serve as a bridge to the career bureaucrats, who are important sources of policy expertise, institutional memory, and administrative stability. In addition, because cabinet members are viewed as less beholden to the president, they can be crucial for selling policy on Capitol Hill and to the public. In the case of the Iraq war, Secretary of State Colin Powell proved to be an effective administration voice before the United Nations Security Council, because he was viewed as someone with independent stature. Finally, when policy goes awry, strong cabinet heads can serve as "lightning rods," channeling public displeasure away from the president.[32] Conservatives, for example, often criticized Powell for what they believed was his failure to faithfully implement Bush's foreign policy vision.

Collectively, however, the full cabinet really serves only two purposes today: it is a visible representation of the president's commitment to a government "that looks like America," and it acts as cheerleader for the president's policies. But these roles are often in conflict. To sell a policy effectively, cabinet secretaries must hide their disagreements with the president. Yet achieving such unity is difficult when presidents feel compelled to select cabinet members on the basis of ethnic, racial, and gender characteristics rather than policy compatibility.

For all these reasons, it is the White House staff, not the cabinet, to whom presidents must turn to take the lead in policy formulation. Despite the frequent references by presidents and others to the cabinet's importance, in the American constitutional system executive accountability is vested in one individual—and for good reason. As the only elected official with a national constituency, the president is best situated to chart a course that addresses the public's interest. The White House staff, and not the cabinet, is most likely to aid in this endeavor.

RESOLVED, psychological character is a powerful predictor of presidential performance

PRO: Stanley A. Renshon
CON: Stephen Skowronek

Only the most resolute historical determinist would deny that individuals make a difference in history. And if individuals matter, then surely character must matter as well. Yet many things are beyond any individual's control. Conditions not of people's own making structure their choices, shape their decisions, and affect their chances for success. On this much all can agree. But truisms are no substitute for political analysis. Can scholars do better at specifying the conditions under which individual character matters in politics?

One of the most influential efforts to do better is James David Barber's 1972 landmark study *The Presidential Character: Predicting Performance in the White House.*[1] Barber insisted that character matters a great deal, but the book's originality lay in its effort to categorize character types and to use those types to predict presidential performance.

Character, for Barber, was "the way the President orients himself to life." Barber identified two key dimensions of character: (1) a president's activity level in office and (2) whether the president "gives the impression he enjoys his political life." Those who are active and enjoy their political life are "active-positive" presidents. Such presidents have high self-esteem and an ability to draw flexibly on different styles of leadership, depending on the situation and the president's goals. These are the presidents who are most likely to be successful. Those most likely to fail spectacularly are the "active-negative" presidents, who compensate for low self-esteem with compulsive activity. Active-negative presidents, according to Barber, work hard with little sense of enjoyment. Because their political actions are animated by personal demons, they become personally invested in policies. When those policies falter, they are likely to feel personally threatened and are thus reluctant to make concessions or corrections. Persevering rigidly in a failed policy is the hallmark of the active-negative president.

Barber's prediction that Nixon's active-negative character would cause his downfall gave his ideas a celebrity status rarely achieved by political science theories. *Time* magazine featured Barber's theory, and some presidential candidates put the book on their reading list (Jimmy Carter claimed to have read it twice). Political scientists greeted Barber's work with more skepticism, asking searching questions about its validity. Do the measures of activity level and attitude toward the job correspond with the psychodynamic patterns and personality needs that Barber identifies? Was Nixon's self-destruction really a product of psychological rigidification? Was Herbert Hoover's rigidification a result of character or of ideology? Where is the line between principled adherence to one's views and unhealthy rigidity? And can that distinction be made without involving one's own political values?

Whether Barber's theory is useful or not, he deserves credit for understanding that if character is to be used to predict performance, the infinite variety of human behaviors must be reduced to a manageable number of character types. If every president is viewed as entirely unique then one can never hope to learn from the past. Prediction requires theory, which, in turn, requires simplification.

Stephen Skowronek's seminal 1993 book *The Politics Presidents Make* has the same sort of theoretical ambitions that animated Barber's *Presidential Character.*[2] Like Barber, Skowronek generates a fourfold typology from two dimensions. But whereas Barber's aim was a theory of character, Skowronek's is a theory of political regimes. Barber hoped to generalize about individuals. Skowronek wants to simplify the types of situations presidents face.

Skowronek identifies two crucial situational dimensions: (1) whether the president is affiliated with the dominant regime, or governing coalition, and (2) whether the regime is resilient or vulnerable. A president's chance of success, Skowronek argues, depends on the president's place in "political time"—that is, in the cycle of regime formation and decay. A president affiliated with a regime that is vulnerable—think of Herbert Hoover or Jimmy Carter, both of whom were saddled with a faltering economy—has little prospect for success. Although the failure of such presidents is not predetermined, the political deck is stacked against them. By contrast, presidents who come to power opposed to a vulnerable regime—think of Franklin D. Roosevelt and Ronald Reagan, Hoover's and Carter's successors, respectively—are in the best position to remake the political order. Their success is not guaranteed, but they have greater opportunities for success than most presidents do. Character and political skill still matter, but, according to Skowronek, success and failure are often attributed wrongly to character and skill when the credit or blame really belongs to the situation the president faced.

Stanley A. Renshon defends the importance of character. Like Barber, he distrusts the deep Freudian psychology—"the couch questions"—but unlike Barber (and Skowronek) he shuns simplifying typologies. The result is a less parsimonious theory, but readers can decide whether it is a less useful way of predicting presidential performance. Readers should ask themselves not only how much character matters, but also how scholars should go about building better theories that will enable them to learn from past presidents and predict the performance of future presidents. This is not merely an academic question; the election of good presidents in the future may depend on it.

PRO: Stanley A. Renshon

This is an auspicious time to be writing about the influence of character on presidential performance. Despite razor-thin margins of victory in 2000 and 2004, President George W. Bush has implemented a set of far-reaching policy initiatives, both domestic and foreign, that have transformed the political landscape. Bush's character—his ambition, his determination, his resilience, his convictions, and his courage to follow them—are at the root of his successes as well as his failures. His presidency thus dramatically illustrates the truth of the proposition that psychological character is a powerful predictor of presidential performance.[1]

I am not arguing that character explains all or, in some cases, even most of presidential performance. All presidents share the stage with other political actors who influence the likelihood that the presidents will accomplish their goals. Moreover, presidents are limited by law, precedent, public opinion, and competing institutional centers of authority. Clearly, then, no president fully controls his own, or the country's, destiny.

But between constraint and fate lies the vast arena of presidential discretion. The president's discretion lies in what he chooses to do or not do, the psychological and political resources that he brings to bear on his political and policy ambitions, and the values and beliefs that shape his decisions. The psychology that underlies a president's discretionary choices is amplified by the office's immense power. That power is set into motion by one force and one force only, the president himself: his ambitions, his degree of commitment to the values he espouses, his patterns of dealing with people, and his judgment. The presidency is an office in which the psychology of its occupant counts for a great deal.

WHAT IS CHARACTER?

Character is the foundation of a president's (or any person's) psychology. It is his basic psychological core, the bedrock of his motives, the ultimate source of the convictions he lives by. It is how he feels about himself as well as about others, his supporters and his enemies, those who can help and those who can hurt him.

Although different psychoanalytic theories abound, all share, regardless of their specifics, certain basic understandings. Together, these understandings constitute *the* psychoanalytic framework. That framework consists of four core elements: (1) the existence and operation of unconscious motives; (2) the view that a person's internal and interpersonal psychology develops and becomes consolidated over time; (3) the understanding that those consolidated internal structures result in patterns of choice that are discernable over time; and (4) the knowledge that these patterns of internal and interpersonal psychology develop in relation to each other and together form a package that is best understood as a person's psychological character.

A psychoanalytic framework does not rest on the assumption that all behavior is shaped primarily by unconscious conflicts and motivation. Indeed, a frequent mistake is to assume that because character runs deep, it requires "couch questions" (how do you feel about your mother?). Character is reflected as much in a president's observable behavior as it is in the deepest recesses of his psyche.

In thinking about the relationship between presidential performance and character, it is useful to identify two core elements of presidential performance—judgment and leadership—and three distinct elements of character—ambition, integrity, and relatedness. Judgment consists of the capacity to understand the essential nature of the problem at hand and devise appropriate solutions. Leadership consists of the ability to mobilize followers and resources in pursuit of those solutions.[2]

Ambition involves a president's range of political and policy aspirations and his level of desire to achieve his purposes. Although ambition has acquired a decidedly mixed reputation, it is absolutely necessary for consolidating an adequately functioning character structure. Without ambition, there can be little accomplishment, and without accomplishment a consolidated feeling of self-worth cannot develop.

One problem with using ambition to distinguish modern presidents from each other is that they all have enormous amounts of it. One cannot endure the grueling nature of modern presidential campaigns without plenty of ambition. Therefore, an important question of presidential character is whether these strong ambitions are in the service of ideals and values that can anchor them.

Integrity refers to the ideals and values by which the president says he lives, and his fidelity to them. Both are critical. Cataloguing a president's public statements about the virtues to which he claims to subscribe is not enough. Rather, integrity is to be found in those instances in which sticking to conviction entails the possibility of real loss, political or otherwise.

Finally, relatedness refers to the basic nature of the candidate's interpersonal relations—that is, how does the president relate to others? Does he level with others or manipulate them? Does he relish being with other people—as Bill Clinton clearly did—or does he withdraw from people—as Richard Nixon was inclined to do?

CHARACTER, SKILLS, AND PRESIDENTIAL SUCCESS

Character affects presidential performance, but a president's success in office also depends on whether he can develop and consolidate a leadership style that enables him to be politically effective. These skills develop in three primary areas: cognitive, interpersonal, and characterological. Cognitively, the president may be especially smart, as John F. Kennedy, Richard Nixon, and Jimmy Carter were. Interpersonally, he may radiate charm, as Ronald Reagan and Bill Clinton did, or be a master of private persuasion, as Lyndon B. Johnson was. Or he may, as George W. Bush does, depend on character traits such as resolve and perseverance.

Character permeates style and the skills that define that style. Consider presidential rhetoric. It is a truism that, to succeed in politics, today's presidents must be able to convey their programs, articulate their beliefs, and promote their virtues. One of Bill Clinton's ambition-supporting cognitive skills was his verbal facility. He was a master of articulation, and he never encountered a question about which he did not or could not have lots to say. By contrast, his opponent in the 1996 presidential campaign, Robert J. Dole, was a smart man, but not an articulate one (people sometimes mistakenly confuse the two).

Articulateness, however, is not the same as insight or good judgment. Nor is it synonymous with character integrity. Verbal facility can mask as well as reveal. "The era of big government is over," said President Clinton in a State of the Union message that then listed copious numbers of new government initiatives. *Nightline* host Ted Koppel once asked Bill Clinton a question to which the president replied with a barrage of words, prompting Koppel to observe that the more Clinton said the less Koppel understood.

For comparison, consider the rhetorical skills of George W. Bush. Articulate he is not. Bush's verbal meanderings are legendary. He is a not a natural speaker, although he can, occasionally, rise to eloquence as he did in speeches to the public and Congress after the terrorist attacks on the United States of September 11, 2001. Nor is he a compelling presence in televised venues; he does not have Ronald Reagan's easy relationship with the camera. In an age in which most people get their glimpses of a president on television, Bush's rhetorical skills and body language do not easily translate into an asset.

What does characterize Bush's speech, however, is his blunt talk. Osama bin Laden? He wanted him "dead or alive." Renegade regimes? They constituted "an axis of evil." Other nations' decisions about whether to support U.S. antiterrorist efforts after September 11? They were either "with us or against us." Bush's blunt talk is a reflection of his character. He says what he means and demonstrates through his actions that he means what he says. Having convictions and being able to follow through with them is the definition of character integrity. Is character critical for presidential performance? Agree or not with his views, Bush shows that it is.

Another dimension of the presidency also illustrates the importance of character—the best presidents see circumstances clearly and act accordingly. Abraham Lincoln is considered great not because he was smart (although he was) or a brilliant public speaker (he was not), but because he acted decisively to save the Union. Franklin D. Roosevelt might have been, as Supreme Court justice Oliver Wendell Holmes famously said, a "second-rate intellect," but FDR understood in the 1930s that the social, economic, and political fabric of the country was in danger of dissolving, and he acted decisively and flexibly to reverse the economic tide. Lincoln and Roosevelt saw the hard facts clearly, as they were, unvarnished by hype or hope, and acted accordingly. Their good judgment rested on the acuity of their analysis, not its brilliance. It rested on their understanding and insight, not the rhetorical superstructure of their explanations.

CHARACTER MATTERS: THE CASE OF SEPTEMBER 11

In his classic book on personality and politics, political scientist Fred I. Greenstein pointed out that some circumstances require a particular response regardless of the psychology of the president.[3] He was right. But most of the situations facing a president, as Greenstein also understood, are not like that. In most situations, there is more than one way for a president to respond.

Consider September 11, 2001. If ever there was a circumstance that required a presidential response, this was it. The United States had been attacked, and no president could have failed to act in response. Yet not every president's response would have been the same. Of the many possible responses, each carried different and enormous political and strategic implications, both domestically and internationally.

In considering what President Bush might have done, it is worth keeping in mind that the attack on September 11 was not the first al-Qaeda attack, either on American soil or against American military and civilian targets. New York City's World Trade Center was bombed in 1993, as were American embassies in Africa and the USS *Cole* in Yemen. Procedures for responding to such attacks were already in place.

President Bush could have framed the circumstances as just an "attack" and responded accordingly by, say, bombing the country that gave safe haven to the culprits. In 1998 Bill Clinton responded to the bombing of American embassies in Nairobi and Dar es Salaam by ordering a cruise missile strike against a reported gathering of Osama bin Laden and his associates.[4] Another president might well have defined the conflict in this limited way and reacted by bombing Afghanistan and targeting Osama bin Laden and his associates.

President Bush also could have framed the attacks of September 11 as a legal issue and demanded that federal law enforcement agencies track down and arrest the culprits. Indeed, this strategy succeeded in bringing many of culprits behind the first World Trade Center bombing to trial and subsequent conviction. President Clinton relied on this framework in issuing a Memorandum of Understanding in August 1998 that authorized the Central Intelligence Agency to capture bin Laden without using lethal force.[5]

The third way in which Bush could have responded was to frame the issue as a diplomatic one. In the period before and after September 11, many voices were raised to urge America to work more closely with international institutions and to rely on them rather than undertake unilateral action. Such a strategy might have entailed a demand that the United Nations pass a resolution condemning this act of aggression.

Each of these three frameworks—September 11 as an "attack," a legal issue, or a diplomatic one requiring international cooperation—would have been consistent with prevailing practice and policy at the time. Each has a certain logic and can be defended by rational arguments. One can imagine a president choosing to define the conflict in any of these ways.

Bush chose to frame the conflict in a startling different way, and that choice has had enormous implications for the nation and the world. "We're at war" was his almost immediate reaction to the news that the World Trade Center and Pentagon had been hit. Bush immediately subordinated foreign and domestic policy to his declared "war on terror." And in the face of intense criticism, both domestic and foreign, Bush stuck to his guns, refusing to change his fundamental policy. His critics said he was stubborn; his supporters said he showed courage and conviction. All agreed that Bush's behavior reflected his core psychological character.

Bush's framing decision, and his willingness to stick with it, are likely to reshape the world for decades to come. It has already reshuffled old alliances, created new ones, and set in motion profound changes in the international system as well as in American foreign and domestic policy. Among the consequences that have flowed, directly or indirectly, from the president's declaration of a war on terror are the overthrow of the Taliban government in Afghanistan and the establishment of a new, and democratically elected, government; the toppling of Saddam Hussein, a ruthless dictator who had ruled Iraq for decades; and the withdrawal of Syrian troops and security services from Lebanon. It is too early to tell how these developments will play out, but certainly all can agree that politics in many Middle East countries, not just

Iraq, have been dramatically transformed because of the choices made by one man, George W. Bush.

It is true that the forces unleashed by Bush's initiatives have not sprung up solely because of him. But even the most rigid historical determinist would concede that his framing of the September 11 attacks changed the course of history in Iraq and probably that of other countries in the Middle East as well. The vast power of the modern presidency means that it matters a great deal who the president is. It matters what he believes and what he values, and how willing he is to stick to his beliefs and values. It matters how he relates to people, if and how he listens to people, and how he responds to criticism and takes advice. Character in the White House matters because the presidency matters, not only to Americans but also to people across the globe.

CON: Stephen Skowronek

When a president succeeds, Americans' natural inclination is to laud the special talents and skills he brought to the office; when things go wrong, they look for personal missteps and character flaws. There is something comforting in these judgments, for they sustain confidence in the office of the presidency no matter what the experience of the particular incumbent holding power at the moment. So long as performance is tied to the personal attributes of the individual president, success is always a possibility; it awaits only the right combination of character and skill. So long as the presidency is a true test of the person, its incumbents are free to become as great as they can be.

Much of what is written about the presidency reinforces these conceits. Typically, analysis of presidential leadership begins by describing an office that all presidents have shared, a position defined by constitutional arrangements that have undergone remarkably little change since 1789. To this is added the trappings of modernity—new governing responsibilities imposed on the office in the wake of the Great Depression and World War II and new resources made available to it. These responsibilities and resources distinguish the leadership situation shared by all presidents after Franklin D. Roosevelt from that of all their predecessors. Setting things up this way, the analysis holds the demands and capacities of the office constant over the latter half of the twentieth century and presents leadership as a problem of how best to apply the resources of the modern presidency to the responsibilities of the modern presidency. In effect, each modern incumbent becomes a new source of insight into what attributes of character and skill work best, what strategies are most effective, what it takes to measure up.

In fact, however, the political demands on incumbents and the leadership capacities of the office of the presidency vary considerably from one administration to the next, and much of what is taken to be evidence of personal flaws and leadership skills can be accounted for by paying closer attention to the particular relationships established between the presidency and the political system by each incumbent in turn. To see how, we first need a clear idea of these changing relationships, and that, in turn, entails thinking about presidential history a bit differently. Rather than set the modern presidents apart from the pre-moderns to treat them as a separate and coherent group, we will need to compare them individually with counterparts in earlier periods. By making better use of the whole history of presidential leadership, we can better assess the contextual conditions under which great leaders typically arise and identify the limitations on leadership possibilities imposed by less fortuitous circumstances.

The alternative history I have in mind charts change in American politics through the recurring establishment and disintegration of relatively durable political regimes. This regime-based structure of American political history has been widely observed by political scientists and historians alike. It demarcates the rise and decline of Federalist nationalism between 1789 and 1800, of Jeffersonian democracy between 1800 and 1828, of Jacksonian democracy between 1828 and 1860, of Republican nationalism between 1860 and 1932, and of New Deal liberalism between 1932 and 1980. Each of these regimes can be identified with the empowerment of an insurgent political coalition whose reconstruction of basic governing arrangements endured through various subsequent configurations of party power. Just as America's fragmented constitutional system has made sweeping political change rare and difficult to achieve, it has worked similarly to perpetuate the ideological and programmatic commitments of the few insurgencies that have succeeded. To this extent at least, the regime structure of American political history may be considered a byproduct of the constitutional structure of American government. It is manifest today in the persistence of the conservative regime ushered in by Ronald Reagan in 1980.

Looking over the course of each of these regimes suggests a number of typically structured relationships between the presidency and the political system, and thinking about the modern presidents in these terms places each of them in a unique analytic relationship with the presidents of the past. I do not mean to suggest that regime formation and decay are processes external to presidential leadership; on the contrary, I mean to show that the active intervention of presidents at various stages in these processes has driven them forward. What I am suggesting is that we try to understand the political demands and challenges of presidential leadership as variables mediated by the generation and degeneration of these political orderings, and that we reverse the standard analytic procedure by holding personality and skill constant and examining the typical political effects of presidential action in the differently structured political contexts characteristic of the U.S. constitutional system.

THE POLITICAL STRUCTURES
OF PRESIDENTIAL LEADERSHIP

Each regime begins with the rise to power of a new political coalition out to construct and legitimize alternative governing arrangements and to recast relations between state and society in ways advantageous to its members. These coalitions will then attempt to extend their claims on power by elaborating and modifying their basic agendas in ways that are responsive to new political demands and changes in the nation at large. Once they are established, however, coalition interests can have an enervating effect on the governing capacities of these regimes. An immediate and constant problem is posed by conflicts of interest within the dominant coalition. The danger here is that attempts to elaborate the coalition's political agenda in ways responsive to new governing conditions will focus a sectarian struggle, weaken regime support through factional disaffection, and open new avenues to power for the political opposition. A longer range, and ultimately more devastating, problem is posed by changes in the nation at large that throw into question the dominant coalition's most basic commitments of ideology and interest. The danger here is that the entire political regime will be called into question as an inadequate governing instrument and then repudiated wholesale in a nationwide crisis of political legitimacy.

Considering the history of the presidency in this light, two systemic relationships stand out as especially significant for an analysis of the politics of leadership. The first is the president's affiliation with the political complex of interests, institutions, and ideas that dominated state/society relations before he came to office. The second is the current standing of these governmental arrangements in the nation at large. These relationships are always highly nuanced, but the basic variations are easily discerned, and when it comes to explaining outcomes, they do a good deal of the work. For the sake of simplicity, the leadership problem can be conceptualized by referring to those institutions with which political regimes are invariably identified in America— namely, the political parties. With the use of this shorthand, the leadership problem confronting each president can be framed by the answers to two simple questions: Is the president affiliated with the political party that has defined the government's basic commitments of ideology and interest? Are the governmental commitments of that party vulnerable to direct repudiation as failed and irrelevant responses to the problems of the day?

Table 11-1

The Political Structures of Presidential Leadership

		Presidents' Political Identity	
		Opposed	Affiliated
Regime party commitments	Vulnerable	Politics of reconstruction	Politics of disjunction
	Resilient	Politics of preemption	Politics of articulation

Source: Stephen Skowronek.

Answers to these questions specify four typical opportunity structures for the exercise of political leadership by a president. In the first, the basic governmental commitments of the previously dominant political party are vulnerable to direct repudiation, and the president is associated with the opposition to them (the politics of reconstruction). In the second, the basic governmental commitments of the previously dominant political party are again on the line, but this time the president is politically affiliated with them (the politics of disjunction). In the third, the governmental commitments of the previously dominant political party still appear timely and politically resilient, but the president is linked with the political opposition to them (the politics of preemption). In the fourth, the governmental commitments of the previously dominant political party again appear to hold out robust solutions to the problems of the day, and the president is affiliated with them (the politics of articulation).

These four opportunity structures are represented in Table 11-1, with the "previously dominant political party" designated as the "regime party" for easy reference. Each of these structures defines a different institutional relationship between the presidency and the political system; each engages the president in a different type of politics; and each defines a different kind of leadership challenge. These differences are summarized in the four cells of the table. Any discussion of the table must be prefaced, however, by two points of clarification. First, the table is a schematic presentation of pure types that are only more or less closely approximated in history. In the discussion that follows, the presidents that best fit each type are grouped together. The objective is to highlight the distinctive problems and dynamics of political action that adhere to leadership in these situations and, by implication, to reconsider the problems and prospects faced by contemporary presidents. The procedure radically delimits the play of personality and skill in determining leadership outcomes, but, in doing so, it may allow a more precise determination of their significance. The second point is that this typology does not provide an independent explanation of the historical patterns on which it draws. There is no accounting here for whether a regime affiliate or a regime opponent will actually be elected (or otherwise come into office), nor for when in the course of the nation's development a regime's basic governmental commitments will be called into question. My purpose is to reorganize the analysis of the politics of leadership by cutting into political history at certain typical junctures. It is to suggest the rather blunt ways in which political structure has delimited the political capacities of the presidency and informed the impact of presidential action on the political system as a whole.

Politics of Reconstruction

The *politics of reconstruction* has been most closely approximated in the administrations of Thomas Jefferson, Andrew Jackson, Abraham Lincoln, Franklin D. Roosevelt, and Ronald Reagan. Each led a political insurgency and rose to power on the heels of an electoral upheaval in political control of the institutions of the federal government. More specifically, their victories were driven by a nationwide crisis of political legitimacy—a tide of discontent with the established order of things potent enough to dislodge a long-established majority party from its dominant position in Congress as well as the presidency. With political obligations to the past severed in this way, these presidents were thrust beyond the old regime into a political interregnum in which they were directly engaged in a systemic recasting of the government's basic commitments of ideology and interest. It is in these circumstances, and apparently only in these circumstances, that presidents are free to do what all political leaders seek to do: redefine legitimate national government in their own terms.

These presidents are widely regarded as the most effective of all political leaders in presidential history, but what is less well appreciated is that they shared the same basic relationship to the political system at large. They are all known as great communicators, but this seems to have less to do with any common training or shared skill than with the fact that they all had the same basic message to communicate. Each was able to repudiate received commitments of ideology and interest outright, to indict them forthrightly as failed and illegitimate responses to the problems of the day, and to identify his leadership with a new beginning, with the salvation of the nation from political bankruptcy.

More important, however, is what the performance of leaders in this situation can say about the structured capacities of the presidency as a political institution. Order-shattering elections do not themselves shape the future, but they vastly expand the president's capacities to break prior governmental

commitments and to orchestrate a political reordering of state–society relations. It is significant in this regard that none of the presidents who reconstructed the terms and conditions of legitimate national government had
much success in actually resolving the tangible problems that gave rise to the
nationwide crisis of political legitimacy in the first place. Jefferson's embargo
policy proved to be a total failure in dealing with the international crisis of the
opening years of the nineteenth century; Jackson's attempt to deal with the
long-festering problem of national banking precipitated an economic panic
and ultimately exacerbated a devastating depression in the late 1830s;
Lincoln's proposed solution to the sectional conflict of the 1850s plunged the
nation into a civil war; and Roosevelt's New Deal failed to pull the nation out
of the depression of the 1930s. But what these presidents could do, that their
predecessors could not, was to define for themselves the significance of the
events they oversaw and to secure the legitimacy of the new governing commitments they brought to power. Released from the burden of upholding the
integrity of the old regime, these presidents were not restricted in their leadership to mere problem solving. Unaffiliated with the old regime, they refor-
mulated the nation's political agenda as a direct response to the manifest failures of the immediate past, presented their solutions as the only alternative to
national ruin, and galvanized political support for a government that eyed an
entirely new set of possibilities.

The leadership opportunities afforded by this kind of political breakthrough are duly matched by its characteristic political challenges. In penetrat-
ing to the core of the political system and forthrightly reordering relations
between state and society, these presidents ultimately found it imperative to try
to secure a governmental infrastructure capable of perpetuating their cause.
The shape of the new regime came to depend on the way party lines were recast
and on how institutional relationships within the government were reorgan-
ized. Reconstructive presidents are all great party builders, and each is engaged
in rooting out the residual institutional supports for the politics of the past.
Court battles, bank wars, a real civil war—great confrontations that dislodged
entire frameworks of governing—are the special province of the reconstructive
leader, and they can be counted on to forge new forms of opposition as well as
support. The reconstructive leader passes to his successor a political system
that is not only reconfigured in its basic commitments of ideology and interest, but also newly constricted in its potential for independent action.

Politics of Disjunction

The *politics of disjunction* has been most closely approximated in the administrations of John Adams, John Quincy Adams, Franklin Pierce, James

Buchanan, Herbert Hoover, and Jimmy Carter. With due regard for the repu-
tations of these men for political incompetence, it is evident in identifying
them as a group that they shared what is an impossible leadership situation.
Rather than orchestrating a political breakthrough in state–society relations,
these presidents were compelled to cope with the breakdown of those relations.
Their affiliation with the old regime at a time when its basic commitments of
ideology and interest were being called into question severely limited their
ability to control the meaning of their own actions, and this limitation ultimately turned their office into the focal point of a nationwide crisis of political legitimacy. This situation imparts to the president a consuming preoccupa-
tion with a political challenge that is really a prerequisite of leadership—that
is, establishing political credibility.

Each of the major historical episodes in the politics of disjunction has been
foreshadowed by a long-festering identity crisis within the old majority party
itself. But the distinctiveness of this juncture goes beyond these simmering ten-
sions within the ranks; it lies in changes within the nation itself that obscure
the regime's relevance as an instrument of governance and cloud its legitimacy
as caretaker of the national interest. The Adamses, Pierce, Buchanan, Hoover,
and Carter are notable for their open recognition of the vulnerabilities of the
establishments with which they were affiliated; each promised to solve national
problems in a way that would repair and rehabilitate the old order. But solving
the nation's problems is a hard test for any president, and in this situation, in
which they have little else to offer, they find themselves in especially difficult
straits. Actions that challenge established commitments in the name of reha-
bilitation and repair are likely to leave the president isolated from his most
likely political allies, and actions that reach out to allies and affirm established
commitments will provide insurgents with proof positive that the president
has nothing new to offer, that he really is nothing more than a symptom of the
problems of the day.

Invariably, these presidents drive forward the crisis of legitimacy they came
into office to forestall. Unable to control the meaning of their own actions, they
find their actions defined by others. They become the leading symbols of systemic political failure and regime bankruptcy and provide the reconstructive
leader his essential premise. Certainly, it is no accident that the presidents who
have set the standard of political incompetence in American political history
are succeeded by presidents who set the standards of political mastery. This
recurrent coupling of dismal failure with towering success suggests that the
contingent political relationship between the presidency and the political system is far more telling of leadership prospects than the contingencies of personality and skill.

Politics of Preemption

The *politics of preemption* has engaged a large number of presidents. Some of the more aggressive leaders among them are John Tyler, Andrew Johnson, Grover Cleveland, Woodrow Wilson, Richard Nixon, and Bill Clinton. The men in this grouping stand out as wild cards in American political history. As their experiences indicate, the politics of leadership in this situation is especially volatile, and perhaps least susceptible to generalization. Tyler was purged from the ranks of the party that elected him; Wilson took a disastrous plunge from the commanding heights of world leadership during World War I into the political abyss; and Andrew Johnson and Nixon were crippled by impeachment proceedings. Of all the presidents who might be grouped in this category, only Dwight D. Eisenhower finished a second term without suffering a precipitous reversal of political fortune, but this exception is itself suggestive, for Eisenhower alone kept whatever intentions he might have had for altering the shape of national politics well hidden.

As leader of the opposition to a regime that still claims formidable political, ideological, and institutional support, the president interrupts the working agenda of national politics and intrudes into the establishment as an alien power. The opportunity for creative political leadership in this situation comes from the independence that the president enjoys by virtue of his opposition stance. However, so long as the incumbent is unable to issue a forthright repudiation of established commitments as bankrupt and illegitimate solutions to the problems of the day, opposition leadership is limited in its reconstructive power. Short of authority to redefine legitimate national government, preemptive leaders exploit their relative freedom from received political definitions. They disavow orthodoxies of all kinds. They offer hybrid political alternatives. Their attraction lies in their unabashedly mongrel appeal, their free mixing of different, seemingly contradictory political commitments.

As a practical matter, preempting the political discourse of an established regime means simultaneously carrying the support of its stalwart opponents, avoiding a frontal attack on the orthodoxy they oppose, and offering disaffected interests normally affiliated with the dominant coalition a modification of the regime's agenda that they will find more attractive. Floating free of established commitments, preemptive leaders look for and play upon latent interest cleavages and factional discontent within the ranks of the regime's traditional supporters. Though these opportunities are not hard to identify, the political terrain to be negotiated in exploiting them is treacherous. Testing both the tolerance of stalwart opponents and the resilience of establishment allies, preemptive leaders provoke the defenders of regime norms to assault the president's highly personalized, seemingly normless political manipulations.

Compared with presidents caught in a politics of disjunction, preemptive leaders have a much greater opportunity to establish and exploit their political independence; all preemptive leaders who were elected to office in the first instance were reelected to second terms. The danger here is not that the president will get caught in a systemic rejection of regime norms per se, but that he will find himself the object of a relentless campaign of character assassination, the effect of which would be to confirm those norms. Compared with a president engaged in the politics of reconstruction, these leaders do not cut into national politics deeply enough to create durable political alternatives, and personal political isolation is the ever-present danger. Preemptive leadership is, in fact, historically unique in its propensity to provoke impeachment proceedings. Probing alternative lines of political cleavage, these presidents may well anticipate future party-building strategies, but they are more effective at disrupting the established political regime than at replacing it.

Politics of Articulation

The *politics of articulation* has engaged the largest number of presidents; in contemporary politics George Bush and his son George W. Bush both fit the bill. Although it may be no more "normal" a situation than any other, this situation does pinpoint the distinctive problems of political leadership that arise when relations between the incumbent and established regime commitments are the most consonant. Here the presidency is the font of political orthodoxy and the president is the minister to the faithful. The leadership posture is wholly affirmative; the opportunity at hand is to service coalition interests, to deliver on outstanding political commitments on the regime's agenda, and to update these commitments to accord with the times. The corresponding challenge is to uphold definitions, to affirm established norms, to maintain a sense of regime coherence and integrity in changing times, and to mitigate and manage the factional ruptures within the ranks of the regime's traditional supporters that inevitably accompany alternations in the status quo ante. These challenges have been met in various ways, and with varying degrees of skill, but a look at the record suggests that the political effects are pretty much the same.

Consider the most impressive of the bunch. In each of America's major political regimes, there has been one particular episode in orthodox innovation that stands out for its programmatic accomplishments. In the Jeffersonian era, it was the administration of James Monroe; in the Jacksonian era, the administration of James Polk; in the Republican era, the administration of Theodore Roosevelt; in the era of New Deal liberalism, the administration of Lyndon B. Johnson. These administrations were not only pivotal in the course of each regime's development, but also emblematic of the problems this situation poses for presidential leadership. These men exercised power in what were, for all appearances, especially propitious circumstances for orthodox innovation. At the outset of each presidency, a long-established regime party was affirmed in its control of the entire national government, and the national posture was so strong at home and abroad that it left no excuses for not finally delivering on long-heralded regime promises. Each president thus set full sail at a time when it was possible to think about completing the unfinished business of national politics, realizing the regime's vision of America, and finally turning the party of orthodoxy into a consensual party of the nation. To that end, each in fact enacted a full and programmatic policy package.

But just as surely as a leadership project of culmination and completion suggests a great leap into the promised land, it accentuates the underlying problem of definition, of upholding fundamental commitments in some coherent fashion and having old allies see the new arrangements as the legitimate expression of their ideals. Each of America's great orthodox innovators found his administration mired in the dilemmas of reconciling old commitments with the expansive political possibilities at hand. Leading a regime at the apex of its projection of national power and purpose, each was beset by a political implosion of conflicting expectations. By pushing ahead with the received business of national politics and embellishing its commitments, these presidents fomented deep schisms within their own ranks; by making real changes in governing commitments, they undercut their own ability to speak for the party faithful. While most fully articulating his regime as a system of national government, each of these presidents was charged with a betrayal of the faith, and each pulled the regime into an accelerated sectarian struggle over the true meaning of orthodoxy. These presidencies were not undermined by the assaults of their nominal political opponents but by the disaffection of their ostensible allies.

CHARACTER AND SKILL IN CONTEXT

Presidential success, in summary, is determined at least as much by systemic factors as by presidential character, decision-making styles, or political skills. All presidents possess a modicum of political competence, but the political challenges they face shift abruptly from one presidency to the next. If this analysis is correct, any evaluation of the importance of a president's personal attributes and skills in leadership must be rendered with great caution.

Take Bill Clinton. Setting Clinton's experience against that of other preemptive presidents recasts understanding of both the typical and extraordinary aspects of his leadership. Although the convulsive character of the Clinton administration stands out among recent presidencies, it fits a recurrent pattern of extraordinary volatility in pursuit of a third way. Independence is the watch-word of preemptive leadership, and in exercising this independence preemptive leaders provoke intense political struggles in which their own personal codes of conduct take center stage. Other presidents may be judged incompetent or misguided; these presidents have been attacked as moral degenerates, congenitally incapable of rising above nihilism and manipulation.

When the attraction of "third-way politics" under Woodrow Wilson and Richard Nixon became evident, opponents labeled them "Shifty Tom" (Wilson's first name was Thomas) and "Tricky Dick." When the same became evident under Clinton, his opponents saddled him with the label "Slick Willy." These characterizations are all of a type—a political type, not a personality type. They are characteristic of the personalization of politics that occurs when an opposition leader seeks to preempt established conceptions of the political alternatives and to substitute a third way. Determined to sustain their contention that Clinton's "New Democratic Party" was really a ploy masking a rearguard defense of liberalism, Republicans deftly transposed the question of ideology into a question of character. Character flaws offered an explanation for Clinton's repeated forays onto conservative ground; they accounted for his use of the presidency to mask his party's true leanings and selectively incorporate his opponents' most attractive positions. As Clinton challenged received definitions of liberal and conservative, of Democrat and Republican, and of left, right, and center, opponents compiled evidence from his personal life to suggest that he really had no standards at all, that he was wholly lacking in principles. By casting Clinton as a man who never cared much for the truth, who had proven incapable of standing by any commitment, and who had no higher purpose than his own self-indulgence, opponents found a way to preserve the truth that they wished to promote—namely, that Democrats remained a desperate party of discredited ideas and debased leadership, while the Republicans remained the only legitimate exponents of national solutions.

Consider, too, George W. Bush, an orthodox innovator negotiating an especially auspicious moment for the established political regime. A look at plausible counterparts in other periods reveals that presidents in these circumstances are all quite accomplished; they are among the most programmatic and expansionist presidencies in American political history. Reframed with reference to other leaders similarly situated in political time, the question of skill becomes quite particular: will Bush do any better than Monroe, Polk, Theodore Roosevelt, or Lyndon Johnson in moving his agenda forward without shattering the political foundations on which his policy accomplishments rest?

The outstanding issue for Bush is whether he will master the leadership dilemma of orthodox innovation. Despite the care with which he has balanced efforts to deliver on the received political commitments of the conservative regime against efforts to build a loftier superstructure on orthodox foundations, the strains on regime definition are, in fact, fast mounting.

It is not just that the party of tax cuts and limited government now supports an administration committed to federal involvement in public education and prescription drug coverage, or that exploding federal and trade deficits cloud the economic future. It is also that this party has come to support an administration that is radically open-ended in its commitments to unilateral intervention abroad and threatening to civil liberties at home. A regime that once declared government "the problem" and that promised to get federal authority "off people's backs" now supports a statist agenda more starkly at odds with its libertarian pretensions than ever before. The great irony is that the extraordinary events that have bolstered Bush's authority and tightened his grip on his party have also pushed him to embrace extreme versions of the competing norms he came to power to reconcile. Holding all this together through a second term would be an extraordinary feat of skill for the affiliated leader of an established regime.

RESOLVED, great presidents are agents of democratic change

PRO: Marc Landy

CON: Bruce Miroff

Presidential scholars periodically receive a letter inviting them to rank the presidents. They are asked to separate the "great" presidents from the "above average" presidents, the "failures" from the merely "average." The effort to rank presidents in this fashion dates from 1948, when historian Arthur M. Schlesinger famously asked fifty-five prominent fellow historians to grade past presidents: "A" signified great; "B," near great; "C," average; "D," below average; and "E," failure. The results were published in *Life* magazine. Believing there to be wisdom in numbers, some subsequent surveys dramatically expanded the panel of experts polled. In 1970, for example, sociologist Gary Maranell published a presidential ranking based on a survey of 571 scholars. And in 1982 historians Robert Murray and Tim Blessing released the results of their survey based on the responses of nearly 850 historians.

In the 1990s, the greatness rankings—not for the first time—became enveloped in partisan controversy. Conservatives were incensed at the low ranking that scholars gave to Ronald Reagan. In 1996 Arthur M. Schlesinger Jr. replicated his father's survey and found that his thirty-two experts ranked Reagan twenty-fifth, just above Chester A. Arthur. Reagan fared just as poorly in a poll of 719 political scientists and historians that was published in 1997. Believing (with good reason) that these surveys were tainted by the liberal and Democratic biases of political scientists and historians, conservatives decided to pick their own panel of experts. *Policy Review* selected a panel of more conservative scholars, which placed Reagan squarely in the near great category. And in 2000 the *Wall Street Journal* and Federalist Society selected an "ideologically balanced group" of 132 scholars who also ranked Reagan as near great.

Although Reagan's standing varied dramatically in these polls, the more striking result was the extent of agreement in all of these surveys, spanning more than a half-century and divergent ideologies, about which presidents were great and which were failures. Virtually every survey identified Abraham Lincoln, George Washington, and Franklin D. Roosevelt (usually in that order) as great. The survey respondents also generally agreed on the failures: James Buchanan, Ulysses S. Grant, and Warren G. Harding. Although the stock of particular presidents rose and fell over time—Dwight D. Eisenhower climbed from the lower end of the average category in 1962 to the top ten by 1996, for example—the great presidents stayed great and the mediocre presidents stayed mediocre. Nobody mistook Harding for a great president, and nobody deemed Lincoln a failure.

Although scholars seem to know presidential greatness when they see it, it is harder to say which behaviors or accomplishments qualify as great. Marc Landy's essay offers one way to define presidential greatness. Great presidents, Landy suggests, inspire "conservative revolutions"—that is, great presidents are those who fundamentally alter the political landscape in ways that align the political system more closely with the nation's guiding constitutional principles.

Bruce Miroff's essay asks readers to think hard about the dangers inherent in the concept of presidential greatness. Waiting for great presidents to arrive and act, Miroff warns, may enervate the nation's democracy by creating passive citizens. Miroff reminds readers, too, of the ways in which presidential action have harmed American democracy. A president granted the power to do great things may also do great harm.

At the heart of the debate between Landy and Miroff lies the question of what citizens want from the presidency. Of course, few Americans would prefer James Buchanan to George Washington or Franklin Pierce to Franklin Roosevelt. No sane person prefers failure to success. But that does not settle the question. One needs to ask as well whether the concept of presidential greatness, and the ratings game that fuels that concept, encourages presidents to do more than is good for the political system. If greatness is defined, at least in part, as transforming the political system, then does the concept encourage presidents to pursue change over stability, recklessness over prudence? And does searching for the grail of greatness encourage presidents to create the kinds of crises that can justify heroic actions? Most of the "greatest" presidents, it is worth remembering, governed in times of war and widespread human misery.

PRO: Marc Landy

Any defense of the proposition that great presidents are agents of democratic change must begin with an explanation of what democratic change is and what it is not. In a democracy the people rule, but ruling is not merely a matter of arithmetic. Indeed, much of the most profound thinking about American democracy, from founder James Madison to French political observer Alexis de Tocqueville to President Abraham Lincoln, has been about coping with the problem of majority tyranny. The principles of republican government embedded in the Constitution represent an effort by the framers to ensure that the inalienable rights of life, liberty, and the pursuit of happiness would not be trampled on by majorities. Democratic change, therefore, is not the same thing as change preferred by the majority.

During the last century, state and national constitutional rules, as well as the procedures of the political parties, have been revised in an increasingly majoritarian direction. Majoritarian simply means decision making on the basis of a majority of voters. Today, U.S. senators are directly elected by the voters and not by state legislatures, which was the practice in most states before adoption of the Seventeen Amendment to the Constitution in 1913 requiring popular election. As a result of new rules adopted by the national political parties in the 1960s and 1970s and by state parties during a similar time span, primaries, not party leaders, now govern the choice of party nominees. Many states also make liberal use of the tools of direct democracy: popular referendums, recalls, and initiatives. In 2003 the voters of California even fired their governor. These majoritarian changes have not proven tyrannical. Instead, they have reflected the debilitating flip side of majority tyranny: majority apathy. The low turnout in most primary and general elections and the meager attendance at town meetings, legislative hearings, and other political forums all demonstrate the people's desire to forego political participation. For a change to be truly democratic, it must do more than increase the opportunities to have a voice in government. It also must improve the capacity of the citizenry to make use of such opportunities and to do so wisely.

Anyone who has ever sat through an academic committee meeting knows that tyranny and apathy are not the only vices to which democracy is prone. Others include indecision, shortsightedness, wishful thinking, vengefulness, irresponsibility, and selfishness. Luckily, as those who have sat through such committee meetings also know, such vices can be mitigated by the mutual instruction that democratic deliberation makes possible. Compelling arguments by my colleagues have sometimes helped me to overcome my own indolence, pettiness, and narrow-mindedness. But American democracy is a sprawling affair; it cannot be squeezed into a committee meeting room. Because the opportunities for genuine deliberation are few, other means must be found to promote democratic virtues and limit democratic vice.

When the Republic has faced its greatest challenges, the chief agent for promoting true democratic change has been the president. At crucial moments in their history, Americans had to be taught how to behave like real democrats. But they proved to be quite educable. The great American presidents were agents of democratic change, because they were great teachers. They prodded and dared Americans to show courage and compassion. But they also accepted democratic discipline: they did not coerce citizens to change, and they submitted themselves to the people's judgment. However audacious their demands, they never interfered in the people's ability to hold them to account, to defeat them at the next election. High among America's democratic moments are the presidential elections of 1864, 1944, and 2004, when in the midst of war American presidents subjected themselves to the verdict of the electorate.

The character of democratic presidential leadership has been obscured, however, because the leading presidential scholars have either underestimated or overestimated the president's ability to lead. The most celebrated of all presidential scholars, Richard E. Neustadt, understood presidential leadership to be essentially an exercise in manipulation. To be politically effective, a president had to court public opinion assiduously. Obsessed with maintaining popularity, the president could ill afford to teach, which often requires imparting unwelcome truths.[1] At the other extreme, James MacGregor Burns defined great leadership as transformational. "The leader can bring about lasting change . . . only by altering . . . the channels in which the stream of events takes place."[2] Stephen Skowronek is closer to Burns than to Neustadt, but his understanding of transformation stresses the role that great presidents play in shattering the existing order. "Time and again the lesson is the same: *the power to recreate order hinges on the authority to repudiate it. . . .* [T]he American presidency has proven itself most effective politically as an instrument of negation."[3]

All leaders must at times be manipulative and must at times work to undermine previously held beliefs. But great democratic leadership aims in a different direction. It seeks to make citizens more *resistant* to manipulation and more able to recognize what elements of the existing order are worth *preserving*. It is not the business of democratic leaders to transform their followers. If indeed such transformations are possible, they are the province of religion, not politics—and especially not democratic politics. As Abraham Lincoln put it in his first inaugural address in 1861, democratic leaders urge citizens to respond to "the better angels of our nature," not in order to escape human limitations, but rather to realize the best possibilities those limitations permit.

In our book *Presidential Greatness,* Sidney M. Milkis and I coined the term *conservative revolution* to describe the kinds of democratic change that great presidents inspire.[4] Such change is revolutionary because it significantly alters the existing regime. It is conservative because it reconciles those alterations with American constitutional traditions and purposes. Conservative revolutions ensure that political innovations go with the American constitutional grain.

Two tools that figure prominently in conservative revolution are rhetoric and party leadership. Presidential words and deeds shape the quality and character of the citizenry. They can either make the public more submissive and self-regarding or encourage it to be more energetic and public-spirited. Just as parents are held responsible for the moral and practical education of their children, so presidents bear responsibility for the education of citizens. Legal scholar (later Supreme Court justice) Felix Frankfurter said of President Franklin D. Roosevelt that he took the "country to school."[5]

Since George Washington's presidency, all the conservative revolutionary presidents have been founders or re-founders of political parties. Over the course of American history, political parties have been the most important source of democratic accountability. Parties have not only held presidents to account, but also have given them a strong popular base for their conservative revolutionary projects. The rest of this essay describes how great presidents have used rhetoric and party leadership to accomplish democratic change by forging conservative revolutions.

THOMAS JEFFERSON

The election of 1800 was the first popularly contested presidential election. Although often called the "Revolution of 1800," it was an exceedingly lawful and merciful revolution, and presidential rhetoric played a decisive role in keeping it that way. In his first inaugural address, President Jefferson reminded the people, including the vengeful among his followers, that "we are all republicans, we are all federalists." He meant that the principles shared by his supporters and opponents, especially their mutual commitment to the constitutional order, were far more important than their differences. Jefferson followed up this plea for unity with a pledge to preserve the general government in its "whole constitutional vigor."

Jefferson's "revolution" had elements of both style and substance. He made the president look like a democrat. He jettisoned the presidential coach and rode his own horse. He ignored distinctions of rank at official functions. He severed the connection between rank and privilege that the Federalists had sought to establish. He presided over a drastic reduction in the size of the national government. To this day, the United States retains a degree of local self-government, commitment to the rights of individuals, mistrust of elites, and lack of centralized rule that is unique among modern democracies. But these profound changes were wrought in a manner consonant with fundamental constitutional principles. Jefferson steadfastly resisted pressure from his more radical congressional allies to destroy the constitutional system of checks and balances by making the courts and the president subservient to Congress.

Jefferson's conservative revolution could not have occurred without his sustained efforts at party building. As the beloved author of the Declaration of Independence, Jefferson might well have been elected in 1800 in the absence of party. But without party support and party discipline, he would have become either a prisoner of the status quo or a fomenter of schismatic change. Jefferson used his party leadership to keep Republican moderates committed to major reforms of the judiciary, public finance, and administration, and to keep party radicals from undermining the form and substance of the Constitution.

ANDREW JACKSON

Andrew Jackson would seem to be a poor candidate for a conservative revolutionary. As a young lawyer and soldier, he was bold to the point of recklessness. He suffered recurrent illnesses and debilitating pain from the bullets lodged in his body from his many duels. Then-senator Martin Van Buren recognized that only the discipline of party could temper Jackson's imperious nature. He set about to reestablish the interregional alliance of Jeffersonians, anchored by the two largest states, New York and Virginia, and to offer Jackson its support in return for Jackson's pledge to conform to party principles. Jackson accepted the offer. Of course, he could have broken with the party after he was elected in 1828, but, to his own surprise, he found the mutual consultation and loyalty instilled through party to be so positive that he willingly succumbed to its discipline.

Jackson and Van Buren grafted a full-fledged party system onto the existing antipartisan political rootstock. By so doing, they preserved the integrity of the Constitution, while endowing American politics with hybrid democratic vigor. Parties were the bulwarks of decentralization. They were localized political associations that linked the people and the national government, thereby providing meaningful popular control of the executive.

Although rooted in locality, parties were knit together nationally. Initially, this unity was solely for the purpose of winning presidential elections. Over time, however, enduring bonds among party loyalists from different regions were forged in the heat of national partisan combat. Both Whigs and Democrats flourished in the South, West, and North. Indeed, the national party ties that developed provided the strongest political counterweight to the sectionalism that continually threatened to tear the country apart. Party provided the president with a national constituency to which he could be held accountable. The Democrats' great success inspired their opponents to create a similar national confederation of state and local party organizations. President Van Buren's reelection defeat by the Whig Party in 1840 ushered in a truly competitive party system, and the alternation in power between two major parties has helped to safeguard American liberty ever since.

Parties also reflected the concern first expressed by the Anti-Federalists that the Constitution did not adequately cultivate an active and competent citizenry. Because the citizens of a great commercial republic like the United States inevitably were tempted to become obsessed with private concerns, political parties were needed to engage them in civic affairs. Parties forge identities that transcend the candidates and issues of the moment and make it possible for individuals to form bonds of civic affiliation. Party loyalty encourages them to honor their public obligations even as they jealously guard their rights. As conceived by Jackson and Van Buren, party provided the vitality and solidarity necessary to complement the formalities of the Constitution.

Jackson also used rhetoric for critical "conservative revolutionary" purposes. In his memorable Nullification Proclamation of 1832, he expressly denied the Jeffersonian notion that the Union was merely a product of an agreement between the states and of which they were the sole constituents. He claimed that the Union actually predates the Constitution and was formed as a result of the joint decision to declare independence from Great Britain and to fight for that independence as a nation rather than a coalition of states. Directly contradicting Jefferson, Jackson claimed that "the people of the United States formed the Constitution. . . . Not only did they establish the federal government but they are its citizens."[6] The right to make treaties, declare war, levy taxes, and exercise exclusive judicial and legislative powers were all functions of sovereign power. The states, then, for all these important purposes were no longer sovereign. The allegiance of their citizens was transferred to the government of the United States; they became U.S. citizens and owed obedience to the Constitution of the United Sates and to laws made in conformity with the powers it vested in Congress.[7]

Presaging Lincoln's later defense of the Constitution, Jackson went beyond rational-legal arguments to declare that "the Constitution is still the object of our reverence. The sages whose memory will always be reverenced have given us a practical and, as they hoped, a permanent constitutional compact."[8] Perhaps nothing so demonstrates Jackson's determination to foster such devotion as his willingness to invoke the name of Washington, "the Father of his Country," in support of it.[9] Such an encomium was a bitter pill indeed to the devout old Republican, who, as a young congressman, had been one of the few members of the House to vote against a congressionally drafted tribute to Washington issued in the wake of Washington's Farewell Address.[10]

The final pages of the Nullification Proclamation contain a hymn to the glories of the American nation state that verges on the Whitmanesque. Jackson implores South Carolinians to

> consider the Government, uniting in one bond of common interest and general protection so many different States, giving to all their inhabitants the proud title of American citizen, protecting their commerce, securing their literature and their arts, facilitating their intercommunication, defending their frontiers and making their name respected in the remotest parts of the earth. Consider the extent of its territory, its increasing and happy population, its advance in arts which render life agreeable and the sciences which elevate the mind. See education spreading the lights of religion, morality and general information into every cottage in this wide extent of our Territories and States. Behold it as the asylum where the wretched and the oppressed find a refuge and support. Look on this picture of happiness and honor and say, we too are citizens of America.[11]

Jackson hardly needed to indulge in such a rhetorical outpouring if all he had wanted to do was mollify South Carolina. But Jackson had more than tariffs on his mind. Although the specific threat posed by the nullification ordinance could have been defused through compromise, to do so immediately would be to lose a crucial opportunity to educate his friends, Van Buren among them. His opponents Daniel Webster and John Quincy Adams already understood the need to preserve federal supremacy. It was the disciples of Jefferson, susceptible to the nullificatory contagion spread by his Kentucky resolution, who needed to improve their constitutional understanding. Jackson's deepest purpose in issuing the proclamation was to teach Van Buren and other Democrats how to combine their zeal for limited government with an equally strong attachment to the Union.

ABRAHAM LINCOLN

Lincoln wielded Jackson's nationalist precedent in the service of the boldest of all presidentially inspired conservative revolutions. In a series of speeches, he explained to the people why a house divided against itself could not endure— that is, why defense of the Constitution actually required a revolutionary act, the freeing of slaves. This stand was no mean feat, because the Constitution actually contained provisions protecting slavery. Lincoln overcame this anomaly by first invoking the key principles of the Declaration of Independence and then claiming that the basic purpose of the Constitution was to bring those principles to life. Drawing on a biblical verse, "a word fitly spoken is like apples of gold in a picture of silver," Lincoln made the Declaration's principle of "liberty for all" the measure of American political life. "The assertion of that principle at that time," Lincoln wrote, "was the word 'fitly spoken' which has proved an 'apple of gold' to us. The Union, and the Constitution, are the pictures of silver, subsequently framed around it. The picture was made not to conceal or destroy the apple; but to adorn and preserve it." [12] Thus Lincoln incorporated the liberty-loving Declaration into the order-providing Constitution, using the former to infuse meaning into the latter. Seen in this light, the "house" of the Union could not possibly endure "half slave and half free." [13]

Lincoln's success in ending slavery and winning the Civil War was also due to his brilliant use of party to mobilize and sustain public support for that difficult and bloody enterprise. Lincoln did not found the Republican Party. Like the Democratic and Whig Parties, the Republican Party grew out of local protest meetings and political organizations. But Lincoln steered the party to success on a national scale and sustained and nurtured it through its time of testing. The Lincolnian Republicans kept what was best about the existing party system and infused it with a greater sense of moral purpose.

In his famous debates with Illinois senator Stephen A. Douglas, a Democrat, Lincoln clarified the essential difference of principle between Democrats and Republicans. Republicans would not accept Douglas's amoral deference to majority rule as the means for determining whether a federal territory should adopt slavery. Lincoln also organized the Republican Party into a formidable political instrument for opposing slavery. He dispensed patronage with a vengeance, removing Democrats from federal offices and giving those jobs to Republicans from all the competing factions of the party. He displayed the same commitment to party unity in selecting and managing his cabinet, which included both William H. Seward, the party's leading moderate, and Salmon P. Chase, its leading antislavery militant. When the tension between Seward and Chase precipitated a cabinet crisis in 1862, Lincoln managed the dispute masterfully, maintaining the loyalty of both statesmen and the party factions they represented. His responsiveness to the needs of his party enabled him to wield it as a powerful weapon of war.

FRANKLIN D. ROOSEVELT

Roosevelt used both party and rhetoric to lead the New Deal conservative revolution. He infused a moribund Democratic Party with new life. Because he had placed the name of New York governor Alfred E. Smith, a Catholic, in nomination at two previous national party conventions, he was able to appeal to Catholics with far more success than any previous Protestant politician and thus to cement Catholic loyalty to the Democrats. By championing the rights of labor to organize, he established the American labor movement as a central element of the Democratic Party and preserved that attachment even when organized labor's top leader, John L. Lewis, deserted him in 1940. New Deal programs also earned the Democrats the allegiance of two previously Republican-leaning groups, blacks and Jews. FDR's greatest electoral victory, however, the one that confirmed the strength and persistence of the New Deal Democratic coalition, occurred posthumously. In 1948 Roosevelt's successor in office, Harry S. Truman, would never have defeated Republican Thomas E. Dewey on his own. But by wrapping himself in Roosevelt's shroud and emphasizing his credentials as a New Deal Democrat, Truman pulled off the greatest electoral upset of the twentieth century.

FDR's mastery of radio, as displayed in his famous "fireside chats," enabled him to explain the significance of the New Deal to the American people in appealing and comprehensible terms.[14] His most comprehensive explanation of his conservative revolution came in a campaign speech to San Francisco's Commonwealth Club. In it, the president declared it was time to recognize the "new terms of the old social contract" in order to take account of how the economy had been transformed by industrial capitalism and the ensuing concentration of economic power. Just as the founders had created the government on a foundation of political rights, it was now time to re-create the economy on the basis of economic rights. The traditional emphasis on individual self-reliance, he argued, must give way to governmental protection from the harshest vagaries of the marketplace. Basic economic security was to be a new government-guaranteed, self-evident right.[15] Thus Roosevelt sought to free the public from excessive economic uncertainty in a manner consonant with American constitutional principles and tradition.

AFTER FDR

No full-fledged conservative revolutions have occurred since the New Deal. But some modern presidents have promoted democratic changes and defeated antidemocratic challenges. They have used rhetoric and party leadership to fulfill Lincoln's promise of political equality for African Americans and to mount a successful defense of liberal democracy against Soviet totalitarianism.

Although the Union victory in the Civil War had ostensibly promised legal and political equality to African Americans, the failure of Reconstruction and the passage of "Jim Crow laws" in the South deprived them of equal protection of the law and of the right to vote. Only presidential leadership could make this democratic promise a reality. If President Dwight D. Eisenhower had not sent troops to Little Rock, Arkansas, in 1958 and President John F. Kennedy had not sent federal marshals to Oxford, Mississippi, in 1962, federal court decisions ending racial segregation in education might have appeared unenforceable, making a mockery of African Americans' efforts to obtain justice through the courts. The Voting Rights Act of 1965 put the power of the Justice Department and the federal courts behind African Americans' right to vote, finally giving meaning to the Fifteenth Amendment, enacted almost a century earlier, which declared that the right to vote could not be abridged "on account of race, color, or previous condition of servitude." President Lyndon B. Johnson spearheaded the act's passage by making effective use of party and rhetoric. His bold 1964 election campaign succeeded in electing such a large number of northern Democrats to Congress that he no longer needed to water down potent voting rights provisions for the purpose of garnering southern Democratic support. In his address to Congress on voting rights on March 15, 1965, Johnson indelibly placed the weight and majesty of the presidency behind the cause of civil rights, even adopting the slogan of the civil rights movement— "we shall overcome"—as his own.

In the realm of foreign policy, the Truman administration, faced with the threat of Soviet domination of Europe and Asia, adopted a strategy of "containment" that committed the United States to wage a "cold war." To wage a cold war, Truman had to commit all the resources necessary to wage real war and deploy them in a fashion that would deter the enemy from instigating major hostilities. Although this strategy promised to keep casualties to a minimum, it required the American people to engage in sustained financial sacrifice and to endure the frustrations and anxieties that decades of continual confrontation with a powerful enemy engendered. From Truman to Reagan, over the course of more than forty years, presidents explained to the American people why such sacrifices and difficulties were necessary and why the patient firmness that containment required was better than either preemptive attack or appeasement.

Terrible mistakes were made prosecuting the cold war. On the home front, Eisenhower failed to confront Joseph R. McCarthy, thereby allowing the reckless Republican senator from Wisconsin, in his pursuit of domestic communist threats, to threaten the very freedoms the cold war was being fought to preserve. The failure of Johnson's strategy for fighting the Vietnam War came close to undermining public support for containment. But these mistakes did not prove fatal. The Senate censure of McCarthy precipitated his downfall and a renewed commitment to avoiding the excesses of McCarthyism. By electing Ronald Reagan in 1980, who opposed a nuclear freeze and supported a massive military buildup, the American people demonstrated their continued support for the cold war. The inability of the Soviet Union to match this buildup undermined its morale and contributed to its implosion in 1991 and to the earlier toppling of the Berlin Wall in 1989.

Victory in the cold war, which owed so much to the presidential leadership exercised over more than four decades, heralded great democratic change. East Germans became citizens of a democratic Germany, and democratic governments were established in Poland, Hungary, the Czech Republic, and the Baltic states. Since Reagan, every president has sought to forge a foreign policy dedicated to human rights and democratization. These principles were at the heart of the coalition President George Bush assembled to drive Iraq from Kuwait in 1991. They were the rationale behind President Bill Clinton's decision to wage war against Serbia in Kosovo in 1999 and to immerse himself in the negotiations that sought to establish a broad-based government in Northern Ireland culminating in the Good Friday Agreement of 1998. Now they are at the heart of President George W. Bush's efforts to establish a free government in Iraq as part of the broader war on global terror. Indeed, Bush is convinced that the only way to defeat terrorism is to bring democracy to places where it does not currently exist—most notably Egypt, Iran, and Saudi Arabia.[16]

This identification of the American president with global democracy is not new; it dates back at least to Woodrow Wilson. But not since Wilson tried to use the post–World War I peace treaty to democratize Europe has a president committed himself so deeply to reforming the politics of foreign nations. In recognition of the profound importance of this development, this essay ends where it began, praising the president as an agent of democratic change while recognizing the dangers inherent in unfettered majoritarianism. To serve the cause of democracy, the president must pair exuberance with caution. He must use the bully pulpit not only to exhort those suffering under dictatorships to throw off their fetters, but also to help them understand that self-government requires self-control, not just self-expression. To find inspiration for this extraordinarily difficult assignment, he can turn to his predecessors in office. He can look to Thomas Jefferson, who, even as he was launching his "Revolution of 1800," reminded both his partisan allies and his opponents that when it came to fundamental questions "we are all Republicans, we are all Federalists." He can look to Abraham Lincoln, who, even as he was demanding that the South acknowledge African Americans as free persons and citizens, insisted that North and South reconcile in a spirit of "malice towards none and charity for all." Thus presidents promote democracy in large part by encouraging citizens to embody the great virtues that democracy can promote.

CON: Bruce Miroff

In the storybook history of the American presidency, great presidents are the champions and promoters of democratic change. Most Americans, especially those who were educated before the recent rise of a more revisionist-minded historical profession, are familiar with the landmarks of presidential service to democracy. Andrew Jackson combated elite privilege and opened government to the common man. Abraham Lincoln emancipated the slaves. Theodore Roosevelt castigated the "malefactors of great wealth" and committed the federal government to a "Square Deal" for all citizens. Franklin D. Roosevelt built a strong national state that offered both opportunity and security to working people. John F. Kennedy and Lyndon B. Johnson placed the weight of the federal government behind the civil rights of black Americans.[1]

Like most such stories that a people tell themselves to inspire pride and instill patriotism, there is enough truth in these tales to make the proposition that great presidents are agents of democratic change plausible. American history includes numerous episodes in which democratic values and practices have been advanced, and in many of these episodes the president's role has been necessary, even indispensable. Where structures of hierarchy and privilege have been deep-rooted and encrusted, the energy and force that presidents uniquely bring to the American political system have played a key part in democratic breakthroughs.

GREAT PRESIDENTS AS AGENTS OF DEMOCRATIC CHANGE

The presidents conventionally accorded the status of "greatness" have acted as agents of democratic change in these episodes, whereas other individuals who might have occupied the executive office at the time would probably not have rendered the same democratic services. Rooted in the republican credo and lineage of the nation's founders, Andrew Jackson's predecessor, John Quincy Adams, favored government by gentry; it took the rough-hewn Jackson to sponsor and symbolize governance by self-made men from modest backgrounds. Harboring a deep revulsion toward the South's "peculiar institution," Abraham Lincoln moved gradually, but ultimately with boldness, to free the slaves; his chief rival for the presidency, Democratic senator Stephen A. Douglas of Illinois, had proclaimed that he did not care whether America embraced or rejected slavery. Theodore Roosevelt thundered and roared against business abuses that did not disturb his predecessor, William McKinley. If President-elect Franklin D. Roosevelt had been struck early in 1933 by the assassin's bullet that missed its target and instead killed Chicago's mayor, Anton J. Cermak, it is unlikely that Vice President-elect John Nance Garner, a conservative Texan, would have inaugurated a New Deal. Barry Goldwater, the very conservative Republican challenger that Kennedy anticipated and Johnson faced in 1964, was opposed to new civil rights legislation.

In advancing democratic values and practices, these presidents had to engage in fierce battles. First, they identified and named the powers and forces that impeded democracy. Second, they mustered the resources and mobilized the allies required to overcome antidemocratic resistance. Third, they institutionalized democratic change in legal forms, whether through legislation, executive orders, or constitutional amendments. Fourth, and perhaps most critically, they established the democratic meaning of the changes they promoted, educating Americans to a fuller and more expansive understanding of the democratic faith.

In light of these contributions to democratic change by great presidents, why is the resolution to which these arguments are directed more wrong than right? Why is the view of great presidents as agents of democratic change a flawed and even misleading way of understanding the history of the presidency?

Although the agency, or instrumental role, of great presidents has often been required for democratic advances, it has seldom been sufficient. Treating great presidents as agents of democratic change promotes the belief that great presidents are the *principal* agents of democratic change. Presidents thus become the heroes of democracy's story, and the agency of other democratic actors, which has been at least as indispensable, is obscured or neglected. When the great episodes of democratic change just described are revisited and examined more closely, it becomes clear that other agents initiated the changes that presidents later sponsored. In fact, at times it has taken the persistent and determined efforts of other actors to overcome presidents' initial reluctance and transform them into the democratic champions that they did not set out to be.

All presidents, even the great ones, operate within a larger field of forces. Andrew Jackson rode a wave of democratization in an expanding nation, and it was the rise of a mass electorate and the supplanting of gentry leadership by plebian politicians that encouraged Jackson to wage war on political and economic privilege. In Lincoln's case, antislavery instincts had to be balanced precariously with political caution and constitutional scruples; it was only the ability of abolitionist educators to prepare northern public opinion for a change that made it possible for Lincoln to come down decisively against slavery with the Emancipation Proclamation. Theodore Roosevelt's break with Republican orthodoxy about the country's gigantic trusts built on public outrage generated by Progressive "muckrakers" and reflected Roosevelt's anxiety that government inaction in the face of corporate abuses might spur the dreaded growth of a socialist movement. Franklin Roosevelt shifted in a more radical direction, toward the "Second New Deal" of social security and union rights, in response to the mobilization of workers and small farmers and as a way to steal the limelight from populist demagogues. John Kennedy and Lyndon Johnson were compelled by the dramatic mass demonstrations of the civil rights movement to side with the cause of racial justice despite their prescient fears of alienating the white South.

In each case, the capacity of these great presidents to advance democratic causes depended on the groundwork laid by other agents of democratization. Without this groundwork, these presidents would not have conceived of the democratic projects associated with their names, nor would they have had the political muscle and momentum to bring these projects to a successful conclusion. Put differently, without pressure from the bottom up, presidents would not have championed democracy from the top down. Presidents, great or not, can accomplish some things on their own, but major democratic change is not one of them.

Some people might ask: what harm is there in offering presidents too much praise, or in overestimating the role of presidents and underestimating the role of others in producing democratic change?

The harm is partly intellectual: when great presidents are portrayed as the principal agents of democratic change and the contributions of others are overshadowed, Americans develop a distorted understanding of how change happens in the United States. Misunderstanding their past as having been driven by the deeds of a few great men, they fail to appreciate the sources and possibilities of change in their own time. The intellectual harm feeds a political and moral harm: a limitation in the public's sense of democratic responsibility. If great presidents have been the principal agents of democratic change in American history, the goal of citizens today should be to vote for and rally behind potentially great presidents. Dependence on presidential greatness, and not citizen activism, then becomes the recipe for democratic progress. Unfortunately, this is a recipe for a passive citizenry and a diminished democracy.

Yet the problem of looking to great presidents as agents of democratic change lies deeper than the distortion in understanding that it fosters. The transformative ambitions that drive great presidents to aim at democratic breakthroughs may also drive them to oversee breakdowns in democracy. The presidents associated with striking the greatest blows for democracy have, in most cases, been presidents who also struck blows against democracy. Presidential scholar Stephen Skowronek has written that the presidency is a blunt disruptive force, a "battering ram."[2] Battering rams open enemy fortresses, but they also wreak destruction. Great presidents have been para-doxical agents of change in American history, and the gains for democracy that they have secured must be measured against the restrictions of democracy that they have imposed. And so it is a good idea to revisit the stories of some great presidents one more time, and in somewhat greater detail, because the undem-ocratic features of the records of the great presidents are less familiar than their democratic accomplishments.

GREAT PRESIDENTS REVISITED

Andrew Jackson was an authentic champion of democratic equality—but only for white men. For Americans of color, his brand of democracy was a disaster. As president, Jackson, the "old Indian fighter," took the initiative to force the tribes residing in the southeastern states to move west across the Mississippi River, opening vast new acreage to land-hungry white settlers and speculators. As biographer Robert V. Remini observes, "Jackson . . . took it upon himself to expel the Indians from their ancient haunts and decree that they must reside outside the company of civilized white men."[3] Endorsed by most whites, Jackson's removal policy meant dispossession and death for many Native Americans.

Jacksonian democracy was no more hospitable to African Americans. A supporter of slavery, Jackson was the first chief executive to face the emergence of antislavery agitation. His response was to attempt to stifle the dissemination of antislavery ideas. When angry southern mobs destroyed abolitionist pam-phlets impounded by the post office, the president made no effort to enforce the postal laws; instead, he proposed new legislation authorizing the post office to prohibit mailing inflammatory writings to the slave states. When antislavery activists flooded Congress with petitions calling for the abolition of slavery in the District of Columbia, Jackson's legislative supporters backed a "gag rule" whereby the petitions were tabled and ignored. Ironically, it was the "elitist" president Jackson had defeated, John Quincy Adams, who, as a member of the House of Representatives, took the lead in fighting the gag rule and defending the First Amendment.

The supreme character in the story of the presidency and democracy, Abraham Lincoln, was also the president who most fully tested the constitu-tional limits to executive power over the liberties of Americans. Acting in the face of the gravest crisis to the survival of the Republic, Lincoln claimed for himself several powers that the Constitution assigned to Congress, sparking furious accusations from opponents that he was a dictator and a tyrant. In per-haps his most controversial move, the president set aside the writ of habeas corpus, a cornerstone of personal liberty whose suspension in times of rebellion or invasion is listed among the powers of Congress in Article I. Under this suspension, Lincoln's military commanders imposed martial law, and many citizens were arbitrarily arrested and imprisoned without charges. As historian Mark Neely Jr. has shown, Lincoln was responding to a very real threat from Confederate spies, agents, and sympathizers, especially in the border states, but he was careful to protect political dissent against his policies in the North.[4] Indeed, compared with later presidents, from Woodrow Wilson to George W. Bush, who would use crises, real or contrived, to expand their powers over the lives and liberties of Americans, Lincoln's curtailment of civil liberties seems the most justifiable expansion of presidential power, as well as the one most tempered by leniency. Nevertheless, he set the essential precedent for the emergency claims of presidents to supercede rights by executive fiat—a precedent all the more dangerous because it was the nation's most revered president who set it.

When Theodore Roosevelt donned the mantle of the people's champion against the "malefactors of great wealth," he assumed for himself the personal discretion to decide whether great wealth had been legitimately or illegitimately accumulated. Appearing before the public as the scourge of avaricious capitalists, Roosevelt would actually become cozy in private with some of the most powerful capitalists in the land. Thus his campaign against the trusts posed less of a challenge to corporate concentration in the economy than his colorful pronouncements suggested. Roosevelt developed a working relationship with the most powerful firm on Wall Street, the financial house of J. P. Morgan. When Morgan executives exploited the financial Panic of 1907 to acquire the largest southern steel company for the Morgan-dominated United States Steel Corporation, thereby extending its near-monopolistic control over a basic industry, Roosevelt, trusting in the executives' misleading claims of selfless motives, assured them that he had no objections. Roosevelt's deference to the Morgan interests has been mirrored in the tendency of many later presidents to placate those who hold great power in the corporate economy to the great detriment of the power of workers, consumers, and small businesses.

For Franklin D. Roosevelt, building a strong state to serve democratic ends justified strong and sometimes high-handed methods against adversaries who stood in the way. As FDR established the presidency as the dominant force in the federal government, he set it on a road to secrecy and covert action that would lead toward the abuses of the Vietnam War and the Watergate scandal that brought the Nixon presidency to an end. Roosevelt developed an alliance with his director of the Federal Bureau of Investigation (FBI), J. Edgar Hoover, that was constrained by neither law nor democratic norms. The president expected the FBI director to obtain any information he sought, and Hoover, in turn, regaled FDR with political dirt about his enemies and even his friends. In the same spirit, Roosevelt's aides hunted for financial improprieties that might bring down a prominent right-wing critic, Father Charles Coughlin, and prodded the Immigration and Naturalization Service to ascertain whether the Canadian-born priest was residing in the United States illegally. Nor was Roosevelt scrupulous about civil liberties amid the crisis of World War II, especially for nonwhites. The greatest twentieth-century presidential champion of democratic advancement for ordinary people also ordered the century's greatest abuse of American liberty: the wartime internment of Japanese Americans. Fighting fascism, FDR dispatched 110,000 Americans who were not charged with any violations of law or acts of disloyalty to prison camps.

The accelerating political and moral force of the civil rights movement led John Kennedy and Lyndon Johnson to endorse the cause of racial equality. But presidents tend to be cautious and calculating politicians, and so both men tried to slow the movement down and regain some degree of White House control. Fearful that civil rights leaders might press for radical change, Kennedy and Johnson ordered their activities to be secretly monitored, which allowed FDR's old ally, J. Edgar Hoover, to pursue covert measures against a movement that he personally despised. Attorney General Robert F. Kennedy, the president's brother, authorized the wiretapping of Martin Luther King Jr.'s home and office phones in 1963 because of FBI information that King was receiving advice from a New York lawyer who had been associated with the Communist Party. Hoover seized on the order to bug and place wiretaps on King everywhere he went, and then the FBI director used the fruits of this surveillance, especially information on King's sexual activities, in a bitter crusade to destroy the civil rights leader.

During Johnson's presidency, the covert FBI war against the civil rights movement was expanded beyond King. In 1967 the FBI began a secret program, known as COINTELPRO, to disrupt and weaken a wide variety of black organizations—from King's Southern Christian Leadership Conference to the Student Nonviolent Coordinating Committee and the Black Panther Party—on the grounds that militant blacks were propagating hate and violence. When Americans today hail the civil rights movement for its democratic victories of the 1960s, few realize how much its leaders were hounded and defamed by federal agents at the same time that they were targeted by violent racists.

Thus even in the hands of the greatest chief executives, the American presidency is an ambiguous agent of democratic change. American democracy often requires the great force of the presidency to break through barriers to democratic advancement. Yet American democracy has also been endangered by that same force, wielded by those same hands. Sometimes, the great presidents have operated on the familiar premise that noble ends legitimize ruthless means. At other times, the rationale for undemocratic actions has been even less defensible. Democratic gains for the majority have been paid for by a despised minority, especially persons of color. Checks upon the powerful have been mitigated by covert cooperation with the powerful. Presidential ambition, aiming at history-making transformation, has been easily converted into presidential arrogance. There is, it seems, an enduring tension between democracy and the institution of the presidency: vested with the authority of the state, occupying a position of unique eminence that is a holdover from the days of monarchy, presidents are set too far above the people to be at one with them.

This ambiguity in presidential greatness has been present since the beginning. Among the founders, Alexander Hamilton was the leading exponent of presidential power. Although Hamilton was a harsh critic of democracy, it appears that the executive energy the great Federalist promised has sometimes been enlisted during the later course of American history on the side of democratic change. But executive energy poses dangers to democracy as well—a point made by Hamilton's Anti-Federalist adversaries. Patrick Henry warned that the proposed executive was a monarchical figure whose "mighty" powers would prove a perennial threat to republican liberty. [5] George Mason argued that more vital to the survival and success of the new republic than executive energy was the commitment of citizens "to their laws, to their freedom, and to their country." [6]

It would be petty of democratic citizens to deny praise to great presidents when they perform historic services to democracy. But it would be debilitating to democratic citizenship if this praise were not qualified by a reckoning with these presidents' undemocratic undertakings. Americans ought to keep in mind the conclusion that George Mason's words suggest: democratic change, in the end, depends more on the quality of the nation's citizens than on the greatness of its presidents.

NOTES

CHAPTER 1: The Framers of the Constitution Would Approve of the Modern Presidency

1. *The Federalist Papers* were originally published as a series of eighty-five newspaper articles (under the pseudonym "Publius") intended to explain the thinking that led to the Constitution and to persuade Americans to adopt it as the cornerstone of the new nation. The essays were written by James Madison, Alexander Hamilton, and John Jay.
2. Michael Walzer, *Politics and Passion: Toward a More Egalitarian Liberalism* (New Haven, Conn.: Yale University Press, 2004), 96.

PRO

1. For the classic description of the modern presidency, see Fred I. Greenstein, "Change and Continuity in the Modern Presidency," in *The New American Political System,* ed. Anthony King (Washington, D.C.: American Enterprise Institute, 1978), 243–244.
2. Max Farrand, ed., *The Records of the Federal Convention of 1787,* 4 vols. (New Haven, Conn.: Yale University Press, 1966), 1:21.
3. Ibid., 1:65–66.
4. Ibid., 2:342.
5. Ibid., 1:68–69.
6. Charles Thach, *The Creation of the Presidency, 1775–1789* (Baltimore: Johns Hopkins University Press, 1969), 101–103.
7. Farrand, *Records of the Federal Convention of 1787,* 2:31.
8. Ibid., 2:29, 230.
9. Ibid., 1:111.
10. See Donald L. Robinson, *"To the Best of My Ability": The Presidency and the Constitution* (New York: Norton, 1987), 82–83.
11. Farrand, *Records of the Federal Convention of 1787,* 2:52.

CON

1. Samuel Kernell, *Going Public: New Strategies of Leadership,* 3d ed. (Washington, D.C.: CQ Press, 1997).
2. *The Federalist Papers,* No. 51 (New York: Penguin Books, 1961), 322.
3. North Carolina and Rhode Island had not ratified the Constitution by the time of the first presidential election and could not participate. See *Selecting the President: From 1789 to 1996* (Washington, D.C.: Congressional Quarterly, 1997), 4.

4. Max Farrand, ed., *The Records of the Federal Convention of 1787,* 4 vols. (New Haven, Conn.: Yale University Press, 1966), 2:52.

5. Jonathan Elliot, ed., *The Debates in the Several State Conventions on the Adoption of the Federal Constitution* (New York: Burt Franklin, 1888), 2:448.

6. *Federalist Papers,* No. 71, 432.

7. *Federalist Papers,* No. 10, 82.

8. *Federalist Papers,* No. 71, 432.

9. Jack N. Rakove, *Original Meanings: Politics and Ideas in the Making of the Constitution* (New York: Knopf, 1996), 267.

10. *Federalist Papers,* No. 51, 323.

11. Rakove, *Original Meanings,* 281.

12. Ralph Ketcham, *Presidents above Party: The First American Presidency, 1789–1829* (Chapel Hill: University of North Carolina Press, 1984), 4.

13. In addition to these two tours, President Washington visited Rhode Island upon its admittance to statehood.

14. As described in Stanley Elkins and Eric McKitrick, *The Age of Federalism* (New York: Oxford University Press, 1993), 49–50.

15. George Washington, "Farewell Address," September 17, 1796, in *A Compilation of the Messages and Papers of the Presidents* (New York: Bureau of National Literature, 1897), 214.

16. Elkins and McKitrick, *Age of Federalism,* 494.

17. Garry Wills, *Cincinnatus: George Washington and the Enlightenment* (Garden City, N.Y.: Doubleday, 1984), 88–89.

18. Fred I. Greenstein, *The Hidden-Hand Presidency: Eisenhower as Leader* (New York: Basic Books, 1982); Robert M. Johnstone Jr., *Jefferson and the Presidency: Leadership in the Young Republic* (Ithaca, N.Y.: Cornell University Press, 1978).

19. James Sterling Young, *The Washington Community, 1800–1828* (New York: Columbia University Press, 1966), 162–163; Mel Laracey *Presidents and the People: The Partisan Story of Going Public* (College Station: Texas A&M Press, 2002).

20. John Quincy Adams, "Inaugural Address," March 4, 1825, http://www.bartleby.com/124/pres22.html (accessed March 12, 2005).

21. Terry Moe, "The Politicized Presidency," in *The New Direction in American Politics,* ed. John E. Chubb and Paul E. Peterson (Washington, D.C.: Brookings, 1985), 235–271.

CHAPTER 2: Political Parties Should Nominate Candidates for the Presidency through a National Primary

PRO

1. Barry C. Burden, "The Nominations: Technology, Money, and Transferable Momentum," in *The Elections of 2004,* ed. Michael Nelson (Washington, D.C.: CQ Press, 2005), 19.

2. States receive more attention from the candidates and the media when they advance the dates of their primaries. See Andrew E. Busch and William G. Mayer, "The Front-Loading Problem," in *The Making of the Presidential Candidates, 2004,* ed. William G. Mayer (Lanham, Md.: Rowman and Littlefield, 2004), 11–12.

3. Ibid., 9.

4. Burden, "Nominations," 2.

5. Broder and Kirkpatrick are quoted in Michael Nelson, "The Presidential Nominating System: Problems and Prescriptions," in *What Role for Government? Lessons from Policy Research,* ed. Richard J. Zeckhauser and Derek Leebaert (Durham, N.C.: Duke University Press, 1983), 42–43.

6. James Bryce, *The American Commonwealth* (New York: Putnam's, 1959), 28–29.

7. James David Barber, *The Presidential Character: Predicting Performance in the White House* (Englewood Cliffs, N.J.: Prentice-Hall, 1972).

8. The phrase is from Richard E. Neustadt, *Presidential Power* (New York: Wiley, 1960).

9. Henry Mayo, *Introduction to Democratic Theory* (New York: Oxford University Press, 1960), 73.

10. Busch and Mayer, "Front-Loading Problem," 33.

11. Burden, "Nominations," 32.

12. Nelson, "Presidential Nominating System," 50; Stephen J. Wayne, *The Road to the White House 2004: The Politics of Presidential Elections,* 7th ed. (Belmont, Calif.: Wadsworth, 2004), 311–312.

13. Busch and Mayer, "Front-Loading Problem," 23.

14. Dean raised more funds than every one of his Democratic rivals in the year leading up to the 2004 election. In the third quarter of 2003, for example, he raised three times more money than his three nearest rivals combined: Senators John F. Kerry, John Edwards, and Joseph I. Lieberman.

15. The Supreme Court, which has already confirmed Congress's authority to govern campaign finance through legislation, would hardly blanch at a national primary law. As for the national parties, the Court has regularly endorsed their authority to establish their own rules.

CON

1. Donald Bruce Johnson and Kirk H. Porter, *National Party Platforms: 1840–1972* (Urbana: University of Illinois Press, 1975), 176.

2. Arthur S. Link, ed., *The Papers of Woodrow Wilson,* vol. 29 (Princeton, N.J.: Princeton University Press, 1979), 7.

3. See Stephen G. Wright, "Voter Turnout in Runoff Elections," *Journal of Politics* 51 (May 1989): 385–396; and Charles S. Bullock III and Loch K. Johnson, *Runoff Elections in the United States* (Chapel Hill: University of North Carolina Press, 1992), chap. 6.

4. For a detailed critique of front-loading, see William G. Mayer and Andrew E. Busch, *The Front-Loading Problem in Presidential Nominations* (Washington, D.C.: Brookings, 2004), esp. chap. 4.

5. See Emily Goodin, "Enough Blame to Share," *National Journal*, December 4, 2004, 3630.
6. See, for example, *Cousins v. Wigoda* (1975); *Republican Party of Connecticut v. Tashjian* (1986); and *March Fong Eu v. San Francisco County Democratic Central Committee* (1989).
7. See *New York v. United States* (1992); *United States v. Lopez* (1995); *Printz v. United States* (1997); and *United States v. Morrison* (2000). The enumerated powers of Congress are those listed in Article I, Section 8, of the Constitution defining the extent and limits of congressional authority. The Tenth Amendment specifies that "[t]he powers not delegated to the United States by the Constitution, nor prohibited by it to the States, are reserved to the States respectively or to the people."
8. See William G. Mayer and Andrew E. Busch, "Can the Federal Government Reform the Presidential Nomination Process?" *Election Law Journal* 3, no. 4 (2004): 613–625.

CHAPTER 3: The President Should Be Elected Directly by the People

PRO

1. John P. Roche, "The Founding Fathers: A Reform Caucus in Action," *American Political Science Review* 55 (September 1961).
2. George C. Edwards III, *Why the Electoral College Is Bad for America* (New Haven, Conn.: Yale University Press, 2004), 81.
3. Ibid., 80.
4. Some think that a true count of the votes in the 1960 election would have given Richard Nixon more popular votes than John F. Kennedy, but the only count available shows Kennedy receiving more popular votes than Nixon. See Edwards, *Why the Electoral College Is Bad for America*, chap. 3.
5. In 2004 the Harris Poll conducted a survey with the extremely large sample size of almost seven thousand voters. In the survey, 64 percent of respondents expressed support for a popular vote to choose the president, while just 22 percent expressed opposition. See http://harrisinteractive.com (accessed April 12, 2005).
6. William Ross, " 'Faithless Electors': The Wild Card," http://www.jurist.law.pitt.edu/election/electionross4.htm (accessed April 15, 2005).

CON

1. Since electors themselves have become subject to the popular vote, the electoral college has never denied the presidency to a candidate with a majority vote. The sole exception is the election of 1876, when a corrupt bargain among elites determined the outcome.

2. In the same way—a wonderful ultimate irony—it is possible to argue that in the absence of the electoral college, those Gore voters who preferred Nader would have voted for him, such that George W. Bush would have won a plurality of the popular vote. But this leads on to a kind of analytic madness.

CHAPTER 4: The Presidential Impeachment Process Is Basically Sound

1. Clinton Rossiter, *The American Presidency* (Baltimore: Johns Hopkins University Press, 1987), 38.
2. Ibid., 39.

PRO

1. Quoted in *Notes of Debates in the Federal Convention of 1787 Reported by James Madison* (New York: Norton, 1987), 56.
2. Quoted in ibid., 332–333.
3. Ibid., 116, 393, 575, 605.
4. In addition to one senator (William Blount in 1799) and one cabinet secretary (Secretary of War William Belknap in 1876), the Senate has tried twelve judges (including Supreme Court justice Samuel P. Chase in 1805) and two presidents (Andrew Johnson in 1868 and Bill Clinton in 1999).
5. These issues are inventoried and evaluated in Michael J. Gerhardt, *The Federal Impeachment Process*, 2d ed. (Chicago: University of Chicago Press, 2000).
6. It seems likely that Richard Nixon would have been impeached and convicted had he not resigned before the House acted.
7. For an example of this common complaint about divided government, see Lloyd N. Cutler, "To Form a Government," *Foreign Affairs* 59 (1980): 126. For a critical examination of this thesis, see David R. Mayhew, *Divided We Govern*, 2d ed. (New Haven, Conn.: Yale University Press, 2005). In parliamentary systems, a majority of the legislature chooses the leadership of the executive branch, and that leadership cannot continue in office when it loses the support of the legislative majority.
8. John Tyler and Andrew Johnson were recent party converts who were added to the presidential ticket to provide balance but surprised party leaders by ascending to the presidency upon the death of their predecessors and breaking from congressional party leaders on matters of both policy and politics. A motion to convene a committee to consider impeachment charges against John Tyler failed to pass in the House in 1843. Andrew Johnson was, in fact, impeached in 1868. The House Judiciary Committee passed articles of impeachment against Richard Nixon in 1974, but he resigned before the full House voted on those charges. Bill Clinton was impeached in 1998.
9. Benjamin Ginsberg and Martin Shefter, *Politics by Other Means* (New York: Basic Books, 1990), x, 163, 162.

10. On the Johnson and Nixon episodes, see Keith E. Whittington, *Constitutional Construction* (Cambridge, Mass.: Harvard University Press, 1999), 113–206.

11. Also see Keith E. Whittington, "Bill Clinton Was No Andrew Johnson: Comparing Two Impeachments," *University of Pennsylvania Journal of Constitutional Law* 2 (2000): 422; and " 'High Crimes' after Clinton: Deciding What's Impeachable," *Policy Review* 99 (February–March 2000): 27.

CON

1. Leonard White, *The Republican Era* (New York: Free Press, 1958), 85.

2. Richard Clarke, *Against All Enemies: America's War on Terrorism* (New York: Free Press, 2004).

3. Jim Rutenberg, "9/11 Panel Comments Freely," *New York Times,* April 15, 2004, A1.

4. Louis Fisher, *Congressional Abdication on War and Spending* (College Station: Texas A&M Press, 2000).

5. Elena Kagan, "Presidential Administration," *Harvard Law Review* 114 (June 2001).

CHAPTER 5: The Media Are Too Hard on Presidents

PRO

1. See Thomas E. Patterson, *Out of Order* (New York: Knopf, 1993); and Matthew R. Kerbel, *Remote and Controlled: Media Politics in a Cynical Age* (Boulder, Colo.: Westview Press, 1999).

2. Kerbel, *Remote and Controlled.*

3. Shanto Iyengar and Donald Kinder, *News That Matters* (Chicago: University of Chicago Press, 1987).

4. Richard E. Neustadt, *Presidential Power* (New York: Wiley, 1960).

5. Tim Groeling and Samuel Kernell, "Is Network News Coverage of the President Biased?" *Journal of Politics* 60 (1998): 1063–1087.

6. Ibid.

7. Center for Media and Public Affairs, "Kerry Gets Best Press Ever," November 1, 2004.

8. Larry J. Sabato, *Feeding Frenzy: How Attack Journalism Has Transformed American Politics* (New York: Free Press, 1991). These figures are derived by adding Sabato's list of feeding frenzies from presidential politics to his list of feeding frenzies from presidential governance.

9. Sidney Blumenthal, *The Permanent Campaign: Inside the World of Elite Political Operatives* (Boston: Beacon Press, 1980).

10. Michael B. Grossman and Martha Joynt Kumar, *Portraying the President: The White House and the News Media* (Baltimore: Johns Hopkins University Press, 1981).

11. Neustadt, *Presidential Power,* 101–102.

12. Ibid., 90, 95.

13. Robert M. Eisinger, *Evolution of Presidential Polling* (New York: Cambridge University Press, 2003).

14. Bruce Altschuler, "Lyndon Johnson and Public Polls," *Public Opinion Quarterly* 50 (1986): 285–299.

15. Seymour Sudman, "The Presidents and the Polls," *Public Opinion Quarterly* 46 (1982): 303.

16. Ibid., 302–310.

17. Altschuler, "Lyndon Johnson and Public Polls."

18. Sudman, "Presidents and the Polls."

19. Theodore J. Lowi, *The Personal President: Power Invested, Promise Unfulfilled* (Ithaca, N.Y.: Cornell University Press, 1985).

20. Altschuler, "Lyndon Johnson and Public Polls."

21. George C. Edwards, III, *The Public Presidency: The Pursuit of Popular Support* (New York: St. Martin's Press, 1983).

22. James A. Stimson, "Public Support for American Presidents: A Cyclical Model," *Public Opinion Quarterly* 40 (1976): 1–21.

23. George C. Edwards, *Presidential Approval: A Source Book* (Baltimore: Johns Hopkins University Press, 1990).

24. Center for Media and Public Affairs, "Kerry Gets Best Press Ever."

CON

1. Doris Graber, *Mass Media and American Politics,* 6th ed. (Washington, D.C.: CQ Press, 2002), 272.

2. Richard Davis, *The Press and American Politics: The New Mediator,* 3d ed. (Upper Saddle River, N.J.: Prentice-Hall, 2001), 249.

3. Stephen Lukes, *Power: A Radical View* (New York: Macmillan, 1974).

4. Bartholomew H. Sparrow, *Uncertain Guardians* (Baltimore: Johns Hopkins University Press, 1999), 123–124; Gaye Tuchman, *Making News: A Study in the Construction of Reality* (New York: Free Press, 1978); Shanto Iyengar and Donald Kinder, *News That Matters* (Chicago: University of Chicago Press, 1997); Robert Entman, *Projections of Power: Framing News, Public Opinion, and U.S. Foreign Policy* (Chicago: University of Chicago Press, 2004).

5. Entman, *Projections of Power.*

6. Roderick P. Hart and Jay P. Childers, "Verbal Certainty in American Politics: An Overview and Extension," *Presidential Studies Quarterly* 34 (September 2004): 516–535; Jon Roper, "The Contemporary Presidency: George W. Bush and the Myth of Heroic Presidential Leadership," *Presidential Studies Quarterly* 34 (March 2004): 132–142.

7. Frank Rich, "Laura Bush's Mission Accomplished," *New York Times,* May 8, 2005, A13.

8. Martin P. Wattenberg, "The Changing Presidential Media Environment," *Presidential Studies Quarterly* 34 (September 2004): 557–572; Jeffrey E. Cohen, "If

the News Is So Bad, Why Are Presidential Polls So High? Presidents, the News Media, and the Mass Public in an Era of New Media," *Presidential Studies Quarterly* 34 (September 2004): 493–515.

9. Stephen J. Farnsworth and S. Robert Lichter, "Source Material: New Presidents and Network News," *Presidential Studies Quarterly* 34 (September 2004): 674–690; Jeffrey S. Peake, "Presidential Agenda Setting in Foreign Policy," *Political Research Quarterly* 54 (March 2001): 69–86.

10. Martha Joynt Kumar, "Presidential Press Conferences: The Importance and Evolution of an Enduring Forum," *Presidential Studies Quarterly* 35 (March 2005): 188, 191.

11. House Committee on Government Reform, *Secrecy in the White House,* 109th Cong., 2d sess., September 14, 2004, http://democrats.reform.house.gov/features/secrecy_report (accessed November 11, 2005).

12. Jeffrey D. Mayer, "The Presidency and Image Management: Discipline in Pursuit of Illusion," *Presidential Studies Quarterly* 34 (September 2004): 620–631.

13. Sean Aday, Steven Livingston, and Maeve Hebert, "Embedding the Truth: A Cross-Cultural Analysis of Objectivity and Television Coverage of the Iraq War," *Press/Politics* 10 (Winter 2005): 3–21. Also see David Domke, *God Willing: Political Fundamentalism in the White House, the "War on Terror," and the Echoing Press* (Ann Arbor, Mich.: Pluto Press, 2004).

14. Aday, Livingston, and Hebert, "Embedding the Truth," 18.

15. Narasimhan Ravi, "Looking beyond Flawed Journalism," *Press/Politics* 10 (Winter 2005): 45–62.

16. John Hutcheson, David Domke, Andre Billeaudeux, and Philip Garland, "U.S. National Identity, Political Elites, and a Patriotic Press following September 11," *Political Communication* 21 (2004): 27–50.

17. David Zarefsky, "Presidential Rhetoric and the Powers of Definition," *Presidential Studies Quarterly* 34 (September 2004): 607–619. Also see Mark Fishman, *Manufacturing the News* (Austin: University of Texas Press, 1980).

18. Hart and Childers, "Verbal Certainty in American Politics," 529.

19. Morris Fiorina, *Culture War? The Myth of a Polarized America* (New York: Longman, 2005).

20. Wattenberg, "Changing Presidential Media Environment."

21. The phrase is from Mayer, "Presidency and Image Management," 629.

22. Matthew Baum, *Soft News Goes to War* (Princeton, N.J.: Princeton University Press, 2003).

CHAPTER 6: The President Is a More Authentic Representative of the American People Than Is Congress

PRO

1. *Baker v. Carr,* 369 U.S. 186 (1962).

CON

1. This dynamic has deep roots in American history. Writing at the end of the nineteenth century, James Bryce, for example, noted that "the nation, which has often good grounds for distrusting Congress, a body liable to be moved by sinister private influences or to defer to the clamor of some noisy section outside, looks to the man of its choice [the president] to keep Congress in order" (*The American Commonwealth,* 2 vols. [Indianapolis: Liberty Fund, 1995], 1:53).
2. Martin P. Wattenberg, "Tax Cut versus Lockbox: Did the Voters Grasp the Tradeoff in 2000," *Presidential Studies Quarterly* 34 (December 2004): 845.
3. Justin Lewis, Michael Morgan, and Sut Jhally, "Libertine or Liberal? The Real Scandal of What People Know about President Clinton," University of Massachusetts/Amherst, February 10, 1998, http://www-unix.oit.umass.edu/~mmorgan/commstudy.html (accessed November 13, 2005).
4. Raymond E. Wolfinger, "Dealignment, Realignment, and Mandates in the 1984 Election," in *The American Elections of 1984,* ed. Austin Ranney (Durham, N.C.: Duke University Press, 1985), 293.
5. On presidents' use of polling, see Diane J. Heith, *Polling to Govern: Public Opinion and Presidential Leadership* (Stanford, Calif.: Stanford University Press, 2004).
6. Edmund S. Morgan, *Inventing the People: The Rise of Popular Sovereignty in England and America* (New York: Norton, 1988), 13.
7. Clinton Rossiter, *The American Presidency,* 2d ed. (New York: Harcourt, Brace, 1960), 18.
8. Ibid., 34.

CHAPTER 7: Presidents Have Usurped the War Power That Rightfully Belongs to Congress

1. Alexis de Tocqueville, *Democracy in America,* trans. Arthur Goldhammer (New York: Library of America, 1966).

PRO

1. Edward S. Corwin, *The President: Office and Powers* (New York: New York University Press, 1957), 201.
2. Alexander Hamilton, James Madison, and John Jay, *The Federalist Papers* (New York: New American Library, 1961), 418 (emphasis in original).

3. Ibid., 417.

4. Max Farrand, ed., *The Records of the Federal Convention of 1787*, 4 vols. (New Haven, Conn.: Yale University Press, 1937), 1:292.

5. That same concept was included in an early federal court case, *U.S. v. Smith* (27 Fed. Cas. 1192 [No. 16,342] [C.C.N.Y. 1806] at 1230), in which the court said that "it is the exclusive province of congress to change a state of peace into a state of war."

6. Louis Henkin, *Foreign Affairs and the Constitution* (Mineola, N.Y.: Foundation Press, 1972), 50–51.

7. Farrand, *Records of the Federal Convention of 1787*, 2:318.

8. The April 1952 executive order was declared unconstitutional by the Supreme Court in *Youngstown Sheet & Tube Co. v. Sawyer*, 343 U.S. 579 (1952). For an analysis of Truman's decision to send U.S. forces to Korea in 1950, see Louis Fisher, *Presidential War Power* (Lawrence: University Press of Kansas, 1995), 84–90; Louis Fisher, "The Korean War: On What Legal Basis Did Truman Act?" *American Journal of International Law* 89 (1995): 21; and Glenn D. Paige, *The Korean Decision: June 24–30, 1950* (New York: Free Press, 1968).

9. Senate Committee on Foreign Relations, 91st Cong., 1st sess., 1969, S. Rep. 129, as reprinted in Peter M. Shane and Harold H. Bruff, *Separation of Powers Law: Cases and Materials* (Durham, N.C.: Carolina Academic Press, 1996), 777–791.

10. Arthur M. Schlesinger Jr., *The Imperial Presidency* (Boston: Houghton Mifflin, 1973), 108. Congress effectively ratified the bases deal retroactively in April 1941.

11. Ibid., 113.

12. There is no better description of this circumstance than Justice Robert Jackson's pointed as well as prescient warning to Congress in his *Youngstown* concurrence: "We may say that power to legislate for emergencies belongs in the hands of Congress, but only Congress itself can prevent power from slipping through its fingers" (343 U.S. at 654).

13. Leonard Meeker, "The Legality of United States Participation in the Defense of Viet-Nam," *Department of State Bulletin* 54 (1966): 474, as reprinted in Peter M. Shane and Harold H. Bruff, *Separation of Powers Law: Cases and Materials* (Durham, N.C.: Carolina Academic Press, 1996), 771–776.

14. Ibid., 772.

15. Ibid.

16. S. Res. 85, 91st Cong., 1st sess., *Congressional Record* 115 (June 25, 1969): S 7153.

17. Senate Committee, S. Rep. 129, 781.

18. Ibid., 781–782.

19. Public Law 93-148, *U.S. Statutes at Large* 555 (1973).

20. Some scholars, such as Louis Fisher and David Gray Adler, would go further, arguing that the existence of the resolution has actually lulled Congress into even greater complacency by discouraging it from using the constitutional tools it already—and always—had, such as the appropriations power, the legislative power, and, ultimately, the impeachment power. See Louis Fisher and David Gray

Adler, "The War Powers Resolution: Time to Say Goodbye," *Political Science Quarterly* 113 (spring 1998): 1.

21. The judicial record is, indeed, a mixed one, ranging from *United States v. Curtiss-Wright Export Corporation* (299 U.S. 304 [1936]), the most expansive interpretation (and an incorrect one, at that) of executive power in foreign policy, to *Youngstown Sheet & Tube Co. v. Sawyer* and *Dellums v. Bush* (752 F. Supp. 1141 [D.D.C. 1990]), decisions that rest on a traditional understanding of the scope of powers allotted to each branch. *Youngstown*, though technically a decision that addressed domestic powers, is clearly applicable to war powers issues, because it includes as a vital part of its consideration the reach of the president's commander in chief power. The record of cases challenging the constitutionality of the Vietnam War that the federal courts refused to decide on the merits demonstrates just how unwilling the judiciary is to counter a sitting president during wartime. See, for example, *Mora v. McNamara* (386 U.S. 934 [1967]); *Mitchell v. Laird* (488 F.2d 611 [D.C. Cir. 1973]); *Orlando v. Laird* (443 F.2d 1039 [2d Cir. 1971]); and *Berk v. Laird* (429 F.2d 302 [2d Cir. 1970]). The judicial response to the war on terrorism under President George W. Bush is a work in progress, although the Supreme Court in its June 2004 decisions in *Hamdi v. Rumsfeld* (124 S. Ct. 2633 [2004]) and *Rasul v. Bush* (124 S. Ct. 2686 [2004]) was more critical of the president's claims than might have been expected during wartime, and it rejected the government's narrow view in those cases of judicial power to review habeas corpus claims from enemy combatants.

22. David Mervin, "The Demise of the War Clause," *Presidential Studies Quarterly* 30 (December 2000): 767–773.

23. David Gray Adler, "The Virtues of the War Clause," *Presidential Studies Quarterly* 30 (December 2000): 777–782.

CON

1. All quotations are taken from *Notes of Debates on the Federal Convention of 1787* (Athens: Ohio University Press, 1966), 475–477.

2. *Prize Cases*, 67 U.S. 635 (1863).

3. *Luftig v. McNamara*, 373 F.2d 664 (1967).

4. *Berk v. Laird*, 429 F.2d 302 (Calif. 2 1970).

5. *Orlando v. Laird*, 443 F.2d 1039 (2d Cir. 1971).

6. *Massachusetts v. Laird*, 451 F.2d 26 (1st Cir. 1971).

7. *Da Costa v. Laird I*, 448 F.2d 368 (2d Cir. 1971).

8. *Da Costa v. Laird II*, 471 F.2d 1146 (2d Cir. 1973).

9. *Dellums v. Bush*, 752 F. Supp. 1141 ([D.D.C. 1990).

10. *Campbell v. Clinton*, 52 F. Supp.2d 34 (D.D.C. 1999).

11. *Doe v. Bush*, 322 F.3d 109 (2003).

CHAPTER 8: The President Has Too Much Power in the Selection of Judges

PRO

1. Senator Thurmond apparently told this story to various law school audiences. The author was present on one such occasion when Thurmond spoke to students at the University of Virginia Law School during the spring of 1988.
2. At the time of this writing, the most recent of those forty-five nominees—Judge Samuel A. Alito Jr.—was still under consideration for confirmation by the U.S. Senate.
3. John O. McGinnis, "The President, the Senate, the Constitution, and the Confirmation Process: A Reply to Professors Strauss and Sunstein," *Texas Law Review* 71 (February 1993): 638–639.
4. Alexander Hamilton, James Madison, and John Jay, *The Federalist Papers* (New York: New American Library, 1961).
5. See Sheldon Goldman, *Picking Federal Judges: Lower Court Selection from Roosevelt through Reagan* (New Haven, Conn.: Yale University Press, 1997), 210.
6. Michael Gerhardt, *The Federal Appointments Process: A Constitutional and Historical Analysis* (Durham, N.C.: Duke University Press, 2000), 145.
7. John Anthony Maltese, *The Selling of Supreme Court Nominees* (Baltimore: Johns Hopkins University Press, 1995), 7.
8. Mark Silverstein, *Judicious Choices: The New Politics of Supreme Court Confirmations* (New York: Norton, 1994), 4.
9. Maltese, *Selling of Supreme Court Nominees*, 93–109.
10. Ibid., 110.

CON

1. Alexander Hamilton, James Madison, and John Jay, *The Federalist Papers* (New York: New American Library, 1961), 454–459.
2. Ibid., 457.
3. Ibid., 456.
4. George Mason to James Monroe, January 30, 1792, quoted in Michael J. Gerhardt, *The Federal Appointments Process: A Constitutional and Historical Analysis* (Durham, N.C.: Duke University Press, 2000), 346, 92n. James Wilson of Pennsylvania likewise argued that presidential nomination "should be . . . unfettered and unsheltered by counselors" (quoted in ibid., 31).
5. Hamilton, Madison, and Jay, *Federalist Papers*, 457.
6. Ibid., 455.
7. This sentence appeared in the original publication of *Federalist* 76 in the *New-York Packet*, but was omitted in the so-called McLean edition (the first collected edition), which serves as the basis of the New American Library edition cited

above. The McLean edition was published in 1788 and was corrected and edited by Hamilton and Jay, but not by Madison. Most online sources of *Federalist 76*, however, include this sentence, including those based on the McLean edition. See, for example, http://usinfo. state.gov/usa/infousa/facts/funddocs/fed/federa00.htm. That cite draws its text "primarily from the McLean edition," but notes that "glaring errors—mainly printer's lapses—have been corrected." That suggests that this sentence my have been omitted in error by the printer.

8. Gerhardt, *Federal Appointments Process,* 21. Other positions were taken by different members of the convention. Some, such as John Rutledge of South Carolina, remained fearful of too much executive power.

9. Quoted in ibid., 22.

10. Quoted in ibid., 24. The convention originally rejected the compromise (which required a two-thirds vote of the Senate to confirm) and voted 6–3 in July to vest the appointment power in the Senate alone. In September, however, the Convention unanimously agreed to the "advice and consent" language for federal judges that ended up in the Constitution (see ibid., 24–25).

11. For an articulation of this view, see, for example, David A. Strauss and Cass R. Sunstein, "The Senate, the Constitution, and the Confirmation Process," *Yale Law Journal* 101 (1992): 1491ff.

12. John O. McGinnis, "The President, the Senate, the Constitution, and the Confirmation Process: A Reply to Professors Strauss and Sunstein," *Texas Law Review* 71 (February 1993): 638–639 (footnotes omitted).

13. Hamilton, Madison, and Jay, *Federalist Papers,* 457.

14. James E. Gauch, "The Intended Role of the Senate in Supreme Court Appointments," *University of Chicago Law Review* 56 (1989): 347–348.

15. These numbers do not include Lyndon B. Johnson's nomination or withdrawal of Homer Thornberry in 1968 or George W. Bush's withdrawal of the nomination of John Roberts Jr. to fill Sandra Day O'Connor's associate justice seat in 2005. Thornberry's name was withdrawn only because the anticipated vacancy in Abe Fortas's associate justice seat failed to materialize. Roberts was withdrawn so that he could be nominated to fill the vacancy left by the death of Chief Justice William H. Rehnquist. The numbers do include Ronald Reagan's nomination and withdrawal of Douglas H. Ginsburg in 1987, even though his nomination was never formally submitted to the Senate. Harriet Miers's nomination was submitted to the Senate in 2005, but was withdrawn before her confirmation hearings.

16. President John Tyler renominated three "failed" nominees in 1844: John C. Spencer (after Senate rejection), Edward King (after the Senate blocked his confirmation by postponement), and Reuben H. Walworth (twice renominated—first after a Senate vote to postpone and then again after no action was taken by the Senate).

The 123 total nominations before 1968 do not include consecutive resubmissions of the same nominee by the same president for the same vacancy, nor do they include the seven nominees who declined. It does include Edwin M. Stanton (who was confirmed in 1869 but died before taking office) and Stanley Matthews (who was consecutively renominated by two different presidents in 1881). Confusion over how to count renominations has led to some confusion about the precise number of Supreme Court nominees. The official U.S. Senate Web site lists eight consecutive resubmissions of nominations of the same person by the same president for the same seat (usually for merely technical reasons).

17. Fund-raising letter for the Free Congress Foundation's Judicial Selection Monitoring Project signed by Robert Bork and quoted in Henry Weinstein, "Drive Seeks to Block Clinton Judicial Nominees," *Los Angeles Times*, October 26, 1997, A3. One could quibble with this claim. Studies of the voting behavior of Clinton's judges—even those appointed when his fellow Democrats controlled the Senate in 1993–1994—suggest a moderate voting record. See, for example, Ronald Stidham, Robert A. Carp, and Donald Songer, "The Voting Behavior of President Clinton's Judicial Appointees," *Judicature* 80 (July–August 1996): 16; Sheldon Goldman and Elliot Slotnick, "Picking Judges under Fire," *Judicature* 82 (May–June 1999): 265; Nancy Scherer, "Are Clinton's Judges 'Old' Democrats or 'New' Democrats?" *Judicature* 84 (November–December 2000): 151.

Until conservative interest groups mobilized in 1997, Republican senators had generally been deferential to Clinton. He had gone out of his way to seek their advice after they took control of the Senate after the 1994 midterm elections. Over all, the Senate confirmed 99 percent of Clinton's first-term judicial nominations.

18. Free Congress Foundation Judicial Selection Monitoring Project, press release, January 23, 1997.

19. Quoted in Michael Kelly, "Judge Dread," *New Republic*, March 31, 1997, 6.

20. Quoted in Ronald Brownstein, "GOP Stall Tactics Damage Judiciary, President Charges," *Los Angeles Times*, September 28, 1997, A1.

21. William H. Rehnquist, "1997 Year-End Report on the Federal Judiciary," Administrative Office of the United States Courts, Washington, D.C., 1998, 7.

22. Sheldon Goldman, Elliot Slotnick, Gerard Gryski, and Gary Zuk, "Clinton's Judges: Summing Up the Legacy," *Judicature* 84 (March–April 2001): tables 3 and 6

23. Statistics for Franklin D. Roosevelt through George W. Bush can be found in a chart accompanying Neil A. Lewis, "Bitter Senators Divided Anew on Judgeships," *New York Times*, November 15, 2003, A1. The Senate did reject two of Nixon's Supreme Court nominees.

24. See George W. Bush, "Remarks after Meeting with Members of Congress on Federal Judicial Nominations," May 9, 2002; transcript and audio available at http://www.whitehouse.gov/news/releases/2002/05/20020509-6.html (accessed December 12, 2005).

25. Because Senator Hatch had, as chair of the Senate Judiciary Committee in the 1990s, allowed Republicans to block hearings of Clinton's nominees, some Democrats cried foul and accused Hatch of manipulating the rules for partisan reasons.

26. Sarah A. Binder and Steven S. Smith, *Politics or Principle? Filibustering in the United States Senate* (Washington, D.C.: Brookings, 1997), 5.

27. Ibid., 33, 37.

28. Martin B. Gold and Dimple Gupta, "The Constitutional Option to Change Senate Rules and Procedures: A Majoritarian Means to Overcome the Filibuster," *Harvard Journal of Law and Public Policy* 28 (fall 2004): 216. Gold served as floor adviser to Senate majority leader Bill Frist in 2003–2004; Gold served in George W. Bush Justice Department.

29. See Figure 2-5 in Binder and Smith, *Politics or Principle?* 48.

30. John Anthony Maltese, *The Selling of Supreme Court Nominees* (Baltimore: Johns Hopkins University Press, 1995), 55.

31. Ibid., 71.

32. Stephen Carter, *The Confirmation Mess: Cleaning Up the Federal Appointments Process* (New York: Basic Books, 1994), 187.

33. *Judicial Roulette: Report of the Twentieth Century Fund Task Force on Judicial Selection* (New York: Priority Press, 1988), 4, 9.

CHAPTER 9: A Broad Executive Privilege Is Essential to the Successful Functioning of the Presidency

1. *United States v. Nixon*, 418 U.S. 683 (1974).

PRO

1. *United States v. Nixon*, 483 U.S. 683 (1974) at 705–706, 708.

2. *Federal Open Market Committee of the Federal Reserve System v. Merrill*, 413 F. Supp. 494 (D.D.C. 1979).

3. *Watkins v. United States*, 354 U.S. 178 (1957); *Wilkinson v. United States*, 365 U.S. 399 (1961).

4. *Senate Select Committee v. Nixon*, 498 F.2d 725 (1974) at 731.

5. Quoted in House Committee on Public Works and Transportation, *Contempt of Congress*, 97th Cong., 2d sess., December 15, 1982, 83n. A classic study of secrecy and legislative inquiry is Irving Younger, "Congressional Investigations and Executive Secrecy: A Study in the Separation of Powers," *University of Pittsburgh Law Review* 20 (1959): 755–784.

6. *Gravel v. United States*, 408 U.S. 606 (1972).

7. David M. O'Brien, *Storm Center: The Supreme Court in American Politics*, 2d ed. (New York: Norton, 1990), 150–151.

8. *Souicie v. David*, 448 F.2d 1067 (D.C.C. 1971) at 1080.

9. George C. Calhoun, "Confidentiality and Executive Privilege," in *The Tethered Presidency: Congressional Constraints on Presidential Power*, ed. Thomas M. Franck (New York: New York University Press, 1981), 174.

10. In 2001–2002 a congressional committee requested Justice Department documents from the 1960s and 1970s that were germane to an investigation of corruption in the Federal Bureau of Investigation's Boston office in its handling of organized crime in the 1960s and 1970s.

CON

1. Quoted in Gerald Guther, ed., *John Marshall's Defense of* McCulloch v. Maryland (Stanford, Calif.: Stanford University Press, 1969), 190–191.

2. *United States v. Nixon*, 418 U.S. 683 (1974).

3. Charles Warren, *The Making of the Constitution* (Cambridge, Mass.: Harvard University Press, 1947), 173.

4. Jonathan Elliot, ed., *The Debates in the Several State Conventions on the Adoption of the Federal Constitution*, 5 vols. (Philadelphia: Lippincott, 1861; New York: Burt Franklin, 1979), 4:14. Citations are to the Franklin edition.

5. Edward M. Earle, ed., *The Federalist Papers*, No. 75 (New York: Modern Library, 1937), 487.

6. Elliot, *Debates*, 2:480 (emphasis in the original).

7. Max Farrand, *The Records of the Federal Convention of 1787*, 4 vols. (New Haven, Conn.: Yale University Press, 1966), 1:70.

8. James Wilson, *The Works of James Wilson*, 2 vols., ed. Robert McCoskey (Cambridge, Mass.: Harvard University Press, 1967), 2:731. In 1791 Wilson referred to the "House of Representatives" as "the grand inquest of the state" (1:415). At the Constitutional Convention, the Committee of Detail also characterized the House as the "grand inquest of the Nation" (Farrand, *Records of the Federal Convention of 1787*, 2:154).

9. Farrand, *Records of the Federal Convention of 1787*, 2:260. George Mason of Virginia, who rarely sided with Wilson, agreed that the provision "would give a just alarm to the people." Others understood that "cases might arise where secrecy might be necessary in both Houses—measures preparatory to a declaration of war" (ibid.). At the Virginia ratifying convention, delegate Patrick Henry demanded to know "why Congress should keep their proceedings secret," and observed that "the liberties of the people never were . . . secure when the transactions of their rulers may be concealed from them." Henry understood the need for temporary concealment from the public of "such transactions as relate to military operations or affairs of great consequence, the immediate promulgation of which defeat the interest of the community." But he declared that to "cover with the veil of secrecy the common routine of business, is an abomination" (Elliot, *Debates*, 3:170). Clearly, the founders were uncomfortable with the prospect of withholding information from the people. To the extent they were willing to countenance secrecy, they trusted Congress, not the executive, to decide what information should be revealed and what should remain secret.

10. The framers, following Madison's observation that presidential powers should be enumerated, extended the enumeration-of-power doctrine to the relatively trivial authority of the president to require in writing the opinions of department heads, a power that, Justice Robert H. Jackson noted in *Youngstown Sheet & Tube Co. v. Sawyer*, was "inherent" if anything was (343 U.S. 579 [1952] at 640–641). It is implausible that the framers would have left to the vagaries of "inherent power" such a formidable power as the claim of executive privilege when they labored to carve out protection for the president to "request" department heads to submit

their opinions in writing. On the framers and inherent power, see David Gray Adler, "The Steel Seizure Case and Inherent President Power," *Constitutional Commentary* 19 (2002): 155, 163–195.

11. *United States v. Nixon*, 418 U.S. at 708, 711. The Court rejected President Nixon's claim of an "absolute, unqualified" executive privilege of immunity from the judicial process. However, in some unfortunate dicta Chief Justice Burger seemed to acknowledge a limited privilege if the president claimed a "need to protect military, diplomatic, or sensitive national security secrets" (706). Nevertheless, Burger made it clear in a footnote that the Nixon case involved judicial, not congressional, access to materials possessed by the executive: "[W]e are not here concerned with congressional demands for information" (712, 19n). In any event, the "generalized constitutionally-based privilege seems to emerge full-bloom from the head of the court." Paul Mishkin, "Great Cases and Soft Law, A Comment on *United States v. Nixon*," *UCLA Law Review* 22 (1974): 76, 83–84. Also see Philip Kurland, "United States v. Nixon: Who Killed Cock Robin," *UCLA Law Review* 22 (1974): 62, 74.

12. *United States v. Burr*, 25 F. Cas. 55 (No. 14,693) (C.C.D. Va. 1807).

13. Quoted in Raoul Berger, *Executive Privilege: A Constitutional Myth* (Cambridge, Mass.: Harvard University Press, 1974), 189.

14. C. de S. Montesquieu, *The Spirit of the Laws*, 2 vols. (Philadelphia: American Translation, 1802), 187.

15. Mark J. Rozell, *Executive Privilege: The Dilemma of Secrecy and Democratic Accountability* (Baltimore: Johns Hopkins University Press, 1994), 33. Of course, assertions of power do not establish constitutional legitimacy, and governmental practice is no proof of an action's legality. As Justice Felix Frankfurter stated in *Inland Waterway Corp. v. Young*, "Illegality cannot attain legitimacy through practice" (309 U.S. 518 [1840] at 524). Similarly, in *Powell v. McCormack* Chief Justice Earl Warren wrote: "That an unconstitutional action has been taken before surely does not render that action any less unconstitutional at a later date" (395 U.S. 486 [1969] at 546).

16. Thomas Jefferson, *Writings*, 10 vols., ed. P. L. Ford (New York: Putnam, 1892–1899), 1:189–190.

17. Berger, *Executive Privilege*, 168.

18. See Louis Fisher, *The Politics of Executive Privilege* (Durham, N.C.: Carolina Academic Press, 2004), 33–39.

19. Daniel N. Hoffman, "Secrecy and Constitutional Controls in the Federalist Period," in *The Constitution and the Conduct of American Foreign Policy*, ed. David Gray Adler and Larry N. George (Lawrence: University Press of Kansas, 1996), 291, 293.

20. Ibid., 294.

21. This view is captured by Connecticut delegate Roger Sherman's comment at the Constitutional Convention that "the executive magistracy [was] nothing more than an institution for carrying the will of the Legislature into effect" (Farrand, *Records of the Federal Convention of 1787*, 1:65).

22. Arthur M. Schlesinger Jr., *The Imperial Presidency* (Boston: Houghton, Mifflin, 1973).

23. For a discussion of the constitutional governance of foreign policy, see the essays in David Gray Adler and Larry N. George, eds., *The Constitution and the Conduct of American Foreign Policy* (Lawrence: University Press of Kansas, 1996), 291, 293; and Louis Fisher, *Presidential War Power*, 2d ed. (Lawrence: University Press of Kansas, 2004).

24. See David Gray Adler, "The President's Recognition Power," in *The Constitution and the Conduct of American Foreign Policy*, ed. David Gray Adler and Larry N. George (Lawrence: University Press of Kansas, 1996), 133–157.

25. See, generally, David Gray Adler, "Constitution, Foreign Affairs and Presidential War-making: A Response to Professor Powell," *Georgia State University Law Review* 19 (2003): 947–1019; and Fisher, *Presidential War Power*.

26. Farrand, *Records of the Federal Convention of 1787*, 1:292.

27. James Madison, *Writings*, 9 vols., ed. Gaillard Hunt (New York: Putnam, 1900–1910), 6:148.

28. Alexander Hamilton, a favorite among extollers of a strong presidency, offered, as Pacificus, a benchmark for the construction of executive powers: "The general doctrine then of our Constitution is, that the Executive Power of the Nation is vested in the President; subject only to the exceptions and qualifications which are expressed in the instrument" (Alexander Hamilton, *The Papers of Alexander Hamilton*, 27 vols., ed. Harold C. Syrett et al. [New York: Columbia University Press, 1961–1987], 15:39). The "exceptions and qualifications" approach suggests, at a minimum, that under the banner of executive power a president may not lay claim to any of the powers, express or implied, that are allocated to either Congress or the judiciary. Thus it seems indisputable that the president may not invoke executive privilege in the face of a demand from Congress for information relevant to its exercise of the war power. See Adler, "Steel Seizure Case," 163–173.

29. Earle, *Federalist Papers*, No. 75, 485–490.

30. Ibid., No. 64, 420.

31. See Arthur Bestor, "Respective Roles of Senate and President in the Making and Abrogation of Treaties—The Original Intent of the Framers of the Constitution Historically Examined," *Washington Law Review* 55 (1979): 4; and David Gray Adler, "The Framers and Treaty Termination: A Matter of Symmetry," *Arizona State Law Journal* (1981): 891–923.

CHAPTER 10: A President's Cabinet Members Should Have a Larger Role in the Formation of Public Policy

1. Robert B. Reich, *Locked in the Cabinet* (New York: Knopf, 1997).

PRO

1. Joseph Kahn, "Bush's Selections Signal a Widening of Cabinet's Role," *New York Times,* December 31, 2000, A1.
2. Reagan quoted in Anthony J. Bennett, *The American President's Cabinet* (New York: St. Martin's Press, 1996), 79.
3. Conversation between Nixon and National Security Adviser Henry Kissinger on April 7, 1971, in James Warren, "More Nixon Tapes," *Atlantic Monthly,* September 2004, 101.
4. Washington is quoted in Richard F. Fenno Jr., *The President's Cabinet* (Cambridge, Mass.: Harvard University Press, 1959), 14. Although President Washington had four cabinet members, including the attorney general, a full-blown Justice Department was not created until 1870. The number of programs cited here (1,170) was calculated by the Bush administration's Office of Management and Budget. See the description in the fiscal 2004 budget message at http://www.gpoaccess.gov/usbudget/fy04/pdf/budget/performance.pdf (accessed December 7, 2005).
5. Most presidents experience a "honeymoon period" early in their term when they enjoy a high level of public and congressional support for their legislative initiatives. FDR's legislative achievements during his first hundred days in office are unsurpassed.
6. Andrew Rudalevige, *Managing the President's Program: Presidential Leadership and Legislative Policy Formulation* (Princeton, N.J.: Princeton University Press, 2002), chap. 4, with 1997–2002 figures updated by author.
7. Robert C. Gilmour, "Central Legislative Clearance: A Revised Perspective," *Public Administration Review* 31 (1971): 152.
8. Rudalevige, *Managing the President's Program,* table 4.5 and figures 4.4 and 4.5.
9. From Katzenbach's oral history of November 23, 1968, accession no. 78-24, Lyndon Baines Johnson Library and Museum, Austin, Texas, 9.
10. Quoted in David Whiteman, *Communication in Congress: Members, Staff, and the Search for Information* (Lawrence: University Press of Kansas, 1995), 47.
11. Jim VandeHei and Glenn Kessler, "President to Consider Changes for New Term: High-Profile Departures Are Rumored," *Washington Post,* November 5, 2004, A1.
12. Rudalevige, *Managing the President's Program,* 113–123. Congressional aide quoted in Mike Allen, "Bush to Change Economic Team," *Washington Post,* November 29, 2004, A1.
13. Rudalevige, *Managing the President's Program,* 146–150.
14. Shirley Anne Warshaw, *Powersharing: White House–Cabinet Relations in the Modern Presidency* (Albany: State University of New York Press, 1996), 174.

15. Richard J. Ellis, *Presidential Lightning Rods: The Politics of Blame Avoidance* (Lawrence: University Press of Kansas, 1994).

16. Richard P. Nathan, *The Administrative Presidency* (New York: Wiley, 1983), 40. Also see Matthew J. Dickinson, *Bitter Harvest: FDR, Presidential Power and the Growth of the Presidential Branch* (New York: Cambridge University Press, 1997), 28–29, 110–112. Note that the staff totals listed here do not include the 225 employees of the Office of the U.S. Trade Representative, which even though an operating agency in most respects is organizationally in the EOP.

17. Nathan, *Administrative Presidency,* 41. Also see Robert Wood, "When Government Works," *The Public Interest* (winter 1970).

18. Richard E. Neustadt, *Presidential Power and the Modern Presidents: The Politics of Leadership from Roosevelt to Reagan* (New York: Free Press, 1990), 280.

19. Sorensen is quoted in Samuel Kernell and Samuel L. Popkin, eds., *Chief of Staff: Twenty-five Years of Managing the Presidency* (Berkeley: University of California Press, 1988).

20. George Stephanopoulos, *All Too Human: A Political Education* (Boston: Little, Brown, 1999), 210.

21. Thomas E. Cronin, *The State of the Presidency,* 2d ed. (Boston: Little, Brown, 1980), 291.

22. Irving Janis, *Groupthink,* 2d ed. (Boston: Houghton Mifflin, 1986); transcript of January 2005 *Washington Times* interview, http://www.washingtontimes.com/national/20050111-114349-9789r.htm (accessed December 6, 2005).

23. Ron Suskind, *The Price of Loyalty: George W. Bush, the White House, and the Education of Paul O'Neill* (New York: Simon and Schuster, 2004), 147–149; Michael A. Fletcher, "Bush Is Keeping Cabinet Secretaries Close to Home: Spending Time at White House Required," *Washington Post,* March 31, 2005, A1.

24. Donald H. Rumsfeld, after his service as White House chief of staff (and before returning to the Defense Department in 2001), noted that "you have all these threads, and the White House staff's function is to see that those threads get through the needle's eye in a reasonably coherent way." Quoted in Rudalevige, *Managing the President's Program,* 34.

25. Bennett, *American President's Cabinet,* chap. 9; Roger B. Porter, *Managing Presidential Decision Making: The Economic Policy Board* (New York: Cambridge University Press, 1980), esp. chap. 3.

26. See Graham Allison, "The Advantages of a Presidential Executive Cabinet (EXCAB)," in *The Post-Imperial Presidency,* ed. Vincent Davies (New Brunswick, N.J.: Transaction Books, 1980). For a somewhat different formulation, see Elliot L. Richardson and James P. Pfiffner, "Our Cabinet System Is a Charade," *New York Times,* May 28, 1989, E15.

27. Porter, *Managing Presidential Decision Making,* 99–100. The effectiveness of the Reagan councils seems to have varied with the president's interest in and attendance at them; they were consolidated into two councils in the second term.

28. Ellis, *Presidential Lightning Rods,* 155–160.

CON

1. Cited in Richard E. Neustadt, *Presidential Power and the Modern Presidents: The Politics of Leadership from Roosevelt to Reagan* (New York: Free Press, 1990), 34.
2. The phrase "separate institutions sharing powers" is from ibid., 29.
3. Data on program numbers are from the Bush administration; see http://www.gpoaccess.gov/usbudget/fy04/pdf/budget/performance.pdf (accessed December 7, 2005).
4. Although there are fifteen executive branch departments with cabinet status, the number of presidential advisers with "cabinet rank," denoted by their Executive I appointment status, is usually larger.
5. Data on independent agencies are located at http://www.opm.gov/feddata/html/2004/ (accessed December 7, 2005).
6. Quoted in Thomas E. Cronin, *The State of the Presidency*, 2d ed. (Boston: Little, Brown, 1980), 237.
7. See, for example, the campaign pledges of Presidents Richard Nixon and Jimmy Carter, both described in Shirley Anne Warshaw, *Powersharing: White House–Cabinet Relations in the Modern Presidency* (Albany: State University of New York Press, 1996), 39, 100.
8. Henry Barrett Learned, *The President's Cabinet, Studies in the Origin, Formation and Structure of an American Institution* (New Haven, Conn.: Yale University Press, 1912), 66–96.
9. Alexander Hamilton, *The Federalist Papers*, No. 70 (Norwalk, Conn.: Easton Press, 1979), 477.
10. Morris Fiorina, Paul E. Peterson, and D. Stephen Voss, *America's New Democracy* (New York: Longman Press, 2002), 314.
11. Although the position of attorney general was created in 1789, the Justice Department was not established until 1870. See Richard F. Fenno, *The President's Cabinet: An Analysis in the Period from Wilson to Eisenhower* (Cambridge, Mass.: Harvard University Press, 1959), 20.
12. Louis William Koenig, *The Invisible Presidency* (New York: Rinehart, 1960), 17.
13. See the "Pacificus-Helvidius Letters," reprinted in Michael Nelson, ed., *The Evolving Presidency* (Washington, D.C.: CQ Press, 1999), 40–44.
14. See *Myers v. United States* (272 U.S. 52 [1926]) and *Humphrey's Executor v. United States* (295 U.S. 602 [1935]).
15. Neustadt, *Presidential Power*, 35.
16. Warshaw, *Powersharing*, 18.
17. See Nelson W. Polsby, "Presidential Cabinet Making: Lessons for the Political System," *Political Science Quarterly* 93 (spring 1978): 15–25.
18. For examples from the two most recent presidencies, see Robert Reich, *Locked in the Cabinet* (New York: Knopf, 1997); and Ron Suskind, *The Price of Loyalty: George W. Bush, the White House, and the Education of Paul O'Neill* (New York: Simon and Schuster, 2004).
19. Fenno, *President's Cabinet*, 247.
20. Cronin, *State of the Presidency*, 274–286.

21. Author's calculation based on data in Jeff Cohen, *The Politics of the U.S. Cabinet* (Pittsburgh, Pa.: University of Pittsburgh Press, 1988), 187.

22. See Harold Seidman and Robert Gilmour, *Politics, Position and Power*, 4th ed. (New York: Oxford University Press, 1986), 251–253.

23. These totals do not include roughly 2,500 additional political appointments that do not require Senate confirmation. These include Schedule C (secretaries performing politically sensitive tasks) and Senior Executive Service positions. Bush's totals from Paul Light, "Late for Their Appointments" (op-ed), *New York Times*, November 16, 2004.

24. On the impact of "thickening government" on policy control, see Paul Light, *Thickening Government* (Washington, D.C.: Brookings, 1995).

25. Neustadt, *Presidential Power*, 34.

26. Data on Bush taken from Light, "Late for Their Appointments." More generally, see G. Calvin Mackenzie, "The State of the Presidential Appointments Process," in *Innocent until Nominated: The Breakdown of the Presidential Appointments Process*, ed. G. Calvin Mackenzie (Washington, D.C.: Brookings, 2001), 1–49.

27. Gordon R. Hoxie, "The Cabinet in the American Presidency, 1789–1984," *Presidential Studies Quarterly* 14 (1984): 224–225.

28. Terry Moe, "The Politicized Presidency," in *The New Direction in American Politics*, ed. John Chubb and Paul E. Peterson (Washington, D.C.: Brookings, 1985), 235–271.

29. The EOP was formally established by Executive Order 8248 (September 8, 1939) under authority granted to the president by Reorganization Plans I and II (July 1, 1939). For details on FDR's intent, see Matthew J. Dickinson, *Bitter Harvest: FDR, Presidential Power and the Growth of the Presidential Branch* (New York: Cambridge University Press, 1996), 45–86.

30. The NSC also included the chairman of the newly created National Security Resources Board, which advised the president on civil defense issues. In 1949 the act was amended to eliminate the three armed services secretaries and add the vice president to the council.

31. The Domestic Council was established in the EOP by Reorganization Plan 2 (March 12, 1970). In 1977, under Reorganization Plan I, Jimmy Carter formally abolished the Domestic Council, replacing it with a White House-based Domestic Policy Staff (DPS). In 1981 Reagan renamed the DPS the Office of Policy Development (OPD). President Clinton formally established two cabinet-level councils—the Domestic Policy Council (Executive Order 12589, August 16, 1993) and the National Economic Council (Executive Order 12835, January 25, 1993). Both councils were located within the Office of Policy Development and were staffed by White House aides and headed by senior-level White House assistants. On October 8, 2001, Bush created a fourth cabinet-level policy council, the Homeland Security Council (HSC), along with a separate Office of Homeland Security within the EOP (Executive Order 13228).

32. On this point, see Richard J. Ellis, *Presidential Lightning Rods: The Politics of Blame Avoidance* (Lawrence: University Press of Kansas, 1994).

CHAPTER 11: Psychological Character Is a Powerful Predictor of Presidential Performance

1. James David Barber, *The Presidential Character: Predicting Performance in the White House* (Englewood Cliffs, N.J.: Prentice-Hall, 1972).
2. Stephen Skowronek, *The Politics Presidents Make: Leadership from John Adams to George Bush* (Cambridge, Mass.: Belknap Harvard Press, 1993).

PRO

1. Those readers with deeper interests in the theoretical, methodological, and epistemological issues involved should consult Stanley A. Renshon, *The Psychological Assessment of Presidential Candidates* (New York: Routledge, 1998); and Stanley A. Renshon, "Assessing the Character and Performance of Presidential Candidates: Some Observations on Theory and Method," in *The Psychological Assessment of Political Leaders: Theories, Methods, and Applications*, ed. Jerrold M. Post (Ann Arbor: University of Michigan Press, 2003).
2. Stanley A. Renshon, *High Hopes: The Clinton Presidency and the Politics of Ambition* (New York: Routledge, 1998).
3. Fred I. Greenstein, *Personality and Politics* (Chicago: Markham, 1969).
4. *The 9/11 Commission Report: Final Report of the National Commission on Terrorist Attacks upon the United States* (New York: Norton, 2004), 115.
5. Ibid., 127, 131.

CHAPTER 12: Great Presidents Are Agents of Democratic Change

PRO

1. Richard E. Neustadt, *Presidential Power and the Modern Presidents: The Politics of Leadership from Roosevelt to Reagan* (New York: Free Press, 1991), 3–10, 73–90.
2. James MacGregor Burns, *Roosevelt: The Lion and the Fox* (New York: Harcourt, Brace, Jovanovich, 1960), 487.
3. Stephen Skowronek, *The Politics Presidents Make: Leadership from John Adams to Bill Clinton* (Cambridge, Mass.: Belknap Press of Harvard University Press, 1993), 27 (emphasis in original).
4. Marc Landy and Sidney M. Milkis, *Presidential Greatness* (Lawrence: University Press of Kansas, 2000).
5. Felix Frankfurter to Franklin D. Roosevelt, August 9, 1937, Box 210, Papers of Thomas Corcoran, Manuscript Division, Library of Congress, Washington, D.C.
6. James D. Richardson, ed., *A Compilation of the Messages and Papers of the Presidents, Prepared under the Direction of the Joint Committee on Printing, of the House and Senate, Pursuant to an Act of the Fifty-second Congress of the United*

States (with Additions and Encyclopedic Index by Private Enterprise), 20 vols. (New York: Bureau of National Literature, 1917), 1211.

7. Ibid., 1213.

8. Ibid., 1208.

9. Ibid.

10. Robert V. Remini, *Life of Andrew Jackson* (New York: Harper and Row, 1988), 36.

11. Richardson, *Messages and Papers*, 1217.

12. Undated fragment written in late 1860 or early 1861, in Paul N. Angle, ed., *New Letters and Papers of Lincoln* (Boston: Houghton Mifflin, 1930), 241–242. Lincoln's reference is to Proverbs 25:11.

13. Abraham Lincoln, "House Divided Speech," Springfield, Illinois, June 16, 1858, http://www.lincolnbicentennial.gov/about/speeches/housedivided.php (accessed December 16, 2005).

14. Transcripts of these radio addresses have been compiled in Russell D. Buhite and David W Levy, eds., *FDR's Fireside Chats* (Norman: University of Oklahoma Press, 1992).

15. Franklin Delano Roosevelt, "The Commonwealth Club Address," in *Public Papers and Addresses of Franklin D. Roosevelt*, ed. Samuel Rosenman, 13 vols. (New York: Random House, 1938–1950), 1:751–752.

16. See especially Bush's second inaugural address, January 20, 2005, http://www.whitehouse.gov/inaugural/index.html (accessed December 12, 2005).

CON

1. Although Kennedy and Johnson may not fit into the category of great presidents as a general matter, they are often placed in that company in the area of civil rights.

2. Stephen Skowronek, *The Politics Presidents Make: Leadership from John Adams to Bill Clinton* (Cambridge, Mass.: Belknap Press of Harvard University Press, 1997).

3. Robert V. Remini, "Andrew Jackson and Indian Removal," http://edweb.tusd.k12.az.us (accessed December 16, 2005).

4. Mark E. Neely Jr., *The Fate of Liberty: Abraham Lincoln and Civil Liberties* (New York: Oxford University Press, 1991).

5. Henry quoted in Ralph Ketcham, ed., *The Anti-Federalist Papers* (New York: New American Library, 1986), 211.

6. Max Farrand, ed., *The Records of the Federal Convention of 1787*, 4 vols. (New Haven, Conn.: Yale University Press, 1937), 1:112.